SHIFTS

More than 30 true stories
and life lessons
from twenty-four years
as a cop on the beat

Stratis Skoufalos

ISBN: 978-1-939237-85-9

Published by Suncoast Digital Press, Inc.
Sarasota, Florida, U.S.A

Dedication

To the memory of all
law enforcement officers everywhere
who have made
the ultimate sacrifice.

Note: While these are all true stories,
many times the names, dates, and locations
have been changed in consideration of privacy.

Contents

Preface

Most of my 24 years with the Philadelphia PD were as a street cop. The stories that follow are about what that was like for me. Some are sad, a few are intense and scary, and some are heartbreaking. Fortunately, a few are humorous. All the stories are based on actual events. As they say, "I couldn't make this stuff up." In some cases, I wish they were made up.

For as long as I can remember, the public's interest in police work has been strong.

It has led to so many TV cop shows that I've lost track. Like a lot of people in the police profession, I don't watch them. Honestly. Mainly because how they depict the job is so far from the reality that I know firsthand. Fill each episode packed with lots of action: fights, gunfire, car chases, and other sensational stuff like that. It may play on television, but it's really not like that. A lot of what police officers do is boring, repetitious, and even unpleasant. But, believe me, a cop's reality *can* be more exciting, dramatic and gripping than any television show. *Any* of them. Obviously, unlike TV, real life police work doesn't have a script, with ratings in mind; it's not predictable. The exciting stuff often happens in the blink of an eye.

So, it's reasonable for those observing from outside the police profession to have uninformed and false opinions and expectations of the men and women who wear the uniform. Yet, these folks, these citizens, are the ones the police serve, the very reason police departments exist. They *should* know the truth about what police officers do, what they think, what they feel and how the job changes them. It's never been more important. That's why *Shifts* came to be written.

Sure, I always rooted for the good guys when I watched TV as a kid. It seems to be in our DNA to enjoy seeing justice being served (there was never a question whether Marshall Dillon would be the hero, saving lives and more in every episode). But I was never one of those kids who wanted to be a police officer from a very young age. Nor did I have a grandfather, father, brothers, or uncles who were cops. My path to the job was twisting and complicated. I'll tell you about it in "Getting There."

In the early 1970s, as a young street cop who found every shift full of surprises and learning opportunities, I started writing things down. It was all fascinating. Just short notes on scraps of paper about people I had encountered on the job, things they did, things done to them, and how they affected me. Eventually, there were pages and pages. I tucked the notes away and forgot about them. To have those notes available to me once I decided to write this book was just incredible. What I captured back then right when everything was raw and fresh always surpassed my memories, though many of those are quite vivid.

It was years after retiring from the department that I scanned through these notes, put them in a pile on my desk, and let them sit for a while. Months later, I went back to them, spread them out and started reading. I couldn't stop.

Those bits and pieces I had written took me back decades, to my days as a young police officer, reuniting me with the people and places from back then. And the events and situations that brought us together. That's when I knew I had to write about those experiences.

So, one day I started. I was surprised how easily I was able to recall so many details; it was like being at each location again. And as I wrote the first story, it led to another and another. I couldn't believe there were so many. A couple of years later, as I looked over what I'd written, I was back there. I could almost see the faces and hear the voices of the citizens and the cops; I could vividly recall the locations and sometimes remember the essence of conversations.

Like being back on patrol, I could practically feel the well-worn seat of the cop car, hear the police radio and the city sounds, and smell and visualize the North Philadelphia streets I had worked. They are a part of me I can't forget and don't want to forget.

This is not a book specifically about true crime, although there is the true crime thread throughout. For me, it is more a book about true life. With some exceptions, the stories don't focus on the violence in the cop's world. Rather, they are recollections that focus on the humanity of my day-to-day encounters. They illuminate the personal side of the experiences—of both the cops and the civilians.

For me, writing these stories was important and necessary. These are the stories about the most significant shifts experienced in my lifetime. My wish is that these chronicles take you with me on patrol so you can get a sense of these experiences, too. I think you'll agree it's quite a ride.

THE STORIES

33rd & Pearl

Rats! Hundreds of them streaked down the alley past my feet, running scared, tumbling over each other in their frenzied escape. They kept coming in never-ending waves; gray blurs, some big as cats. Now I believed the persistent rumor that the occupants of the house intentionally fed and sheltered rats. The size and speed of the stampede was epic. Out from the rear of the property, through the yard and into the alley where I was standing, they streamed squealing and drenched, darting by where I had been for the last three hours, waiting for I don't know what. It registered that the rat exodus must be the result of the deluge of water the fire department had been power-spraying for two hours through the front doors and windows, flooding the basement.

This was not a typical scene where first responders are called to a house on fire. In Philadelphia, there were two separate and serious confrontations between a group known as "MOVE" and the city police department. I was one of about 300 cops assigned to the first incident. This story is about that episode.

The philosophy of MOVE, a back-to-nature group founded in Philadelphia in the early 1970s, rejected man-made laws as problematic. For a while, their interactions with others were mostly peaceful. Then, from 1973 to 1978, MOVE members adopted a radically unconventional, "nature-based" lifestyle. They also took a more aggressive stance in many interactions with citizens and city officials. It was in 1974 that they acquired a duplex on 33rd Street, knocked out walls, and created one large compound to house who knows how many people.

My first experience with MOVE was in early 1978 when I, along with about two dozen other cops, was assigned to a detail in the Powelton Village neighborhood of West Philadelphia. For the police department, it was an ongoing assignment, 24/7, with different officers rotating in every day. We were there to keep the peace between the occupants of the MOVE compound and their neighbors.

Powelton was a normally quiet area of West Philly, with beautiful large Victorian-era homes. But it hadn't been quiet lately. The MOVE family had moved into one of those once-grand, now dilapidated mansions in 1973.

About two years later, their behavior became unruly, with constant vulgar, philosophical and political proselytizing and bellowing of their vitriol over loudspeakers that literally shook the ground. There were also issues with extremely unsanitary conditions and concerns about the MOVE children, who were stuck living without public utilities and in other disturbing, risk-ridden conditions.

The situation was affecting the entire neighborhood and folks continued to demand that the city take action. Normally, such behavior and conditions would prompt the police to issue multiple warnings that if unheeded would (at most) result in citations for disturbing the peace. And attempts would be made to correct the issues with the utilities. That's how it *should have* been handled. But, that's not what happened. The back and forth went on for years. And during that time, MOVE was quietly acquiring firearms. Lots of firearms. We all knew there would be a reckoning someday.

What follows is my account of how I experienced the events that occurred on that day—August 8, 1978—one of the darkest days of my career and of the City of Philadelphia and its police and fire departments. That was the day it became the City versus MOVE. It would not end well for either side.

On the morning of August 8, 1978, the city showed up at the house at 33rd and Pearl Streets to serve arrest warrants and to enforce a court order.

What I know of the department's strategy for arresting the MOVE offenders and evicting the rest is that it's anything but a solid plan. We'll show up, announce ourselves, and then what? No chance they would just come out with their hands up, saying, "Hey man, no problem, we were just kidding…"

We—I and hundreds of other cops, arriving here before dawn on what was already a steaming hot August day—were set up in concentric perimeters, moving outward from the MOVE property to the barricaded outer limits where the reporters and crowds of thrill-seeking onlookers were gathered. We were scattered in the area, standing by. Those were our orders: Just stand by. It would turn out that the planning for the city's annual Mummers New Year's Day Parade (a shitshow on a *good* day) was light years ahead of this deal.

Now I stand stunned and unnerved as the last of the cat-rats scurry away, some into nearby basements as the neighbors could only watch. Some tried to shoo them with brooms and other tools, a useless exercise. These guys are looking for a new home and they like the neighborhood.

Standing in the filthy alley behind the MOVE house, I'm acutely aware that it stinks really bad back here!! The hot air is heavy with terrible smells, human and otherwise. These MOVE folks would do better on a farm, where composting in vast quantities is encouraged and useful. No wonder there are so many rats. I can't imagine what it's like inside. I'd heard that an anonymous sympathizer had actually offered a large farm to the group, no charge, which they had strongly rejected.

"That was gunfire, Tom," I say to my partner. He nods, eyes darting. The echoing sound of the shots makes it hard to fix the location, but it's close. About ten yards away from where we are standing by the backyard of the MOVE house, I see a SWAT officer pop up in the second-floor window of the abandoned house facing the action. He's hauling up a rifle, shouting at us to get down. Get down? Is he kidding? We're in a shit-littered alley next to a splintering wooden fence that is probably a hundred years old and is more down than up. My partner and I hunch down and scoot to a nearby cinderblock wall and wait, guns in hand. Now, it's important to know these are the days way before the Philly PD went to semi-automatic pistols. So when I say guns, I mean revolvers, only six-shooters, even though the gunshots I was hearing from inside the MOVE house were from automatic weapons.

It's like a goddam war back here! The shots are all around us. The damn MOVE guys are actually shooting at our guys and the cops are shooting back! Is it coming from the front of the house? Can't tell. I'm watching the SWAT guy to see what he does. He's got his rifle ready, but he doesn't fire. I'm praying the bad guys don't decide to escape through the back and come our way. If that happens, Tom and I are in deep shit. So many shots; it seems like the battle is taking forever.

Then it's over. Supervisors suddenly appear and shout orders to regroup on the far side of the street, down the street from the front of the property. Grim faces tell me what I suspected—we have casualties. One officer is dead, and more than a dozen others—cops and firefighters—have been struck in the hail of bullets.

Then…*what's that smell? Familiar*. Suddenly, I get it. In the eyes, the nose, the throat. Tear gas. It was coming right at us. No one had checked the wind! None of us has a mask. *Some plan!*

As I recall my own experience with the gas from my Army days, a WWI image hits me as a line from a Wilfred Owen poem: "Gas! Gas! Quick, boys! – an ecstasy of fumbling…" (Some things haven't changed much since 1918.)

Painfully slow, the air clears. Through the hazy residue, I'm coughing as I watch the blurred strobes of the fire rescue and police vans as the casualties are taken away. I am numb as the sirens fade.

Leaning against a patrol car, listening to the bosses, I realize that this thing *is not* over. The MOVE members are still inside. There's no way we're leaving here until they're all removed and locked up. Or dead. Besides, the mayor has a plan.

The next few hours grind by. SWAT teams move in and, one by one, the radicals are arrested and brought out. Finally, the last and the biggest loudmouth surrenders, holding a baby as a shield. Even so, he screams obscenities as he strolls slowly and defiantly across the filthy front yard of the once grand, now infamous, MOVE house.

While this is going on, about 20-30 captive dogs see their chance to escape the house. All types and sizes, their flight is frantic as if someone might catch them and put them back into that hellhole. I wish I could grab them all and take them home; make them know that everything is okay. I think they know it's not.

Once we know that the house is finally empty, I relax, just a little. About an hour later, I see the cranes, bulldozers, and dump trucks rumbling up the street in formation. Now, I get the mayor's plan: We will take this building down and remove all traces of the evil that occupied it. By the time I report off duty much later that night, all that remains of the place is the raked-over dirt of a vacant lot. As if doing that really changed anything.

For me, the memories persist.

It is sad that the proper lessons were not learned on that terrible day. None of us could have imagined how relatively mild the horror of August 8, 1978, would be compared with the city's next battle with MOVE, seven years later. And the City of Brotherly Love will bear the burning scars forever.

Getting There

It was about that time. I would hear him before he arrived. The white Harley pulled up in front of our store and there he was: the biggest policeman I'd ever seen. Not just tall—huge. He stopped in about once a month, filling the doorway as he entered, and all he wanted was…to look at the comic books. He knew when the new shipment would arrive, refreshing our large selection. He always came in uniform and on his motorcycle. (I don't think I'd have recognized him in civilian clothes.) I was only nine or ten when I first saw him. Dad loved him coming in; he said it made him feel safe.

I would quietly and slowly walk around him, checking him out while he perused the comics, careful not to get too close. I'd study him like he was a strongman superhero come-to-life out of one of the comic books and when he would occasionally catch me, he'd just smile. I remember his gun, dull wood and shiny steel. I had never seen one before (well, other than on *Gunsmoke* and such). And all those bullets on his belt. Wow! His leather gear was always shiny, especially his boots, and you always heard creaking when he moved.

I never got up the nerve to ask, "Hey Officer, did you ever shoot anybody?" even though I considered it every single time I saw him. And here he was, a customer in our store! I never thought about the obvious paradox—what's a giant cop doing looking at comic books?— until years later.

When he was finished, he would bring about a dozen comics to the counter to buy. I can't say for sure, but I think he liked mystery and action ones like *Superman*. I didn't pay attention to the titles because I was too busy stealing looks at him—his badge, his handcuffs, that white helmet. I would sometimes follow him outside to his bike and watch as he opened the storage compartment and threw the books inside, slamming it shut quickly as he watched me watch him.

"Can I see inside?" I once asked him.

"No, son," he said with that smile. "That's secret police stuff in there." I know now that it wasn't, but we both liked the mystique he created for me.

On the job years later, I ran into a cop outside a courtroom in City Hall. I did a double-take because he looked just like my comic-book-buying motorcycle cop, only about 25 years younger. The resemblance was so remarkable that I walked up to him and asked him if he had a dad on the job. "Yeah. He was with the Motor Bandit Squad." (An elite unit, their job was to look for stolen cars and respond to crimes in progress.) I told him who I was and about the store and my memories of his dad and the comics. He broke into a great big smile and said, "I always wondered where he got them! I asked, but he never told me." *More secrets.*

"How is he?" I asked, holding my breath, a little afraid of what the answer might be.

"Great. He's been retired for about 15 years now and still reading those damn comic books."

"Please tell him Nick's son asked about him." He said that he would.

⚊⚊⚊•◉•⚊⚊⚊

I was never one of those boys who had a career plan. Not one who wanted to be a fireman or a cop or lawyer or doctor since he was five. Nope. Year to year, the plan was always for that day, and always the same: go to school; get the best grades; work in the family store. Once I got to high school, I started thinking about what I would do next—after college, that is. Not optional, that.

Now, it's important to know that my parents didn't have a career plan for me either. They were born in a small island village in Greece and neither went past the 6th grade. For them, work was what your parents said it was, and for Dad in that village, that meant going neighborhood to neighborhood with their old, worn-out donkey, *Palia*, who was loaded down with household goods and some foods. My dad, like his father, was a peddler. So, it made sense that he would do the same when he came to the states: open a variety store. The only difference (besides not having Palia) was that the customers came to him, which he loved. Mom, like most girls there, was taught that it was *her job* to find and marry a good man.

Later, I was Mom's main interpreter and her favorite child (at least I thought so), and we would sometimes have heart-to-heart talks when we were out, usually grocery shopping or looking for bargains in the center city department stores like Gimbels, Lit Brothers, and Strawbridge's.

Riding on The El train on our way downtown, I mentioned to my mother that I might want to become a lawyer. It seemed honorable and a way to earn a good living, I thought. Before saying anything, she faced me and taking hold of my hand said, "OXI!"["NO!"] I looked at her, very surprised. I thought she'd be happy that I would be so ambitious. Instead, her face dropped and she just sat there and shook her head. I said nothing more about it then.

After a few days, I asked Mom about it, still not knowing what caused her reaction to my comment. She looked into my eyes and said, "Strataki, lawyers are liars. I don't want you to become a liar." Disappointed with this assessment and that I probably wouldn't be going to law school, I just walked away.

For days I was angry, and nobody, not even Mom, knew why. After all, I had shared and she had ruled. Done. That's how it was. I just stewed and thought about it and then let it go. After all, I was just a high school junior; I had time.

In my senior year, I had made up my mind: I would become a doctor.

After planning the timing, I again tested the parental-approval-of-my-career waters as my mother and I were walking to the grocery store on a rainy Saturday morning. Once more, a horrified reaction. Shaking her head and in her perfect Greek, she said, *What if you kill somebody?"*

What??? Again, I had not expected that response and had nothing to say in reply.

There were no more discussions of career plans. But I had to figure this out.

In time, it came to me: all their lives, my parents were focused on doing what they were told and what they knew. This was just ignorance about the opportunities that were available to me and their beliefs about some lawyers and doctors. Not valid in my vision, but it was their reality.

But I still thought, *What will I do?* Thankfully, my school had a co-op program which placed seniors with local businesses. So in my senior year, I was able to get a job as a messenger with a large advertising firm.

Eventually, this led to a position at a local Sears, working in the Customer Service Department. It was okay. But, no problem, I would go to college soon and see where that led.

High School graduation: a happy day for all of us. My parents' joy was based on my grades and awards; they were so proud. Mine was just looking to the next part of my life.

At Sears, I settled into a work routine. I liked being a problem-solver, which is what the job description was—Customer Service. Mom and Dad were happy. In their eyes, I was already a success.

I started college soon after and, without a car, I took a train, two buses, and then walked nearly a mile three days a week to get to the remote Penn State campus in Abington, a northern suburb of Philadelphia. I didn't mind; I knew this was just part of the necessary stuff at the beginning of the journey that would take me to my career, whatever it was going to be.

All along, my folks were proud. This was familiar territory for them: I go to school, do my homework, study, and get good grades. We were all rolling along.

I should mention here that I always sucked at science courses. Capital "S." Nevertheless, I had to take at least one science course in my first two years, so I picked chemistry. I still scratch my head over that decision, but in my defense, at the time it seemed to be the least formidable. It all started out okay, but quickly went bad. I struggled to understand and fell way behind. The professor was no help: "This is college, son, not high school. Just do the work." I flunked the course. I had a hard time approaching my folks about this. It was a big deal and I knew they'd be disappointed. I sure was.

When I told them, they let me know how unhappy they were. Neither I nor my brothers had *ever* failed a course. It was a disappointment for us all, but no one asked me how I felt.

The following week, I signed up to take a biology course with thoughts about that medical career I was still considering. I would do things differently this time; I'd get ahead of the coursework and, if necessary, find a tutor.

Not so fast, pal…

This was 1966. There was this place called *Vietnam*.

One of the conditions for an educational deferment from the military draft at the time was passing all courses. Fail even one and Uncle Sam wanted you—now.

I didn't have to wait long to find out how bad my Uncle wanted me. The letter, also known as "Greetings," arrived within three weeks. Funny how efficient bureaucracies can sometimes be!

Within two months, I was on a train to Columbia, South Carolina, and to Fort Jackson for boot camp, the US Army's Basic Training. Small comfort, but there were several hundred other guys there who looked like I felt—lost and scared to death. The ordeal of basic was about two months, but felt *much* longer.

Of course, I survived. I even felt good about myself, having gone through eight weeks of psychological torment and physical hell. Little did I know basic had been just the introduction. More fun was still ahead.

After Basic, I was sent to Fort Hood, Texas, for A.I.T. (Advanced Individual Training). Like the other soldiers, I was assigned to training for a job that allegedly matched the results of my aptitude test. Imagine my surprise: Military Policeman. *What?*

"There must be some mistake," I explained to the intake sergeant as soon as I arrived at Fort Hood. He just stared at me with a look that said that the mistake was me bothering him with bullshit.

So, I became a military policeman, learning all there was to know in eight weeks. Our drill instructor was Sergeant Hodges (first name not available to us), a former member of the Old Guard, the select few who protected the Tomb of the Unknown Soldier. He could have been on a poster for the Army, one of the people in your life you don't forget. He was tough; he also made us into good M.P.s.

During our training, we all kind of ignored the elephant in the room: we were being prepared to go to Vietnam. As young 20-somethings, we knew it and were not happy about the prospect, but we dealt with it and got ready. Then we learned that M.P.s, whose duties included organizing convoys, troop transports, and security for the bases, were among the favorite targets of the enemy. Not great news.

I learned patrol work. On the base, we patrolled in jeeps in the remote wooded areas and pulled gate duty. In Killeen, just outside the gates of Fort Hood, a pair of us drove the streets of the town in a brown army sedan marked with "Military Police" decals and what we called a red bubble gum machine rotating light on top. Our job was to look for soldiers in trouble or causing trouble in places like bus stations, bars, and restaurants.

Fortunately, my number to travel to Vietnam was never called, so I remained stateside for my entire tenure. Not so for so many of my friends and colleagues in the 518th M.P. Battalion. I still wonder how they made out.

About seven months before my required time was up, our commanding officer called us together and announced that we might be eligible for a six-month early-out of the army. He had our attention. "Because so many young men are committed to the military, the pool of police officer candidates is very low in many cities and towns. So, if you are interested in joining the police department in your hometown, you may be eligible. Let me know and we'll see about getting you there." Before leaving, he added, "You will need to commit to the police force for at least three years in order to get the early discharge."

No thanks, not for me, I said to myself. I never thought about it again. After all, I wasn't crazy about the structured life of the army or the lousy hours, and thought that law enforcement would be more of the same. Besides, I had a good job at Sears waiting for me back home.

My time in the Army, while sometimes challenging, was, overall, a positive and life-changing experience. It helped me learn self-reliance, discipline, and teamwork. I still miss many of my fellow soldiers.

In August of 1968 I returned to Philadelphia and civilian life, including my position at Sears. My old job was not available, so they offered me one selling floor coverings, promising me more earning potential, commission and all that. I took it.

One of my fellow salesmen was Dave Timmons, and we became friends right away. Dave was about my age, highly energetic and always ready with a good joke. I soon figured out that he wasn't a great salesman. After a couple of beers with him one Friday afternoon after work, I learned why. He wasn't really interested in sales. Never had been. But he had a family and needed a job. "I *really* want to be a cop," he said. I could feel it. When I started to tell him about my Army M.P. experience, he put down his beer and moved closer.

"*That's* what I'm talking about, Strati!" he said. "I want to join the Philly P.D."

"Good for you, Dave," I replied, toasting him with my beer. "Sounds like a plan. Good luck."

That's how it started.

After that, about three times a week, Dave asked me to go take the police test with him. Sometimes he begged. Even after I had told him about my not-so-fun M.P. experiences.

"No, Dave, not for me," I would tell him over and over again. But he persisted.

"Come on, man, just go with me. We can do it on our lunch hour. Don't you want to get away from Andy?"

Hmmm. Our pain-in-the-ass boss, Andy, huh?

In those days, because of the war, the city was so strapped for cops, they would give the test almost daily. Those who passed and met all the other requirements—background check, physical and psychological exams— could be sitting in a police academy class within months.

Dave kept after me and I kept saying no.

Until one day when the boss outdid himself and ranted at all of us because our sales numbers were down. He did this publicly and so loudly, I was embarrassed. And he was yelling as some of us were with customers and in the middle of writing up some decent sales. Our customers looked at him, then at us and some of them walked.

As bad as it was, this worked in Dave's favor. I was so pissed and disillusioned that, later that day, I told him I'd go with him to take the test. I thought he might kiss me.

Five days later, with the boss off, we took an extended lunch and he drove us to the Municipal Services Building, across from City Hall, in downtown Philadelphia. When we walked into the testing room and signed in, I noticed that there were only three other guys there.

I finished the exam in about 20 minutes and took my booklet to be scored. They asked if I was a veteran and I said yes. They added 10 points to my score, giving me 108. The clerk congratulated me and told me I would be hearing from the Police Department in about a week. I just looked at her. *What the hell did I just do?* I thought to myself and went outside to wait for Dave. He, too, had scored high on the test.

After much thought and internal debate, I accepted the city's offer. On June 21, 1971, I entered the Philadelphia Police Academy for recruit training.

Dave wasn't there; he didn't make it past the background check. Something about some minor trouble he'd been in when he was a juvenile. The detectives told him they had to check it out further.

Great. The guy who wanted this so bad, who pushed *me* to apply, didn't get it. And I, the one who did it for all the wrong reasons, was sitting there, embarking on a career I'd never dreamed of. Thanks, Dave.

Sitting there in the academy classroom, another thought hit me, hard: three years prior, I had dismissed the early-out option the Army had offered. "No way. Not for me. Are you kidding?" I had said. Oh really? *You dope.*

As I sat waiting for the orientation to begin, I wondered what my parents really thought about all of this. They were worried, sure, but weren't saying much. All they'd said was that they thought that Sears was a good place to work.

I wondered what they thought about lawyers and doctors now.

⟶•●•⟵

Dave's background issues were resolved quickly and, within a year, he was hired. He became a great cop. In a few short years, all that becoming-a-cop desire resulted in Dave's promotion to Police Detective, a position in which he exceled.

Lessons Learned

During our last week at the Police Academy, we were given one of the most important—and jolting—lessons of all. It came from one of my favorite academy instructors: "You new officers don't *really* know *anything* about police work." The statement wasn't made with the arrogance of a veteran talking down to rookies. It felt more like a heads-up. I remember sitting up straighter in my chair, listening. The instructor looked just over forty, with military-cut brown hair. His dark blue eyes seemed to intensify as he spoke. His crisp uniform and posture reminded me of drill instructors I'd had in the army.

Physically, he was in pretty good shape, considering all his years working in the cold weather, getting in and out of squad cars, standing on parade lines in every kind of weather, mixing it up with drunks and cop-fighters and those who didn't agree with him that they were under arrest.

My classmates and I had been sitting in these same rooms, in these same chairs, for so many days and weeks, listening and learning what we thought was all we needed to get out there and do the job. We were *really* looking forward to graduation day and to finally being street cops. And here was our instructor telling us…what? It had been a waste of time?

"When you get to your districts next week, that's when the real training and learning starts," Officer Harry Jackson said with a slight but knowing smile. "The guys you'll be working with, the veterans, they're the ones who'll give you a lot of what you need." Jackson had been an instructor for just a couple of years. Before that, he had spent twenty plus years on patrol, accumulating the experiences he'd been sharing with us. He went on: "God gave you two ears and one mouth." We nodded, having heard this proverb from him dozens of times before. Somebody in the back of the room finished it: "We know, sir. You need to listen twice as much as you talk."

Jackson nodded in agreement. "You're all sponges, remember that—sponges," he said, moving out from behind the old, scarred wooden podium with the large Philadelphia PD decal on the front. He stood there looking around making sure he had everyone's attention.

Agreeing to share his knowledge and experience with raw police recruits wasn't at the top of Harry's to-do list. He had a reputation as a great cop, but he preferred working alone. He wasn't one of those guys who liked to tell other cops how to do the job. But he was always there to provide back-up and to help. On the job, his reputation was golden and everyone knew he was a dedicated family man, a straight-home-after-work guy. Veterans who'd worked with Harry all told the same story: "He could be the poster boy for police officers." Everybody liked him, even the bad guys—by all reports, they respected him, too.

So, when he talked to us about being new street cops, we listened. We asked questions. And we listened to his answers. It turned out that Harry was a pretty good instructor, I would even say great. He had not sought the position for status or as alternative to patrol time, but simply because he *cared* and wanted to share what he'd learned. And he was a natural.

Quickly taking to his new role as teacher, he regularly shared with us the hard and sometimes scary lessons he'd learned over more than two decades on the Philly streets.

During the months of our training, Harry Jackson had been one of our lead instructors, teaching us about the Pennsylvania Crimes Code, Report Writing and Patrol Procedures and Practices. For police recruits, the latter was like taking a peek through a curtain at the strange and ugly side of society, something most people never see. Not given to regale us with "war stories," he would share his real-life experiences only to illustrate a point or principle, such as how to approach a vehicle you'd stopped. He also shared what he'd learned about reading a person's body language. Always well-prepared in his lessons, he focused more on the safety and policy-following side of handling situations than on the tough guy method. "Consider this," he said, pausing to look at each one of us to be sure he had our attention. "Every time you—a uniformed police officer in a marked vehicle – approach a driver or occupant of a car or a pedestrian, or step into someone's home, one thing is *always* for sure: they know who you are, but you know nothing or next to nothing about them."

Wow, I thought. *Hadn't even thought about that.*

One of my most memorable "Harry lessons" had nothing to do with arresting bad guys or heroic actions. "Remember, people are always looking at you, always watching," he'd said one afternoon, talking about how he thought cops should conduct themselves. "Your appearance is the start of it. If you look good, you feel good; if you feel good, you act professionally. People notice that, they respond to that." He continued, "Always try to do things the right way—not just the way you learned, and not always the way somebody else does it, but the way *you* know is right. It may sound trite, but those few words formed the basis of my approach to my new profession and my new world. "You never know who you're talking to," he reminded us, "so talk to everyone the right way, with courtesy and respect."

Harry was the one who taught me the importance of proper documentation. "The report you write today may not go past the corporal in your own district. But it *might*. You can never be sure if an incident report you wrote might end up on the Captain's or even the Commissioner's desk. Or it could lead to an arrest and be part of court proceedings read by prosecutors and defense lawyers and maybe even a judge." He stood there looking out at us, letting the words sink in.

During our time together, he emphasized this point again and again. "Your report is a reflection of you. How do you want to be seen?" Then, "How will you be seen?" He cemented this with the following: "Imagine that you were one of the two Phoenix Arizona police officers who arrested a male for rape and kidnapping in 1963. The guy's name was Ernesto Miranda." Again, he paused for effect. "Sound familiar? Pretty sure those officers never expected what the case would become. But today, we know that Miranda's arrest led to one of the most significant landmark cases in history. Will your report stand up to that kind of scrutiny?"

I promised myself that mine would.

Harry Jackson worried about us. I could tell. We watched movies about cops making car stops, cops investigating burglaries, and cops responding to domestic disturbances. Though the films were dated and the actors were not movie stars, the scenes were based on real incidents. The potential for danger was everywhere, we learned, and *anyone* could be a threat. For example:

Respond to a call for an abusive husband where a bruised and hysterical wife wants him arrested; go to lock him up, and you may end up fighting both of them. I learned first-hand that this happens all the time.

Or this: You stop a car for a minor traffic violation and come face to face with a desperate individual who has just robbed a bank or shot someone. He thinks you know this, and that's why you're stopping him.

Or you approach a teenager who's hanging around on a corner to give him some friendly advice about the risks of being in an area known for drug activity, only to be confronted with a gun pointed your way by a scared kid who's been watching too much television.

Great lessons, all of them. But Harry was right when he told us what little we still knew during that last week in the classroom. It was true—we had no context. There's no way we could have expected or even imagined what any of these situations would be like for us when they happened for real.

We had no way of knowing what we would face starting the day after graduation. They say that somewhere between his academy training and completing the first year of duty comes that moment when each policeman knows in his heart if he's going to be able to do the job. It's inside that first year that he will experience so much of the anger, frustration, evil, and violence that are part of a cop's everyday world. We didn't know that yet. How could we? Even Harry couldn't teach us that.

He once told us, "Guys, people call the cops when they don't know who else to call." It didn't take me long to find out how right he was.

So, on a late June morning, it finally arrived: Graduation Day. In the Academy gymnasium/auditorium, I, along with my twenty-eight classmates, received a diploma and a handshake from the Police Commissioner. As I left the stage, I saw Harry Jackson standing in the rear of the auditorium, watching. He was in his dress uniform, looking sharp and proud. Afterward, I went to thank him and say goodbye. He shook my hand and congratulated me. Then he told me to be careful and to be the best cop I could be. I felt his sincerity in that handshake. I still remember that. Before I walked away, he looked into my eyes and said: "Officer, never forget you were a civilian before you became a cop."

And I never did.

As I left the Academy building on that last day, I wasn't sure about what would happen, how I would do. Didn't know much about anything, I realized. But what I *did* know was that I would try to do my best, and that Harry Jackson's words would help with that. I also remember thinking that, if it were possible sometime, years from then, I would like to be an academy instructor – to try to help recruit officers get ready for their turn to serve and protect. That is, if I was, in my mind, good enough. Like Harry.

I hit the streets, working in the 26th District, a busy, busy place; a good place to learn. The veterans, every one of them, had something to teach in his own way. I listened and watched, keeping my mouth closed (most of the time). And I learned.

I would see Harry from time to time. Sometimes, he'd ask me about the job and how I was doing. I thought he was making conversation and being polite. He was. But I also realized that he was keeping in touch with the streets. He wanted to know how things had changed since the days when he was on patrol. He wanted to know the latest information and new trends about crime and criminals from out there, so he could better prepare his lessons for the new cops.

Ten years later, I stood quietly in the front of classroom A and looked around, waiting. In a few minutes, I'd present my first lesson as a Philadelphia Police Academy Instructor. The subject: Patrol Procedures. I saw the wide-eyed faces of the newest police academy recruits looking back at me as they took their seats.

I ran the lesson plan through my mind one more time and remembered Officer Harry Jackson. I was ready.

Shifts

Soon after becoming a cop, my brain changed. I learned to pay attention and to think differently. Some things that weren't important before, now were. I needed a new perspective; to realize that *everything* mattered. It took me a while to make the mental transition to life as a cop. It didn't happen in an instant like some *ah-ha!* moment; it was a series of profound and permanent shifts.

Out of the academy just a couple of weeks, I was riding with the veteran, Ike, when a call for gunshots in a nearby apartment building came out. He was driving, so I was in charge of the radio. I didn't hear the call. They were calling our car number, but I was clueless. As a brand-new rookie, the radio chatter was confusing to me, nothing but noise. All I heard were car numbers and street addresses jumbled and blended together, hard to make out. In time, I'd learn how to listen right.

"Put us in on that," said Ike.

"What?" I said, looking over at him.

"The call they just gave us. Just say '2614, we got it' and that's it." I did that, still not knowing where we were going or what the assignment was.

How come I didn't hear that? I asked myself. *This guy is driving* and *paying attention to the radio. I'm just a slug.*

Ike made a screeching U-turn on Columbia Avenue, then sped west. I heard another car (2616) come on. "2616, I'm in on the gunshots." As the dispatcher acknowledged him, I looked over at Ike who was concentrating as he zoomed through the narrow, crowded streets, siren howling.

"Ike, where're we going?"

"Skoufalos, we got a job. Didn't you hear them call us?"

"I answered the call. But, no, I didn't hear what it was. You're telling me we got the job '16's going to?" *We're racing to where people are shooting?* I thought, sitting up straighter.

He looked at me. "Yeah."

"Why?"

Getting it now, he said quietly, "That's what we do."

Feeling like an ass, I mumbled, "Yeah." *What was I thinking? Or not?* Still using my civilian brain.

The call was unfounded. As we sat there and I wrote the report, we weren't talking. I felt like a total loser, wondering what Ike must be thinking. I didn't know what to say. He did. "Skoufalos, you've been on the job, what, about ten days now? The Academy don't count, that's just class work."

I nodded, still not looking at him. "But I…."

He put up a hand, stopping me. "Just listen, okay?"

Another nod.

"Was that your first 'gunshots' call?" he asked.

"Yeah," I said in my smallest voice.

"Think you're the first cop who did that? Had to make the adjustment? No. We all do it. Hell, *I* did too. You'll be fine. You'll see."

Of course he's right, he has to be, I said to myself. But, as we rode around, I wasn't sure I believed that. I kept thinking about it. It wasn't logical. It still seemed counterintuitive for me to race to a place where people were shooting. But in some deep down, still-strange place, I knew that doing those kinds of things was my job now, my new reality. Later that shift, we got a call for a man with a gun and this one was founded. We got there first and arrested the guy. Frisking him, I found a loaded revolver in his coat pocket. My first pinch. I did okay and I could tell Ike thought so too. I was gonna be fine.

Ike and I worked together a lot my first year. And we talked a lot. About the job and, in time, about him growing up in a neighborhood much like the one we patrolled. Riding around, he told me and showed me a lot of good stuff I could use, stuff that made me a better street cop. Like how some bad guys act when the cops ride by, and why a good way to get along is to make friends with the neighborhood. He taught me how to look at people, watch their hands, their eyes, their body language. He kept telling me how important it was to be as safe as I could, all the time, not just when the call was dangerous.

I listened and learned. I never forgot that first call for gunshots, or one of the first things Ike told me about being a street cop: "Remember, you're in uniform, in a marked car with lights on top. People always know who you are. But you can't tell jack about them." My academy instructor Harry Jackson's words came back to me.

There were other cops, in those early days, who taught me things I'd need. I appreciated it, very clear that they all knew more than I did. One of them was Rob, a ten-year veteran who liked to make a lot of car stops. He told me he could sense if a car or driver were "wrong." Most of the time, he could. After a while, I learned what to look for. He was a high-energy guy, always looking around, talking a mile a minute, going in on calls all over the place, even when they weren't our jobs. I liked that; I liked being busy.

Officer safety was big with Rob. One of the things I learned from him was that you *always* let Radio know when you were making a car stop—or were out of the car for any reason. Sure, our academy instructors had hammered the same thing into us, but in reality, it didn't always happen. Cops had handy excuses like, "Radio was busy" or "The car was trying to leave." It was true that sometimes things happened so fast that notifying the dispatcher wasn't always possible, but we all knew we were taking a chance every time we didn't call it in. Hell, we took a chance every time we stopped anyone for anything.

Anyway, I noticed that whenever we made a car stop, Rob wrote the tag number on the border of the "hot sheet," the daily listing of stolen and wanted cars. Before getting out, one of us would check the sheet to see if our pulled-over car was on it. That way, if the car got away or if something happened to one of us, we'd have the tag number. Funny how things don't always work out the way you plan, even when you try to do everything right.

It was about 9:00 p.m. on a busy Friday. It was a nice fall evening and there were lots of people outdoors. And lots of cars. As we drove around our Emergency Patrol Wagon's three-sector area, Rob and I were discussing the Eagles and their chances that year. Suddenly, he stopped talking, mid-sentence, and picked up the hot sheet, checking the car we were driving behind. "These guys are bad. I'm gonna stop them," he said, focusing, his usual smile gone. I could see two occupants in the front seat. I had the mike in my hand, trying to tell Radio we were making the stop, but the air was too busy; I couldn't get through. As he pulled them over, Rob sensed something was up and started getting out, but the two guys were thinking way ahead of us. They had already jumped out of the car and, without looking back, took off west on Master Street from Franklin. Rob took off after them. I jumped behind the wheel and tried to keep track of where they were heading. Then I couldn't see Rob anymore. "2603, priority." The words and my louder-than-usual voice commanded immediate silence on the radio.

"Go ahead, 0-3."

"My partner's in foot pursuit of two males, last seen west on Master from Franklin." I was talking fast. After giving their descriptions, I slowly drove around, every sense on high alert. I had lost my partner.

Calm down. Figure this out. You're gonna find him! I was trying to believe it.

"2603, reason for pursuit?"

"Possible stolen car. We were gonna pull 'em over and they bailed." I said, telling them the description of the car and the suspects and where we'd tried to make the stop. Another unit got on the air and said he was heading our way. Every other available car in the district started over to help find Rob and, if we were lucky, the two runners.

Crawling along, working the wagon's spotlight, I noticed a small group of people standing on the sidewalk in the middle of the 900 block of Master, the general direction I'd seen Rob headed. As I got closer, I saw that they were looking my way. *Could be something*…I notified Radio, pulled up and got out.

Like in many inner-city neighborhoods, the police weren't the most popular folks on the west side of the 26th District. I still had to try. Putting on my best "nice guy" look, I walked up. "Hi folks, did anybody see a cop come running this way?" Figuring it might help, I added, "He's a pretty big Black cop." I didn't expect an answer. I didn't get one. Some of the people glanced my way; most of them just walked away. Nothing like a cop to make a group of citizens disappear. I stood there looking around, thinking, trying to figure out which way Rob had gone. I had no idea.

I called in an update, advising Radio of my current location and that I was still trying to locate my partner. The dispatcher confirmed what Rob had suspected: the car was stolen. Other cops started showing up. I listened as the cars chirped their sirens and came up the street, tires squealing. I grabbed my flashlight and a few of us headed into the alley, which was pitch-black and filled with tons of garbage, filth, and piles of what was probably dog shit. Another group headed to the other end. We slogged through the trash as fast as we could, flashlights going back and forth. We kept calling out for Rob and finally got an answer about a third of the way through that dark, disgusting obstacle course.

After a few anxious minutes, we found Rob. He was in the yard of an abandoned house. He had caught up to one of the guys (turned out it was the driver of the car) who was nearby, cuffed, and on the ground. Rob was leaning against the building's half-demolished wall, bent over, out of breath. Of course, none of the alley lights were working, so I used my Maglite to give my partner a once-over. Other than his muddy, torn pants and filth-caked shoes, he looked okay.

"You all right, man?" I asked him.

He nodded. "Car stolen?" he asked, breathing heavily.

"Yeah. Rob, what about the other guy?" I asked. "He around here?"

Shaking his head, he told us, between short puffs, that the two guys had split up and he'd gone after the driver. Smart. If he'd caught the passenger, the guy could say he didn't know the car was stolen. The driver couldn't really use that excuse.

Two of the cops with me were a wagon crew; they pulled up the prisoner by the arms, stood him up, frisked him, and started walking him back to their van. "We'll take this guy up to Front and Westmoreland [East Detectives] for you. And we'll make sure the stolen car gets to headquarters, okay?"

Before heading to East, ignoring Rob's protests, I drove us to St. Luke's Hospital ER. I told him he should get cleaned up before heading to the detectives for the tons of paperwork we had to do. But I really wanted to get him checked out by the staff. He was okay.

We finally made it to East and were met by Lieutenant Andy Jenkins, a no-nonsense cop and a good boss. Too many guys who got promoted forgot where they came from. Jenkins never did. "Gentlemen, about time you got here," he said to us with his trademark straight-faced look, and acting all annoyed. "Hey Detective Alvarez, your two cops are finally here!" Joe Alvarez, a detective for just a couple of years, was going along with the gag, sitting at his desk, arms folded, with the blank arrest report sitting in the old manual Smith-Corona. Like he'd been waiting hours for us to show up. Once I got it, we all had a chuckle, then Rob and I got a coffee and sat down with Alvarez.

Before we got there, the detective had interviewed our prisoner and run him through NCIC, the national crime information database. He was only 23 but was a pretty bad dude; he already had a string of felony convictions. The car they had been driving was not only stolen, it had been used in a robbery earlier that day. The prisoner wasn't talking, denying he'd even been in the car we stopped.

Using the "you're-in-deep-shit-here-kid-so-you'd-better-help-us-find-your-partner" approach, Alvarez eventually wore the guy down, made him see the light. What finally did it was the detective telling him that if we didn't catch his partner, *he* was going to be pinned for everything: the car, the robbery, the attempted escape from law officers–everything, all by himself. Scared, he gave up his buddy. That's how it worked.

At the District, the wagon crew, did an inventory of the stolen-recovered car and found a little piece-of-crap gun under the front seat. Probably the one used in the robbery. All in all, a good day's work.

Even so, after reporting off duty, and on the drive home, I replayed the whole scenario. Rob's good work habits not only led to the arrests of these two bad guys, he had kept us safe.

Still a relative rookie, I realized that in this new world of policing I'd entered, there were new rules—lots of them—and if I wanted to survive, I needed to learn them all as quickly as I could. That day's lessons: look out for your partner and your other colleagues; never give up; and, whenever you could, do your best to engage with the community.

For, as I learned along the way to a meaningful police career, the folks in the neighborhoods really do care about their cops, so long as the care is mutual.

Street Smarts

It was a quiet Thursday morning, and I was just rolling around my sector. As I pulled over to update my patrol log, the piercing *whoop-whoop* of a siren and the sound of an accelerating car came from a couple blocks over—sounded like American Street. I hadn't heard any priority calls come out so I headed that way to see what was going on. Turning the corner, I caught the tail end of 265 car, emergency lights flashing and siren still blaring. *Ah, it's Frank*, I said to myself. I honked and sped up to catch him; he pulled over, turned off the siren and lights and sat there.

Frank Monroe was the squad's practical joker. He was always looking for new ways to lighten things up, especially when it was slow with few calls for police service, which was rare in the 26th District, one of the busiest in the City of Brotherly Love.

U-turning the squad car, I stopped so we were drivers' window to window. "What's up?" I asked.

"Nothing, just fooling around."

"Whaddya mean?"

His face lit up in a big smile as he thought about it. "Joe Gall," he said, pointing back the way he'd come. I looked back and saw another police car sitting at the curb.

Joe was one of our squad's old-timers. He'd been a cop in the 26th for his whole career—more than 25 years. He was low-key and every time I looked at him I thought of Barney Fife from *The Andy Griffith Show*: thin, a little nervous, and always hitching up his pants where the gun belt weighed it down. But, unlike Barney, he wasn't always out looking for something, letting his imagination get him into trouble. Quite the contrary; he liked to park and wait for calls. And he always seemed to park in the same spot:

the 1500 block of American Street. So I was curious what Joe Gall had to do with Frank's high-visibility driving. "What about Joe Gall?" I asked.

"Wanted to see if he was paying attention. When I rode by, he was sittin' behind the *Daily News*, not even looking."

Frank shook his head at my puzzled look. He leaned out of the car window toward me and said, "So I put on my lights and siren and zoomed by him." I still didn't get it. "Strati, don't ya see? I wanted him to think something was going on, that he had missed a call."

"Really?" I asked. "Does that work? Joe's been around a while."

"Yeah, he has, but he's not always payin' attention to the radio, so…"

Shaking my head, I smiled at his thinking. "You're crazy," I said, getting ready to leave.

He bellowed his deep, hearty laugh. "Wait – listen," he said, leaning further out of the car window. "I've done this with him a couple of times before, so last week, he tried to pull the same thing on me, right? I was sitting down on Jefferson finishing up a report when he drove by me with his strobes on, going about ten miles an hour. And he was looking over at me, nodding and grinning, like he was sayin' *'gotcha!'*"

Smiling, I tried to picture the scene: Joe getting even with Frank, using his own slow- motion version of Frank's gag. Except that in all my years in the 26th, I'd never seen Joe Gall drive faster than 20 miles an hour. And he *never* used his siren. Now I laughed as I imagined our very own Barney Fife trying to match wits with a world-class jokester.

I put the car in gear and started pulling away when Frank yelled, "Hey Strati, wait up. Let me tell ya about what happened with my partner in the 39th."

Unable to resist, I backed up to his window and put it in park. Frank's stories were always great and made me laugh. So I asked, "Was it like what you just did with Joe?"

He waved his hand, dismissing the idea. "Nah, this was better!" he said, half-turning in his seat to face me. "Wait'll ya hear…" He started by setting up the scene: a cold and rainy January night on the midnight shift. He and his longtime partner, Bill Helms, were working their usual patrol wagon, and Frank was driving. "It was around 3:30 a.m., and we'd just closed two clubs and went to headquarters and turned in our paperwork. Bill got comfortable and settled back in the warmth. It was real slow."

What is this, a mystery story? I thought. There's nothing better than a warm wagon on a cold night, especially when you're not the driver. You get relaxed and let your partner navigate, just driving nice and slow. Sometimes, you might even doze off—which is exactly what happened that night.

"It's really quiet, right, and I'm just drivin' around, checking things out. Meantime, right, Bill gets all comfortable and nods off. Then, about 45 minutes later, I floor the gas and turn on the lights and siren. I tell Bill 'put us in on that.' Bill, waking from a dead sleep, grabs the radio and says, '3903, put us in on that!' He's wide awake now, sitting up, excited. Then he asks me, 'What do we got?' I slowed down, turned off the lights and siren, pulled over, and just looked at him, smiling. At the same time, the dispatcher breaks the silence with '3903, put you in on what?' It was great!"

I can't imagine how embarrassed Bill Helms must have been. I made a mental note that if I ever worked a wagon on midnights with Frank Monroe, either I would drive or I would do whatever it took to not fall asleep.

"So how did Bill take it?" I asked.

Frank put his car in gear and smiled over at me. As he pulled away, he said, "He was fine. Where do ya think I learned that?"

Even though Frank Monroe's pranks were, hands down, the best and most original I'd ever seen, there were lots of others, played by plenty of cops and even some supervisors. It was all part of the game, cops just being cops. And I never saw or heard of anybody getting mad about being the target of jokes played by a fellow officer.

One of the most common tricks was also one of the most important street lessons. It usually involved a rookie who had recently been assigned to a solo car and a patrol supervisor. It went like this: the young cop would pull up to a restaurant, go in for a coffee and leave the police car running. If the sergeant saw this, he would take the car, drive it around the corner lock it and pocket the keys. Then the sergeant would drive away. Imagine the young cop coming out of the restaurant and finding his car missing. What would he do?

Back then, we didn't have handheld walkie-talkies. He'd usually stand there, looking around, a little panicked, not knowing *what* to do. Eventually, he'd go to a pay phone, call the Radio Room and ask for a trusted veteran to meet him at his location, where he'd explain his dilemma. The old-timer, who'd probably had the same experience early on in his career, knew exactly what to do. "What the hell were you thinking, huh?" he'd ask, playing it up so the kid would get the full effect and to make sure the lesson was locked in. Eventually, the sergeant would return and act like he knew nothing about the car. The veteran would urge the new cop to explain, which he'd do with head down, mumbling. The sergeant would act pissed off and, after making sure the mortified officer understood the seriousness of having his patrol car "stolen," would then produce the keys and tell him where his car was parked. Lesson learned. I never heard of a guy having that happen to him twice.

And then there was the disappearing hat trick. We had all learned during our first days at the Academy that when you got out of your car, you put on your hat. It was part of your uniform and the *frontispiece*, the badge on the front of the hat, signified your official rank. Still, many rookies would either forget their hats in the patrol car or just decide to not wear it when they stopped in to headquarters. Mistake. Enforcing this rule was open to anyone who happened to see its violation. When the hatless officer went into the building, the observer would retrieve the abandoned hat, usually in an unlocked car, and deposit it into the freezer in the district's kitchen. Then he'd watch as the rookie would come out and sometimes even leave, only to return shortly, thinking he'd left his hat in the building.

The expression of confused alarm was quite humorous to watch—a lost hat with frontispiece was a reportable policy violation and could result in disciplinary action. Eventually, the hat thief would direct the young cop to the kitchen and remind the relieved officer to always wear his hat. How cool was that? Wearing a hat that was frozen stiff with ice chips coating the brim? Unlike the missing car lesson, this one sometimes took multiple remedial sessions to sink in.

Sometimes, the lessons that veterans taught rookies about how things should be done involved driving home the point of why they should always lock their car. If a vet observed a new guy leaving his car unlocked again and again, he'd go to the cops who worked inside, the guys taking care of the paperwork side of police work. The veteran cop would ask for and receive the "dots" that were created by the hundreds of documents that were hole-punched and filed in binders. In fact, these tiny paper circles were in such demand, they were kept in large plastic bags to be used for such occasions. A few handfuls of the paper bits were then quickly inserted into the defroster vents of the rookie's unlocked car. Of course, the "teacher" would switch the defroster to "on" and the fan to "high." A confettI blizzard resulted when the unsuspecting officer returned and turned his car key to "on." The snowstorm instantly covered the front seats, floors, and, of course, the ill-fated rookie. Oh, what fun!

Occasionally, veteran officers were the targets of pranks. And supervisors were not exempt. Sometimes it was all in fun; other times it was the cops' way of telling a guy that he's an asshole, and that his behavior or attitude towards his subordinates needed to change. I can assure you that cops can be very creative in such situations.

As a patrol lieutenant working the 1st District in South Philly, I had under my command a sergeant who'd been around a long time—too long, in my opinion. And the guy was a knucklehead. He saw his stripes as a way to annoy and even intimidate the cops he supervised. I'd had many talks with the guy and advised him that his way was not my way and that he'd better straighten up. Discipline was the next step and I told him so. He'd be better for a while, then, usually when I was off, he'd go back to his bullying ways. The cops knew I was keeping an eye on this sergeant, and they knew that eventually, he'd fall off his own high horse. But, given the opportunity, they decided to send a message of their own. And theirs was way better, much more fun.

On a warm spring afternoon, along with this sergeant and a few officers, I responded to a house to check on the well-being of an elderly woman who lived there alone. Her son, who lived in another city, had called and said he'd not heard from his mother for a few days and that he was concerned. We got no answer at the door and were checking the property when a neighbor came over and said that she hadn't seen the woman for several days and that wasn't normal. We walked around the property and found an unlocked window. I directed one of the officers to climb in and unlock the door. The sergeant and I, along with a couple of cops, walked through and found the place empty. While we were inside, dispatch notified us that the woman's son called back. He had heard from his sister who lived nearby and learned that their mother had shown up at her house. Mom was okay. We secured the property and walked to our cars.

The sergeant, however, was NOT okay when he got back to his vehicle. The opportunity had presented itself and the cops had been ready. Seems that a couple of the sergeant's cops who'd been waiting outside had located a good-sized wild rabbit in the park across the street. They decided that their sergeant needed a partner for the rest of the day, so they placed the poor thing on the floor of his unlocked car. "Watch this, Lieutenant," one of them whispered as the sarge got in. We all watched. The unpopular sergeant started the car and pulled away from the curb. About 20 feet later, we could hear him scream as he jammed on his brakes and opened his door. A brown, furry blur flew from the car and landed on the grassy median about ten feet away. I was glad to see that the poor rabbit seemed okay and quickly hopped into some nearby bushes. The cops and I all hoped that the sergeant was more scared than the rabbit, which, we later learned, had jumped into his lap when he'd started driving away.

For months, the sergeant blamed me; I was glad to keep the secret. He swore I'd put the rabbit in his car and I always denied it, although I said it with a smile. I don't think he believed me, but I didn't really care. I wanted him to remember that he'd been the brunt of a joke, and nobody else would let him forget it, either. After that, every time he'd walk into the District Operations Room, *The Bunny Hop* would be whistled or hummed by everybody. Lesson reinforced.

Eventually, I was reassigned away from the street to an administrative position and I lost touch with the members of my 1st District squad. I missed my folks and I missed the street. But I hoped that, like the officers I'd known over the years who had left their cars unlocked and those who forgot their hats, the lesson presented to the self-important sergeant by some good cops and an unsuspecting rabbit was received and remembered.

Children's Night

The call came in at 11:15 p.m., just before quitting time. "Investigate the well-being of children." Other than the address, the dispatcher gave no additional information. That meant I could be walking into anything from an unfounded call to a family disturbance, or possibly something worse. I tossed my coffee out the car window, which I quickly closed halfway against the brutal cold and wind. As I started toward the 1500 block of Franklin Street, a nearby patrol car reported that he'd back me.

As I drove through the decaying neighborhood on the icy March night, it felt like I was working in a junkyard. All around me I saw abandoned and burned-out carcasses of cars, vacant lots, and run-down properties.

Rolling through the empty, trash-filled streets, I reflected for the thousandth time about how pathetic life is for so many of the children who live here. They are Black, brown, and white and they're just living their lives. Crime and poverty compete daily with their children's games. This sorry condition is all they know. Part of me wonders if they are happy, being kids and all, not really aware of their situations. But the other—the real part—doesn't buy that. For the most part, they look sad, resignation reflected in their downturned faces, and especially their eyes. I'm not sure they even know it.

I'd learned that most of this neighborhood's poor kids accept the police. A few of them even admired us. But many clearly fear the man mommy regularly warns will "…take you away if you're not good." What terrible images of handcuffs, torture, bread and water, never-to-see-mommy-again are in their little heads?

As I approached the block, I tried to remember if I'd been here before. It didn't register. I stepped into the apartment building and noticed that, despite the very late hour, several young children appeared on the stairs between the first floor and my destination on the third. Like it was their (unsupervised) playground. Some were half-dressed and some were crying. They all were curious about why my backup and I were there. One or two reached out to touch us as we passed, perhaps a temporary distraction from their miserable lives.

The small, nervous woman who opened the door looked scared. She avoided eye contact as she told us, in halting English mixed with Spanish, that she had not called the police. Reluctantly, and after several requests, she let us in. I quickly surveyed the small apartment and saw four children, all under six or seven, scattered around the place. There were no other adults that I could see, so I took a quick look to make sure we wouldn't be surprised by someone concealed. The place was shabby and sparsely furnished—no rugs, just ancient, worn out, wooden-planked floors; a beat-up sofa facing a tiny TV sitting on a milk crate; a small back room filled with small beds; and a miniscule kitchen that actually smelled like a tasty meal had been made there recently. It was reasonably clean; it looked like the mother was trying to do her best.

Speaking in poor English, she gave me her name, Ana, and said she was twenty-three. She looked forty. Looking past her grim, worn-down features, I could see that Ana had once been a beauty. Life as a single mom, raising a bunch of little kids, had taken a heavy toll. And it would not likely be getting any better, I thought. Her long, wavy black hair and big dark eyes were the only remnants of that once-upon-a-time Ana. "Where's your husband?" I asked, trying my rusty Spanish and moving away from the wall to avoid a couple of quick-moving roaches.

"No se," came the answer, the standard Spanish "I don't know" reply to police. I spoke with Ana some more, trying to get a sense about how things were here in this tiny apartment, to understand what might be going on. I needed to figure out if this call was founded, whether or not the kids were somehow at risk. As we talked, my partner and I looked at the children, who'd come closer to investigate us. I noticed that all of their faces were tear-streaked. Thankfully, there were no visible signs of injury.

"How many people you kill, cop?" The boy was about five, dressed in shoes too big and pants too small and raggedy. The dirt on his hands and face looked days old.

"None," I said calmly and removed his tiny, sticky hand from the butt of my revolver. Disappointment showed on his face as he wandered off to play with his little sister.

I returned my attention to the young mother and she began to tell me about problems with her neighbors. The conversation was tough, with her very limited English and most of my high school Spanish long-forgotten. I could see that our being there made her uncomfortable. At the same time, she also seemed relieved. *Why?* I wondered. *Maybe she thinks—hopes—we can somehow help her?* Concentrating to understand, I thought I heard her say that she believed that some of the other building residents were breaking into her apartment when she was out, stealing her food. She had no proof and no suspects. Vague complaints, maybe to deflect our attention from the original call. Maybe not.

"They say I beat my kids. They call policia all a time," she said softly. "I try to do what is right, but I have no help." As she spoke, she began to cry. With tear-filled eyes, this woman, who was so overwhelmed by her circumstances, apologized. Her pride and frustration had collided with the hard realities of life in this tattered apartment and she felt helpless. So did I.

Before leaving, we checked the doors and locks. There was some damage, but it could have been fifty years old. I told her to contact the landlord to have him replace the lock on her front door, then realized how absurd that sounded, even to her. She thanked us and we left.

As I sat in the cold cruiser, my report reflected that the call was unfounded, that there was no child abuse at that location. But was that really true? The abuses were evident, from the poorly dressed babies to the hopeless mother to the horrible, decaying rooms they shared. Sadly, it was all perfectly legal.

I promised myself that I would keep an eye on this family, to stop by once in a while, to check on them. I would add them to my list. I meant it. But in just the last two years, the list had grown so long.

—————•●•—————

Two, maybe three years later, I got a call to the same address. The same apartment. It was late on a Friday afternoon, overcast and chilly. This time, it was to back up the Department of Human Services (DHS) personnel who were there to remove the children. Ana's children. I stood outside the place as the man and woman, both fluent in Spanish, politely tried to explain (without success) that it would be for just a little while, until she was able to find herself and the kids a better place to live. Ana's keening and sobbing made the kids join in. Their distress and pain dominated the scene. The social workers handed her a list of city offices to contact for help. That was putting her on a merry-go-round ride that would send her all over the city, to countless agencies, who would all assure her that they would put her on a list. I'd seen this routine before. Hardly ever worked out.

As she followed them down the steps, Ana was helplessly reaching out for her kids, and they for her. They were all hysterical. I stood by outside on the sidewalk, preferring the frigid air. I wanted it all to be over. I knew, though, that this was just the beginning for her and for her kids.

Ana continued her pleading and crying all the way down the stairs and outside. Once there, she stopped, finally recognizing me. I *had* gone back a few times, checking on her and the kids. I'd made sure that she was in touch with the local food banks and other folks who could give her some assistance with day-to-day challenges. I had also tried to get her help with housing and employment, advising her of agencies she could contact. I don't know if she ever did. I got the feeling that nothing had changed. I supposed that whoever had made the original complaint had finally succeeded in separating her from her kids, tearing the family apart. Maybe it was the father, maybe not. Didn't matter. They were being removed from her care.

Maybe seeing me as her last hope, Ana ran over, grabbed hold of my arm, and in rapid-fire Spanish pleaded with me. I'm sure she wanted me to stop these strangers from taking her children. I didn't understand most of what she was saying, but I got every bit of her anguish. And there was nothing I could do. We both knew that. Knowing it didn't make it any better.

What a lousy day, I thought as I watched the old green DHS station wagon pull away, the kids still screaming for their mommy. Ana sat on the front steps of her building, head in hands, rocking and crying softly.

I walked over to where she was sitting and stood there for a minute or so. I tried to get her to go back inside. She never looked up, never moved.

I got in my patrol car and started it, waiting for the heat to kick in. I was shivering, suddenly feeling the chill of the day. More than that. I had to get away from here and sit somewhere quiet for a few minutes, calm down. Pulling down the street, I wanted to look back, but couldn't. I hated this shit. I *really* did.

Mr. Nice Guy

The Philadelphia neighborhood where I grew up in the 50s and 60s was typically blue collar. The people who lived around us in the Kensington section of the city were working folks, men mostly in factories or offices, women mostly as housewives. It was a little different for us: my mom and dad owned a corner variety store, where we lived and where my two brothers and I worked alongside them. Those were happy, innocent times for me. The area felt safe and, as a boy, I never thought much about leaving, didn't think much past what was happening that day, that minute. But, as time passed and I grew up, I did move away. After the army and working in sales at Sears for a few years, I became a police officer, a spontaneous decision I never regretted.

Looking back, one of the many things my parents taught me with words and deeds was that most people are good and trustworthy. It was a principle that had served me well. I believed it and still do. But a cop is not a storekeeper. That said, I still held onto the tenet Mom and Pop had instilled in me, even as I came to know some good people who did horrible things.

Riding The El back to headquarters, I was debating whether or not to work the rest of the day. In 1980, the Patrol Division of the Philadelphia Police Department was so short-staffed that plenty of overtime was available.

So, if an officer had a court appearance on his day off and finished early, he was usually asked to complete his eight-hour tour of duty—all considered overtime with overtime pay.

The lieutenant spotted me and called me over as soon as I walked into the 26th District and offered me the time. I liked working with Lt. Johnson's squad, so I said okay. Besides, the extra money was a good thing and I had nothing else going on. The duty was usually a piece of cake, just backing up the other cops in the squad, picking up a few radio calls. And it would only be for about four hours.

I found 267 car, put my equipment in the back seat and headed north to my sector. Before I could stop for my usual start-of-the-shift coffee, the dispatcher called my number and sent me to a fire location about six blocks away. I acknowledged the call and proceeded, with lights and siren. A minute later, I was redirected to a location a block south of the fire scene for traffic control. Sure wish I'd had a minute to get that coffee.

So, there I sat, my car across the roadway, blocking northbound traffic, the flashing red and blue strobes doing their job. I decided to stand out in the street to head off the occasional driver who tried to squeeze around the police car and thought I was sitting there to decorate the neighborhood.

On graduation from the Academy nine years earlier, I had been sent to the 26th and I was happy with the assignment. This was the part of the city where I'd grown up. My parents still lived here and ran their small corner store, which was just a few blocks from where I was.

I watched the fire activity and listened as the dispatcher announced that the fire had been declared under control. Other than that, the radio was pretty quiet.

Then, ten minutes later, it wasn't.

The dispatcher, Lou Frankel, preceded the call with three loud beeping tones – indicating that what followed was a priority message. Then Lou said, "In the 26th District, Emerald and Cumberland, man with a gun; we're getting multiple calls." That last part meant that, almost certainly, the call was founded.

And the radio call was for the intersection of my parents' store.

Lou was an experienced officer and an excellent dispatcher, putting in more than 15 years on the street before being reassigned to Radio. He understood cops. I always listened to the tone of his voice – a clue to his read on the job. He sounded excited. When no one responded, he repeated the call.

Still, no one answered. I put the car in drive, and radioed that I was enroute. I told Lou that it looked like the fire department was wrapping up and there was very little traffic at my location. Leaving my assignment without radio approval was not permitted, but *not* responding was out of the question. Lou acknowledged and again called for other units to back me.

Within three minutes, I had the location in sight and saw the man in the middle of the street. He was waving a big revolver at another guy who was backing up, his hands in the air. I don't think either one of them saw me coming.

I screeched to a stop a few feet behind the man with the gun, which made him turn away from his victim and toward the sound. I quickly exited the car, my pistol in hand and ordered him to place the gun on the ground. Thankfully, he did it without hesitating. I retrieved the weapon, cuffed him and placed him in the back of my car.

Once I advised radio of conditions, another car, 268, arrived and, at my request, took the other person involved to the detective division to sign a complaint and give a statement, while my backup and I waited for an Emergency Patrol Wagon to transport my prisoner. Radio sent 266 car to back me up until the wagon arrived. A few minutes later, Lou, the dispatcher called. "267, there are no wagons available. Transport your prisoner to East Detectives. 266, follow 267 to East with his prisoner." We acknowledged and headed to East.

As we drove the two miles to detectives, in the rearview mirror, I watched the cuffed man in the back. I had learned along the way in my short career that things weren't always what they seemed. The guy was about thirty-five, tall, well-groomed and dressed in a suit. His head down, shoulders slumped, he looked beaten. I'm not a psychologist, but something just didn't seem quite right with this whole deal. I had the feeling that this wasn't just a typical "man with a gun". This guy seemed way, way out of his element; he didn't seem at all comfortable with the whole situation. In my mirror, I saw that he was quietly crying. I asked him if he was hurt, was he okay? He said he wasn't hurt, just upset. Then he told me the story.

His name was Alan Schmidt (not his real name) and he was in real estate. He'd been married for about eight years and he and his wife were having problems, arguing all the time. He didn't know what was going on, but suspected she was seeing someone else. He blamed himself because of the long hours and weekends he worked. Then, after a couple of hang-up calls, he followed his wife to a bar where she met the guy – the same guy he'd been close to shooting. As he spoke, he was upset at first, then seemed to become calm and continued in a matter-of-fact way. He had tracked the man down after he learned where he worked. He said he never intended to hurt the guy, whose name he didn't even know. He just wanted to send him a strong message: "Stay away from my wife!"

I believed him. Alan seemed to be an okay guy, recent events aside, but one never knows. A records check confirmed my hunch that he'd never been arrested before. He didn't know what he should do next.

I sketched out how the process worked and suggested that he find a good lawyer and, no matter what, to stay away from the other guy. I explained that at the preliminary hearing, he should let his lawyer explain the situation to show him in the best possible light. After all, he'd had the opportunity to shoot the man, but just wanted to scare him away from his wife. As I turned him over to the detectives, he thanked me and I said I'd see him at the hearing.

Within an hour, the paperwork was completed and my part in the arrest process was done. I met with the assigned detective, Joe Alvarez, and he reminded me of the date of the preliminary hearing, the following Monday, handed me a subpoena, and said I could go.

When I got home, I called my dad to check in. "Hi, Pop, how are you? How's Mom?" They were both fine. We spoke for a little while, Mom making me promise to come over soon for dinner. As it turned out, they hadn't seen or heard any of the action right outside their door. They'd been eating lunch at the time, in another part of the house. I said nothing about it, just vowed to myself to again speak with my brothers and figure out how we were going to get Mom and Pop to sell the property, retire, and move—it was time. The neighborhood had become too dangerous for them to be by themselves.

The day of the hearing, I stood waiting in the back of the 24th/25th Districts roll call room, which doubled as a courtroom for divisional preliminary hearings three days a week. It was packed wall-to-wall with cops, lawyers and civilians. I was going to be here awhile.

Two hours later, when the Schmidt case was called, there was no response. No lawyer, no Alan Schmidt. I looked across the room at Detective Alvarez who gave me an "I don't know" shrug. The bailiff repeated the call for parties in the Schmidt case. Again, no answer. The judge immediately issued a bench warrant for Mr. Schmidt's arrest and moved on to the next case. I was really surprised that Schmidt was a no-show. I'd gotten the impression that he was going to follow through and do the right thing. I signed out with the court clerk and left.

On a Wednesday, about seven months later, I reported for duty on the 4:00 p.m. to midnight shift. After roll call, the corporal called me into the Operations Room and gave me a phone message slip and said that I should return the call ASAP. I didn't recognize the number and the area code wasn't local. Curious, I dialed the number and a woman answered, a receptionist for a law firm in West Palm Beach, Florida.

Since I'd never been to West Palm Beach, and didn't think that I'd been involved in anything that would prompt a lawyer's call from there, I was even more curious. Besides, we always dealt with the District Attorney's office, not directly with private lawyers. When I gave my name to the receptionist, she put someone on the phone who said he was an attorney representing Alan Schmidt. At first, the name didn't register, but as he explained, I remembered. The lawyer was being very nice to me. As a cop, I wasn't used to that, especially when it came to defense attorneys. I sat down and listened as he explained the reason for his call.

By the time he was finished, I thought that Alan probably wouldn't have to worry about that bench warrant for not showing up in the gun case. That was now minor stuff. Schmidt had made it to the majors. *Congratulations Alan,* I thought. *You've hit the big time.*

Alan Schmidt, the "nice guy" who had impressed me as someone who would take the high road and see this thing through, had done something I would never have guessed. Right after his arrest in Philly, his wife left, presumably with the guy Alan almost shot. Instead of going to court, he tracked them to Florida and, in the very early morning hours of Christmas day, broke into their motel room and shot them both dead. Wow! I couldn't believe it. At my request, he shared a few more details as I sat there shaking my head. I said to myself, *Alan, buddy, I thought we had a deal!*

After his arrest, he confessed to everything. In preparing his defense, his lawyer asked Alan for names of potential character witnesses. He gave him mine!

Now, his attorney was asking if I would come to Florida and testify as to his restraint in the Philly gun incident and, in doing so, support his defense in this double homicide. Me, a character witness for a killer. Hah! Fat chance. I explained that, while I appreciated Mr. Schmidt's faith in me, it was not normal procedure for police officers to provide testimony on behalf of those charged with crimes, especially murder. He said he understood my position, then asked me a question that I was sure would get me out of this whole thing: "Officer, if I can get the DA to approve your testimony, will you come?" Knowing that the hardass Philly DA would *never* go for this, I said, "Sure."

I was way wrong. Three weeks later, on a cold Philadelphia afternoon, I flew into West Palm Beach. The next morning, I met with Schmidt's lawyer who told me there had been a plea agreement earlier that day and my testimony wouldn't be needed. The prosecutor had agreed to manslaughter charges because of Schmidt's lack of a criminal history.

So, after two warm and relaxing days in Florida, I headed back north. I never got to see or talk with Alan Schmidt during my time in the Sunshine State or ever again. And although I made several calls to the attorney and the Florida law enforcement agencies involved in the case, I never learned the final outcome of the sentencing. I sometimes think about Alan and wonder...

My brothers and I kept after Mom and Pop, and within a few months, our folks realized that it was time to make a change. They retired and found a nice apartment in a safe and quiet neighborhood. I never told them or my brothers about what had happened that day.

As a cop, I have been involved in other terrible incidents over the years. There is no doubt that the Alan Schmidt matter gave my powers of perception an edge that helped me stay safe. Still, I have often wondered about how things can go so bad for some good people.

Years later, after I'd left the 26th District, I drove by Emerald & Cumberland. Our corner was now a vacant lot; with no sign of the store or the house where I'd grown up.

In that moment, I missed those good old days and a young boy's innocence. I still do.

Sinatra and the Mummers

I hate sequins and feathers and have for many years. Alright, separately, they're okay, but, in combination, they remind me of some days I'd rather forget. Long, cold days. And although I like most music, please don't play "Golden Slippers" around me. That song brings back unpleasant memories I've been trying to shake for decades.

The Mummers Parade. It was a day-long event—sometimes 15 hours—that showcased three different types of performers marching in large groups, or brigades: Comics, Fancies, and String Bands, in that order. A large presence of working cops was part of the tradition.

The whole thing made little sense, at least to me. There was so much about this I just didn't get. Men getting dressed up in brightly-colored satin and lace costumes? Thousands of them, marching down the street—for miles—wearing gold or silver shoes? What was *that* all about? They'd do it every year, year after year; they had been doing it for more than a century. Some even dressed in drag. What made it worse was that they'd do it on what usually turned out to be one of the coldest days of the year—New Year's Day.

For the record, I'm not a party-pooper. Look, I like a parade as much as the next guy. But *this*? It's more like a competition of the absurd. There were so many groups of these guys and they *competed* against one another. For prizes, and money, BIG money. But mostly for bragging rights.

I know what you're going to say: "Strati, you hated it because you weren't there as a spectator. You were only there because you had to be." Well, yes and no. Along with about two thousand other cops, I stood on the cold streets of South Philly watching the crowds who were watching the Mummers Parade.

To be fair, the majority of folks – mostly families – had come to enjoy the spectacle. They were typically well-behaved, happy to just be part of a mildly raucous crowd celebrating this traditional, uniquely Philadelphia event. *They* made the whole thing bearable, especially the little kids, whose wide-eyed, open-mouthed looks made me smile every time.

So, although I *was* technically a spectator, I just didn't like what I saw the most: drunks. Some were just tipsy. Then, there were those who were *beyond* drunk; they were smashed, plastered, soused. And usually obnoxious. They were the ones I'd mostly be dealing with, parade-goers who'd had too much celebration and showed up cruising for trouble. They were, gratefully, very few in number, and they typically started their nonsense behind the crowd or people who were trying to get a good look at the passing parade. When discovered, the scoundrels were usually corralled by a couple of nearby cops and hustled off to a waiting Emergency Patrol Wagon and taken to a quiet cell to sleep it off.

But if dealing with an occasional drunken spectator had been the only challenge, I'd have been okay with the whole parade scene. But then there were these self-named Comics, who always seemed to screw things up. I got to observe them up close and personal. They'd come right up to the street side of the barricades, checking out the scene, hoping for a kiss from squealing young girls behind the barricades, who, for reasons I couldn't fathom, were apparently enchanted by these falling-down, stinking drunk, tiny-umbrella-carrying Romeos.

Occasionally, a pickled Comic would stumble into the barricade and knock into a few people which would sometimes lead to a little skirmish. But the best part? The best part was when the guy was close enough for *me* to smell. Without fail, he'd stumble up, shake my hand with a filthy, stinking paw and utter the inevitable "Happy New Years, officuh", slurred and slobbered in that unmistakable South Philly dialect. *Yeah, Happy New Year, you drunken toad,* I'd say to myself, giving him a hard look he was either too smashed to notice or just ignored. I'd then watch the guy stagger away, as he eyed up his next willing young female victim. This would be repeated again and again throughout the march of the Comics.

Don't get me wrong. I fully appreciated the effort most of the Mummers put into their costumes. I'm talking about the Fancy Brigades and the String Bands whose members spent tons of money and an entire year preparing for that one day. It was serious business. The competition was always fierce and driven by tradition. Even today, a great percentage of participants are just the latest generation of Mummers since the first parade in 1901. There is great pride in Mummer families. Every year, the patriarchs of each brigade would carry the newest additions to the family, fully dressed in miniature versions of the club's themed costume, thus initiating the babies into Mummer madness. Anyway, I was pretty okay with the Fancies and the String Bands.

Like I said, the ones I had issues with were the Comic Brigades. I gotta tell you, I just didn't get the name. To me, they weren't funny. Ever. To me, they should've been called the Sillies. All they did was walk up Broad Street, wearing bright satin costumes (most of which I couldn't tell what they were) and usually carrying small multi-colored parasols that they would juke up and down as they shuffled and spun in circles, dancing and staggering to the music. And you could see their drunken, glazed eyes as they whirled, twirled and staggered in the street.

By the time they got to my area, their painted faces were smeared all over by the many smooches they'd garnered from the screaming young girls they'd encountered earlier. And get this: even if they'd lost or forgotten their little umbrellas – and that happened a *lot* – they'd still do the crazy up-and-down moves, known by purists as the "Mummer's Strut." I figured that large amounts of alcohol helped in this regard. It was from these comic groups that the drunkest guys would break away and stagger over to kiss and rub their smeared, painted mugs on the face of an eager young miss screaming from the crowd.

But it wasn't just the Comics that made me an unhappy camper. It was the cold. Biting, endless, painful, never-ending cold. And, no matter how prepared I *thought* I was, I wasn't. Thermal underwear, check. Heavy wool trousers, check. Wool sweater and scarf, yup. Three-quarter length leather coat *with* liner, got it. Two pairs of wool socks inside rubber-soled, thick leather boots, yes. Finally, army-issue wool gloves inside fleece-lined leather mittens. Topped off with a lined, over-the-ears cap. All warm and toasty. Ha! After ten hours out there, none of it mattered.

We'd arrive early, just before 7:00 a.m. The preliminary fun was setting up the miles of wooden barricades to keep the throngs at bay. Okay, that was part of the job. And it helped us stay warm. At least for a while. Then we'd stand by for a couple of hours, waiting for the parade to kick off at about 9 o'clock. We would sip coffee or hot chocolate from the Second Alarmers trucks. They were manned by cheerful volunteers and always showed up when police and firefighters were posted at a location for an extended time, usually protracted fire scenes and events like the Mummers parade. It was during this lull that the early-bird spectators would start showing up.

When the weather was nice (above freezing), it wasn't bad – yet. People from all over the city, some visiting from other states and even other countries, would crowd in to get a front row spot behind the yellow and blue wooden barricades for the oldest such event in America. Sitting in beach chairs, cocooned in blankets, they would chat with us, always wishing us a Happy New Year. Sometimes, cops' families would show up and watch from the area their cop was working.

As far as the parade itself, there really wasn't much for us to do. All the cross streets were blocked off and each section in the procession—Comics, Fancies and String Bands—had its own set of marshals who saw to the movement and pace of the various groups. So we'd stand there, supposedly facing the crowd, looking for any trouble. Usually, other than a few fights between drunken revelers – both in and out of costume – it was a peaceful crowd. The Comic divisions always started things off, each club with their small floats and kids of all ages, all decorated and painted up, leading the way.

You could hear them coming a few blocks away. The 'regular' Comics usually had recorded music they danced to, blaring from inside an accompanying pace car. Some comic clubs would march to music provided by small, un-costumed bands, which often included Black musicians, at the time the only non-white participants in attendance. And they all carried the traditional decorated umbrellas, some multi-leveled.

Then, there was the other part of the Comic division: the Wench Brigades. These guys would typically wear the dress-and-bloomers costumes, carry decorated umbrellas, and sport painted and otherwise garishly-decorated versions of golden slippers on their feet. The Comics, including the Wench Brigades, would be loosely formed and were the only Mummers who ventured close to the barricades, showing off their costumes and Mummer's Strut skills. And their level of intoxication.

I was always glad when the Comics were through, although I knew we'd see them again. Once they passed the reviewing stand at City Hall, miles north, they would disband and make their way back to South Philly where most of them lived, and where the after-parties were. They'd make their homeward trek, behind the crowds, somehow always managing to find more alcohol to refuel their inebriated state, raising a little New Year's hell. Like seeing them once today wasn't enough…

By the time the Fancy Division started their march up Broad Street, both sidewalks were packed, curb-line to house-line. The Fancies' presentations – large, elaborate and color-coordinated – always showed style and creativity. They clearly showed the amount of money and time their members had invested. It was nice to watch. Their bands were also costumed and were bigger and better than those of the Comics.

Even so, the day dragged on and a cold, stiff breeze was all it took to remind me how miserable I was. The only thing that made it worse was cold rain, drizzle or sleet – not enough to call the whole thing off, just enough to glaze my face and uniform with ice. And by now, all my careful survival preparations of good, warm clothing were starting to feel useless. The familiar tingle of pre-numbness had set in, beginning with my toes and fingers.

Whenever I could, I'd take an occasional break to get off Broad Street and walk to a side street, looking for a sunny spot, trying to get warmer than freezing. Once in a while, a kindly South Philly resident, seeing me passing by, would come out of the house, grab me by the arm, and guide me into a blissfully warm house where the dining table was packed with food and drink. I confess there were times I was talked into a small brandy. God bless those folks. Then, after a break that felt way too short, it was back to the barricades. And I'll tell you, coming out of that warm house made it feel twice as cold.

Hey, we're getting there, I would keep telling myself. As the Fancies wound down, it meant we were moving along, getting to the String Bands and the end. It wasn't true, though, just wishful thinking, because there was always at least a half-hour break in the action between the last Fancy Brigade and the first String Band. Nobody knew why.

Finally, many hours later, looking south on Broad Street, I could see the red and blue strobes of the traffic district cars, leading the first of the String Bands. Rejuvenated by the sight, I'd think, *Hey, It's okay! I'm gonna make it*. Then I'd remember last year and the year before and all the years before that I'd stood out here and done this. There were usually between 15 and 20 string bands. And they all kept a healthy distance between each other to give themselves the best chance of presenting a memorable performance for the judges waiting all the way up by City Hall. *Strat I don't get too excited, there're still hours to go.*

Regardless of how on-schedule the parade was, by the time the String Bands began their musical march up the street, the sun was usually setting. This meant that any hint of warmth, real or imagined, was also going away. So, I'd stand there on the cold blacktop of Broad Street stamping my feet, moving my fingers inside my now-useless gloves, hating my job.

Trying to stay upbeat, looking for the bright spot, I turned to the music. The talented musicians of these bands, along with their ornate, well-crafted costumes, would take my mind off my misery for a few minutes at a time. Their outfits, usually based on current events and trends and always themed to the music they played, emphasized to the spectators that the city had truly saved the best for last.

On and on and on they came and went. As well as they played, as entertaining as their presentations were, after a few of them, I couldn't help feeling the biting cold creeping in again, now worse than ever. *I'm never gonna get warm again.* I thought. *Never!* I could tell that the other cops all around me were freezing, too. Small comfort but, as they say, misery loves company, and I had a couple thousand cops for company.

When the last of the String Bands had passed our location, the crowds quickly disappeared. One minute they were there, and then they were all gone. Great! We were almost done. But not quite yet. We watched as the Sanitation Department trucks moved in to collect the piles of trash left behind, and waited for the police commanders to give us the word to start breaking down the barricades. Now feeling like the Tin Man with stiffened joints in urgent need of oil, I really didn't mind it because it was body-warming and told me I'd be going home soon. Home to warmth – and sitting down.

Those are my *typical* memories of the annual Philadelphia event called the Mummers Parade. And, by the late 80s, I'd already done it more than a dozen times. Then came the year it all changed for me.

As usual, we got there about 7:00 a.m. And, as usual, the day was cold and breezy. If it had been just a *little* windier, they would've postponed the thing. But it wasn't. So, there I stood on already half-frozen, wooden legs, in the middle of a block deep in South Philly, going through the first couple phases of the parade – the Comics and Fancies so far. I remember that the crowds that day had been happy and friendly; even the drunken clowns had sort of behaved.

The Fancies were just about done when my corporal, Gerry Walker, walked up behind me and said, "Hey Strati, there's somebody here to see you. Over there," pointing me northward toward the corner. I walked up, glad to be moving. *Who can this be? I don't know anybody from South Philly,* I thought. But *this* girl I knew. Monica was smiling that big smile of hers, standing there in her long, warm-looking coat and knitted cap. I walked over to the barricade and gave my wife a long hug and a kiss. "What're you doing here?" I asked, so glad that she was.

"Wanted to see you, so here I am!"

"Great, but aren't you cold?"

"Not really, this is my grandmother's coat and it's really toasty." Then she told me she was going to stay till the parade was over. Good deal.

We'd talk and visit in between the times I would move off to check my area. Finally, *finally*, the last of the String Bands was past us and we got the word to take down the barricades. About an hour later, we were dismissed.

When I got to where she was waiting, she put her arm in mine and we started walking up Broad Street. "Hey," I said, slowing down, "my car's back there."

"We're not going home right away, are you okay with that?"

"Huh?" I didn't understand.

"We're invited to a party, right down the street."

"Really?" I said, trying to think who we knew down here.

Reading my mind, she said, "It's my friend Mary's house. She's a nurse I work with." Then she turned to me and asked, "You up for it? You're not too tired, are you?"

"No. I'm into it," I said, knowing she was really looking forward to it. And, hey, she'd come all this way to surprise me. "I'm good, let's go," I said pulling her closer.

We walked a while then stopped in the middle of a long block as she checked the house addresses against the slip of paper from her purse. "Here it is." She grabbed my arm tighter as we walked up the front steps of a beautiful three-story brownstone and rang the bell.

"Wow," I said. "This is great!" Music was pounding from inside and, through the big front window, I could see people laughing, some of them decked out in brightly-colored cardboard New Year hats.

Mary welcomed us in with a hug then showed us to the large living room, where a dozen or more folks were partying, not one of them put off by a cop in full uniform. "Happy New Year!" wishes all around as we were introduced to the rest of Mary's guests. In the dining room, we helped ourselves to some food and found seats in the corner. After a little while, I had forgotten about the drunks and the cold.

We ate and drank and danced and had a great time. But the *best* part was when we all spontaneously joined arms and, circling the dining table, did our own Rockettes-like dance to Frank Sinatra's "New York, New York," the whole crowd belting out every word.

Ironic. What turned out to be my last Mummers Parade was also my best. Of course, I didn't know then that it would be my last, but nothing could have topped that day. It was the perfect confluence of good things, and a happy ending. All the negative stuff just melted away.

Driving home later that night, I was going over it all in my head. *Maybe the Mummers Parade wasn't so bad after all. Maybe it was me. Maybe I hadn't given it a chance.*

Or maybe I'd been looking at things from the wrong side of the barricades.

The Bavarian Connection

Monica and I had been walking the narrow, cobbled streets of Mittenwald, Germany, for about an hour after our lunch, moving at a slow pace, trying to work off the hearty meal of wurst, potatoes and red cabbage. Not to mention a couple of half-liters of excellent *Mittenwalder*.

We strolled past a bakery, then a place that had been making and selling violins for two centuries. At the very end of the street, we stopped at a woodcarver's shop. "Look at him," I said, pointing to a large, hand-carved, beautifully painted drummer boy, proudly standing in the center of the window, drumsticks at the ready.

"He's great!" she said, pulling my hand. "Let's go in."

As in all our travels, we'd been looking for a souvenir from this charming alpine town, something to bring home as a remembrance of this particular trip. This fellow might be it. Pushing open the heavy wooden door, a small but loud cowbell clanged our arrival. Once inside, we didn't know where to look first. Beautiful carvings were everywhere; from gnomes to horses and deer, to shelves of religious figures and scenes. The shop owner came from the back, smiling and wiping his hands on his stained leather apron.

"*Guten abend,*" he said, welcoming us. From behind the large wooden counter, he told us he was one of two craftsmen who'd created these works of art. We walked around and, like kids in a toy store, called out to each other as one of us discovered a new and amazing carving. But we always came back to the drummer boy. We huddled as Monica, much better than I with numbers, calculated the cost, translating deutsche marks to dollars. He was expensive! But he was a true work of art.

"His face is so real and his eyes look right at you," Monica said. "And look at that little smile!"

"He *is* beautiful," I agreed. "Let's think about it, okay?" But I knew we'd be back for him.

Since we'd seen everything and admired the drummer boy several more times, we thanked the shopkeeper and stepped back out into the cold March afternoon. The brisk alpine air was warmed just a little by the late-day sunshine that was reflecting off the remnants of that morning's snowfall. Arm-in-arm we continued our stroll, window-shopping and enjoying the moment. A few days later, our last in Mittenwald, we came back and bought the drummer boy. He has been the centerpiece of our Christmas decorations ever since, wowing all who see him.

After leaving the store, we turned the corner and were heading back to our hotel when I saw him—I could tell right away by his uniform that he was a policeman. "Let's go talk with this guy," I said, picking up the pace. (I could converse a bit, but Monica's fluent German allowed us to adventure freely and engage anyone in conversation—often easy because many Germans spoke perfect English.)

He stood outside an old brick building that had a wooden *PolizeI* plaque hanging over the doorway. We walked up and I introduced myself and Monica. I showed him my wallet badge and ID card from the Philadelphia PD. Throwing down the cigarette he'd been smoking, he grabbed my hand and shook it vigorously. He greeted Monica in the same way, talking excitedly in a combination of German and English. He entered the old building and motioned for us to follow. "Come in, come in, please," he said. I returned his broad smile as my wife and I moved into the warmth of the police station. He was dressed in short black boots and woolen slacks and wore a heavy blue police sweater over his light blue uniform shirt.

As he walked us back through the building, he told us his name was Hans and that he'd grown up right there in Mittenwald. "So, you are a policeman from America?" he asked when we got to the open office area of the small station. The space contained three gray metal desks and matching file cabinets lined two of the walls.

"Yes, Philadelphia," I said, taking off my gloves and unzipping my parka. "Monica and I are here for about ten days. Are you working alone?"

"Yes, we usually work alone; there is not much for us to do. But at least one of us has to be here in case there is a call or a problem." Then he asked, "Is this your first time in Mittenwald?"

"Oh, no, it's our third," I said. "We love it here." I thought back to the first time we'd found the small Bavarian village, years ago, quite by accident. After visiting King Ludwig's fairy-tale *Neuschwanstein* castle in Füssen, we headed south, just driving the scenic drive. We never worried about finding accommodations. With Monica's excellent German, finding a hotel wasn't a problem, but we preferred to stay in a *zimmer frei*, a room for rent in a private home. It was a common practice in Germany, a way that some folks supplemented their income by renting a room to travelers. We'd done it many times and liked the *zimmer freI* option because we got to know local folks, whose hospitality was warmer than any hotel. Often, we'd sit at the dining table with our hosts and share excellent meals and, if we were lucky, we'd even get to spend time with the family pet.

One of the things I usually did when we traveled was to bring along some Philadelphia Police Department shoulder patches—in case I met a local cop in a town that we were visiting. I reached into the pocket of my coat and pulled out the small plastic bag I'd remembered to pack at the last minute. "Hans, these are for you, from my police department." I handed him the bag containing several of the cloth patches. He thanked me and opened it, laying the embroidered pieces on the counter. They included a couple of the standard departmental shoulder insignias, the ones that were worn by every officer. But the ones he focused on were those worn by members of the Philly PD special units, such as Highway Patrol, K9, Academy staff, firearms instructors and SWAT officers. His beaming face as he held up each one told me he was pleased.

Hans spread the patches out on a desk, touching each one, remarking on the variety. "Thank you so much! There are so many."

"Oh, these are just a few of them," I said. "There are many, many patches; probably dozens."

"Really? How many officers are there in Philadelphia?"

"About sixty-five hundred or so," I said.

"Six thousand?" he exclaimed.

"Yes, Philadelphia is a very big city and, unfortunately, has enough crime to require thousands of officers."

He nodded in understanding. "I apologize that I do not have any patches to give you in return. I wish I had known you were coming." I loved listening to him speak. His English was perfect. He spoke the language better than many Americans. My father-in-law, Manfred, had told me that German kids study English as part of their basic education from elementary through high school. Many learn it well and use it properly.

"Don't worry about it. Really. I'm just glad we got to meet you." Then, returning to our previous topic, I asked, "How about Mittenwald? I'm sure there's not very much crime, so what kinds of things keep you busy?"

"Well, here it is not like in America." He paused, perhaps searching for the right words. "True, there is not so much crime here. We are in the Alps, you know. So much of what we do is connected to the mountains and the weather…you know, auto crashes and hikers getting hurt up there." He gestured to the high snow-topped mountains that surrounded the village. Then, he said, "Come with me, I want to show you something." He led the way to a room in the back of the building. He flipped a few switches and fluorescent light filled the room. Hans stood back and let the pictures on the walls speak for themselves.

"You see, our mountains are very beautiful. But they have a part that is not so beautiful. Look around." I started with the wall closest to the door. There were poster-sized photographs, close-up shots of various sections of the mountainsides. Each showed lots of snow that was interrupted by giant outcroppings of rock, sticking up, partially snow-covered. Drawn in red on each photo were lines and other marks that ended with an area that was circled. Every picture also had German writing at the bottom with dates and other numbers; I guessed these were the case numbers and the descriptions of the incidents.

"Look closely," said Hans, moving to the photo I was looking at. He pointed to the spot on the picture that was circled. "This man fell down from halfway up the mountain. We didn't find him for days—you know, a blizzard. His family called us when he didn't return to his home." Hans went on to explain that they sent helicopters and expert climbers up when the snow stopped, but it still took several days to locate his body.

All around the room, it was more of the same, each giant photo documenting many ill-fated climbers. "Were these people all visitors, or are they locals?" I asked.

"Most were from this part of Germany and many had been climbing for years." He shook his head as if he were still trying to figure out how these accidents happened. "We have no way of controlling when they go up. Here in Germany, hiking is like jogging in America. It is very popular and many people enjoy the fresh air of the mountains. But, you know, sometimes they make mistakes, things happen and…" He trailed off, his arms silently gesturing to the photos on the walls, his head down. We all stood quiet, thinking.

Standing there, I wondered how these sudden deaths affected the police who were charged with investigating these cases and retrieving the poor souls who didn't make it back down the mountain. Surely, it was something that, over time, had to get to them. I started to ask, then thinking better of it, I let it go.

As Hans walked us back to the cell area of the police station, he explained that because the winters were so long in this part of Bavaria, there were also a number of suicides. He said that there was a local phenomenon— the *föehn*—that led to depression and sometimes suicide. The *föehn* was a low, mournful sound made by a warm wind moving downward through the mountains and could last for days at a time during the winter months. "Some people go crazy with the sound," said Hans, shaking his head. "Some of those pictures I showed you were *föehn* victims." More heavy-duty stuff for these cops to deal with. So, even in a pristine, virtually crime-free place like Mittenwald, there was a dark side behind the beauty, and plenty to wear down the cops. He showed us the rest of the station, with the only thing of note being the detention area. Looking into the two open, unoccupied cells, I thought how clean and unused these were compared to the worn out, overused lockups in every one of Philly's 23 districts.

We then made our way back to the main office area and put on our coats. "We have to get back to the hotel, it's almost dinnertime," I said as we shook hands and opened the front door. "We're walking up and it'll take about half an hour. Hans, thank you so much for the tour."

"It was my pleasure. May I ask where you are staying?"

"Hotel Lautersee," I said.

"Ah, Lautersee. It's a beautiful place, and very quiet, yes?"

"It is, except sometimes the cowbells wake us up." I wasn't complaining. I thought the ringing bells were part of the appeal of Mittenwald.

He laughed. "Yes, of course, the cows don't always sleep at night like people."

We left, and after a brisk walk from the center of Mittenwald to the lakefront hotel, we washed up and made our way to our assigned table in the dining room. As always, the view of the lake, the skyscraper-tall pines and the snow-covered mountains made me stare in amazement.

Once again, our host and chef, Josef, had prepared a magnificent three-course dinner, all served by his sister, Kathe. Hearty salads to start, then schnitzel for me and trout for Monica, accompanied by a nice local Riesling. Then the house specialty—warm apple strudel with homemade vanilla sauce. The view, the wine, the food…it was perfect. It had been a very good day.

Our hike down to the village and back up had worn us out. After another hearty meal, we waddled back to our room. No TV, but it didn't matter. We were instantly asleep and slept like a couple of logs. Maybe the cows were tired too; I didn't hear a single cow bell.

We were up early, not wanting to miss out on chef Josef's hearty breakfast. Entering the huge dining room, we greeted some of the other guests as we made our way to our spot. Seeing us, Kathe hurried over with a big pot of coffee and filled our cups. As usual, the buffet was packed with local cheeses, sausages and other breakfast meats, soft-cooked eggs, and warm bread with butter from a local farmer. And lots of good hot coffee. I wished we could start every day this way.

Sitting back and enjoying a third cup, I heard a murmur in the room. Hearing it too, Josef came out of the kitchen, drying his hands on his long white apron. Hearing what was being said by some of the German-speaking guests, he walked to the large windows that fronted the dining room and looked out. From the hotel's elevated location, the one road that twisted up from the town of Mittenwald was clearly visible. And that's where Josef, Kathe, and most of the others were pointing and looking. I went over and looked too.

Two police cars were making their way up the winding road, heading our way. I smiled. I knew why they were coming. I returned to the table and filled Monica in.

As we waited, I asked Monica to translate what the German-speakers were saying. She told me that one woman had said in a worried voice, "I wonder what kind of trouble there is?" An older man sitting near us was wondering if the police officers were coming to breakfast. Josef looked around the room, trying to figure out if one of the guests was missing, perhaps sick.

None of the above.

The cars pulled up and parked. Three uniformed officers, with Hans in the lead, walked into the place and started looking around. I gave a slight wave and, seeing me, he waved back and headed to our table.

"*Guten morgen*, Officer Skoufalos! *Guten morgen, Frau* Skoufalos." said Hans, shaking our hands. He introduced us to the other two officers as Josef and Kathe and the rest of the diners stared, wondering what was going on. The officers declined our invitation to join us for coffee, saying they had to get back.

I understood: Police officers, no matter where, always welcome other policemen. And while I'd seen it in our travels in America plenty of times, this was the first time I'd experienced it in another country. And it was exactly the same. I wasn't surprised—the police fraternity really *was* worldwide.

Then Hans said, "When I told my comrades about your visit, they said they wanted to meet you and, look, we brought you some patches for your collection." He pulled a few beautifully embroidered *Polizei* patches from his pocket and handed them to me.

Huh! I thought, *even in Europe, in this small village in the Bavarian Alps, the police brotherhood thing is the same.*

I thanked them all and told them how much I appreciated their thoughtfulness, even though their arrival had scared the shit out of everybody else. They laughed at that and shook our hands; then they were gone.

After observing this brief get-together, Josef, clearly relieved, came over and sat down. He wanted to know why the police officers had come up from the village. I told him about meeting Hans the day before. Then I tried to explain about the closeness, the connection of police officers—*all* police officers—no matter where they found one another. He nodded like he understood. I smiled and nodded back, but in reality, I knew that only another cop could get the connection.

In that moment, I understood that we'd be bringing home much more than a wooden figurine and a few cloth patches. A much deeper shared meaning remains with me, always.

The Rookie

When I graduated from the Police Academy in the fall of 1971, I was assigned to the 26th District, one of the busiest in the city. Like all rookies, my assignments were limited, like walking foot beats or keeping an eye on crowds at church bazaars, or standing in the freezing rain at an intersection and trying to stop people from driving over the fire department's huge hoses. *I'm wasting my time,* I thought to myself whenever I was relegated to any of these assignments, which was almost every day. But I knew this was the drill and kept looking forward to the day I could, in my mind, be *a real cop.*

Whatever the orders, I did what I was told for my first six months—the probationary period during which rookies were watched closely and weren't allowed to drive a police car. The best times were when, once in a while, the sergeant would call my name at roll call and assign me to work with one of the veterans (compared to me, pretty much every other cop there was a veteran). Usually, it was as a partner to an old, crusty officer who wasn't happy to have me along for the day in the Radio Patrol Car or Emergency Patrol Wagon. His brooding silence told me how unwelcome I was, loud and clear.

He would always drive, which left me as the recorder, answering the radio and documenting what we did. Like all rookies, I was expected to just sit there…period. *Except* for writing incident reports—the vets hated to do them, so the new kid got to write them all. But, nothing got turned in until the veteran approved it; and the rule was—the shorter, the better. He'd say, "Don't give 'em too much in the 48." (The "75-48" was the basic report for all incidents and activities we were involved in.) "The more you write,"" the experienced guy would explain, "the more the corporal has to read. He don't like it. You don't wanna piss off the corporal." Such a conversation by the veteran would be considered long-winded, especially when spoken to a rookie.

The corporal was the Operations Room Supervisor and he was in charge of activities inside the district headquarters—like processing all incident reports turned in during the tour of duty, monitoring any prisoners (usually local drunks) who ended up in one of the district's three ancient cells, and, most importantly, submitting the daily attendance report so we got paid.

Back to the veterans. Most communications by the senior guys would be a stony glare. For the fortunate rookie, there might be a head shake. And if the veteran was feeling truly magnanimous, he might respond with a grunt. It would be normal for hours to go by without a word from the old-timer. This was true even when they were asked a job-related question.

Just before graduation, one of our Academy instructors had told us, "Your real training starts when you hit the streets. Listen to the veterans, they'll teach you what you need to know." *So,* I wondered, *how am I supposed to learn anything when this guy won't talk to me?*

In addition to report-writing, my job as recorder included answering the radio. But I risked an injured hand or an elbow to the ribs if the veteran driver saw me even *reaching* for the microphone to pick up a call. After a few times, I figured it out: *he* would decide which calls we'd answer. Sometimes he would wait for the dispatcher to call at least twice before answering – hoping for somebody else to pick up the assignment. *Wow!* I thought. *Hope I never get like this.*

In time, though, I figured it out: the veteran's communication and social skills aside, all I had to do to learn was to watch and listen. So I did. These guys had it down. They could read a situation right away and tell if a loudmouth was harmless or if he was a real troublemaker that had to be straightened out or taken in. They might be low-key when they were driving around, but sure knew what to do when they had to be the guy with the badge.

I didn't know it during those first six months, but when I got through probation and was eventually on my own, I realized that what I'd learned riding with the veterans had given me some pretty good cop skills. Being assigned your 'own' or steady car was the sergeant saying you're *probably* ready to work alone. It could also mean that there were new rookies to bring along, and you were no longer at the bottom of the seniority food chain.

It was early the next spring when the sergeant finally turned me loose, to work by myself. I was like a kid with a new toy. My own car on my own sector, making decisions about how and where to patrol, answering as many calls as I could, and writing reports, like I'd learned. Like a real cop.

One morning, about 3:00 a.m., after I'd been on my own for just a few weeks, they called me and a couple of other cars to respond to a factory burglar alarm. I was only about four or five blocks away and the streets were actually deserted, so I would get there in seconds. Still, I turned on my lights and siren and sped to the location. As I pulled up, the other cops who were already there all turned and looked at me. *What's their problem?* After we had checked the building and determined it to be a faulty alarm, my sergeant, John McArthur, a gruff ex-marine, called me over.

With his ever-present stogie sticking out of his jaw, he said, "Skoufalos, do that shit again, and you'll be walking Germantown Avenue 'til Christ comes back." My puzzled look led to his next comment, which became one of those important early street lessons. "Lights and sirens are for getting through traffic." He paused for effect, then held out both arms to the side and looked around. "Do you see any other cars? Do you? Huh?"

My head down, I said, "No, sarge. Sorry."

He wasn't finished. He wasn't just yelling, he was teaching. "If there had been a burglar here, you let 'em know we were coming."

I nodded. "I didn't think about that."

"All right, just remember…" he said, looking at me hard.

I never made that mistake again.

And so it went. Day after day, months and years passed. The 26th was a perfect learning ground: so many calls and so much crime meant that I was exposed to every part of the job. I loved it. Years after years, no longer a rookie, I still learned by watching, listening and doing. In time, I became one of the veterans the sergeant assigned the rookies to. *Was I that weird and stupid?* I asked myself as I helped break them in. I didn't give them the silent treatment, though; that must have been a generational thing. Anyway, I remembered how it had been for me, and was glad to help the new cops get started. Like me, most of them eventually figured things out.

Every day, I would take a spin through my sector as soon as I hit the street to see what was going on. I checked out my area street by street to get the vibe of the place and try to find anything different from my last shift. And, I looked for trouble: people who didn't belong or were lurking in the dark, drivers that were acting wrong, or young people who were doing things that could get them into trouble.

There were lots of kids around because most of the 26th was residential, and there were way too many auto-pedestrian accidents. I was sick of taking banged-up kids to the hospital—or the morgue—because a speeder didn't see him crossing the street. So I made a lot of car stops.

Some of the drivers I stopped were drunk. Like any cop who was paying attention, I could usually smell the booze as soon as I walked up to the driver's window. Over time, I had locked up enough drunk drivers so that I was pretty good at picking them out in traffic and, if warranted, locking them up. I spent my share of time in court testifying in these cases and was proud of my record of DUI convictions.

Going to court, I got to know many of the Assistant District Attorneys (ADAs). I made it a point to always be prepared for court and most of the overworked ADAs were grateful.

On the other side were the lawyers who represented the defendants. I also had met some of them and knew them well enough to chat when we met in the courtroom. Most of them were okay. Experience had taught me some things about their approach to a DUI defense. Serious cases involving offenders with multiple DUI convictions required a more aggressive and skillful approach by the defense. Most cases involving repeat offenders led to pre-trial discussions between the lawyers and usually resulted in plea bargains—a compromise I didn't always agree with.

Walking into City Hall Courtroom 195 one rainy morning years later, I spotted one of my favorite ADAs, Bill Summers. He was sitting, jacket off, at the prosecution table in the front of the still-empty courtroom, a spread of case folders around him fanned out like a huge deck of cards.

"Morning, Counselor," I said, coming up next to him.

"Hey, Strati, you in here today?" he said, looking up from his work. "I haven't had a chance to look over all these cases yet."

"Yes sir. Name's Walters. DUI."

He shuffled through his pile and pulled out and opened one of the brown folders.

"Let's see…" he said as he scanned the arrest report and the guy's arrest record. "Man, this guy's a regular, counting up the DUIs. Was this an accident or just a car stop?"

"Car stop. The guy stopped at an intersection where he had the green light and was waving me through the red light. Believe that?"

Bill nodded and said, "After a while, I believe anything." Then, "I gotta get back to this stuff. See you in a while."

I found a spot in the back of the courtroom and sat looking over a day-old *Philadelphia Inquirer*, killing time. A couple of hours later, they were only about ten cases into the docket. The judge was trying to move things along, but wasn't having much success. I sat there hoping my case would be heard before lunch. Otherwise, I could be here past five.

Finally, just before noon, the court clerk called, "Commonwealth versus Joseph Walters." My case.

"Mr. Summers, is the prosecution ready to proceed?" asked the judge.

The veteran ADA stood up and said, "We are, Your Honor."

A sharp-looking young man in a well-tailored gray suit stood up from the defense table. "Good morning, Your Honor. I'm Jason Miller, representing Mr. Walters, who is present in the courtroom."

I didn't know this lawyer and didn't recognize his name. He had the *trying harder* look of a new lawyer, maybe a court-appointed public defender.

"Okay gentlemen, let's proceed," said the judge. "Mr. Summers, call your first witness."

That was me. I was called up, sworn in, and took my seat in the witness chair.

Bill Summers walked up and asked me the usual introductory questions: my name, rank, badge number, and assignment. Then, "Officer, please go on in your own words and tell the court the circumstances which bring you to court today."

Looking up at the judge I said, "Your Honor, if it please the court." Then I related my encounter with the defendant. As always, I had reviewed my reports and notes the night prior and again that morning. I laid out the facts which had led to Joseph Walters's arrest.

Apparently satisfied with my testimony, ADA Summers walked back to his seat and said, "Thank you, officer. No further questions, Your Honor."

Looking over at defense attorney Miller, the judge said, "Counselor, your witness."

Miller got up quickly and walked toward the front of the courtroom, stopping a few yards from where I was seated. "Officer, would you tell us what the weather conditions were on the night you arrested Mr. Walters."

Okay, getting right to it, I thought. Most lawyers start with a "good morning" but I could see Miller was nervous. Maybe he was new to the game, or maybe he was just anxious in court. *I'll cut him some slack.* "Yes, sir, good morning," I said, now glancing down at my notes. "It was clear and cold."

"And what were the lighting conditions?"

"It was dark, about 9:30 p.m. There were street lights at the intersection where I first observed Mr. Walters. And, my headlights and Mr. Walters's headlights were on." These were typical defense questions, especially in cases where the prosecution's evidence was strong and the defense was looking for a mistake from the cop, something he could challenge. Not a bad strategy. But, apparently not getting the answers he wanted from me, he seemed stuck, just standing there, studying his yellow legal pad, flipping pages.

The silence was interrupted by the judge's booming voice. "Mr. Miller? Are you finished with this witness?"

"No, Your Honor. I just have a few more questions."

"Alright. Proceed."

"Thank you, judge." Then to me, "Officer, was my client inside or out of the car when you first approached him?"

"He was out of the car."

"Did you notice anything unusual about Mr. Walters when you walked up to him?"

"Yes, he seemed to be unsteady, so I grabbed his arm and asked him to lean against his car, which he did."

Miller asked a few more seemingly pointless questions and I answered them. We went back and forth, on and on. He was all over the place and I felt that some of what he was asking had nothing to do with the case. I guess the ADA felt the same way; so, after a minute or two, he stood up and objected. "Your Honor, these questions are irrelevant".

The judge overruled the objection then asked, "Mr. Miller *is* there a point to this line of questioning?"

"There is, Your Honor. I'm getting to it now. Officer, you say in your report that Mr. Walters was slurring his speech and seemed dazed, is that right?"

"That's correct." *Why is this guy asking questions I've already answered? And they're questions that help the prosecution.*

"Officer, had you ever met Mr. Walters before the day you arrested him?"

"No, sir."

"So, you didn't know if he suffered from some condition that caused him to speak in an unclear manner; and that his condition could create the impression that he sometimes appeared confused?"

Wow, this guy's reaching, I thought. Straightening up, I said, "I was not familiar with any medical condition that would cause the defendant to act in the way described in my reports. And, Mr. Walters never mentioned any such condition to me."

He seemed to not hear me and rolled on. "So, officer, you're telling us that, based on my client's dazed appearance and his inability to speak without slurring, you made the decision to arrest him for driving under the influence?"

"Yes, that, *and* the strong odor of alcohol, *and* the way he was driving." Miller looked at me for a second. Then he asked me to explain. *Oh boy,* I thought. *You really want me to do that? Weren't you listening earlier when I described your client's erratic driving?* I repeated my testimony about Walters's stopping at a green light and waving me through the red. I could see Miller's wheels turning.

I knew that a rule for lawyers was, "Never ask a question you don't know the answer to." Maybe Mr. Miller didn't know that rule or it had slipped his mind, because his next few questions definitely took him down a rabbit hole.

"Officer Skoufalos, how long have you been a police officer?"

"About nine years, sir." I shot a questioning glance at ADA Summers, waiting for an objection. But he was leaning back in his chair, hands folded, a slight smile on his lips. He knew what Miller was going for. I didn't, not yet.

"Do you consider yourself an expert in the area of DUI detection?"

"Well, sir, I'm not sure what you mean by 'expert.'" I spoke slowly, cautious of the question.

"Officer, in your nine years as a police officer, have you made any other arrests for DUI?" He seemed pretty sure of himself now as he moved closer.

"Yes, I have."

"Would you please tell the court approximately how many?"

I thought for a minute, trying to come up with a number. Now I knew where he was headed. For a second, I felt a little sorry for him. "Maybe about twenty-five or thirty, not exactly sure." I said, looking right at him. He stepped back, just a little. If he'd stopped his questions there, he might have been okay. But he didn't.

"And of those, officer, how many have resulted in convictions?" Now, he didn't seem so confident.

I looked at him. "Let's see… pretty sure it was all of them." I said quietly. That backed him up and sat him down.

The judge: "Mr. Miller, I believe you were trying to ascertain whether or not the officer is an expert in DUI enforcement. In my opinion, you've succeeded. Any further questions?"

Miller's shrunken-in-his-seat posture was accompanied by a barely audible, "No, your Honor."

The judge found Joseph Walters guilty and, based on his prior convictions, sentenced him to jail time and ordered his license suspended.

Mr. Miller had a few hurried words with his shocked and angry client before the Deputy Sheriff cuffed Walters and led him out of the courtroom. Clearly, the guy had been expecting probation. Then Miller quickly gathered his papers and was gone.

Before making my way to the courtroom exit, I walked over to ADA Summers who was sitting at his table, getting his next case ready. I leaned over and asked him, "Bill, what the hell was *that*?"

He grinned. "Rookie mistake."

Here's Looking at You, Kid

I was quickly running out of breath. No way I could keep this pace much longer. The kid I was chasing was now barely in view, a good fifty yards ahead. He looked about sixteen and ran like a scared rabbit. It was almost full dark and he was little more than a shadow in the alley. His path was covered in trash and dog shit, but bad as the going was, he was way better at it than I was.

My pursuit of this young man started as the result of another officer's call to the police radio that *he* was chasing the male, with no specific reason given. This was typical of the day—the early 70's when my police career was just getting started. The dispatcher would broadcast the location and description of the person being pursued and, too infrequently, the reason for the pursuit. He could be a suspect in a crime, someone for whom an active warrant existed, or a kid who saw the cops coming and ran. No other reason.

The kid was pulling away from me now. I was navigating the alley alone since we didn't have walkie-talkies back then; none of the cops on the scene knew one another's position. We had driven to the location where the suspect had last been seen, jumped out of our patrol cars, and gave chase. It was wacky, not-well-thought-out, and dangerous. As was often the case on calls like this, my adrenaline was pumping up the red alerts to where my own heart rate surely matched that of the frightened kid trying to get away.

Of course, the overhead street lights were out and, of course, I'd left my flashlight in the car. As I tried to gain on him (unsuccessfully), I couldn't remember if the dispatcher had given a reason for the pursuit. I had nothing. So, this kid could be anything from a curfew violator, to a thief, to a shooter, to a corner drug dealer. Or he could just be a scared kid, running as fast as he could.

And, given all the possible reasons he was running, the thing that made him most dangerous was the fact he was *scared.* Dangerous for us and for the public in this area. But mostly dangerous for the kid. I imagine his mind was a kaleidoscope of the cop horror stories he'd heard or even experienced in his young life. It was certainly conceivable that, in his mind, he was being pursued by terrible monsters who meant him harm.

Exiting the alley, I heard the excited shouts of other responding officers and I ran in that direction, toward a vacant lot halfway down another dark street, where they were focusing on a nearby abandoned house. I slowed down, exhausted now.

Walking up to the area, I saw that there were several neighbors standing around. I figured they'd heard all the commotion and came out to see what was going on. Not unusual. I stopped just short of a group of women where I noticed a little girl who was standing next to a woman whom I presumed was her mother. The woman was holding the girl's hand as she and another woman chatted. My first thought was that the kid should have been in bed hours ago.

As I walked toward the place where the other officers had begun their search for the runner, the little girl—she was about five or six, I'd say—looked right at me. For a second, I forgot why I was there, just taken by this child, so beautiful and innocent. She wore a flowered dress and someone had taken care to braid her hair and tie it with ribbons. She slid behind her mom's skirt, shy and hiding, then peeked out and gave me the tiniest smile. I smiled back. *Why is she looking at me so hard?* It was clear that she was not afraid, worried, or upset.

She turned halfway away from her mother and was doing something with her free hand, kind of hiding it behind her mom. I could see one tiny finger of her free hand, purposely pointed to the left, at a *different* abandoned house than where the police were searching. She was looking at me as she pointed. I quickly guessed that she didn't want her mom to see, but that she was telling me where the young man had gone.

She thought she was *helping*, but her mother, who had seen the gesture, had a different view. She yanked the little arm so hard I thought she might dislocate the child's shoulder. "Don't you be talking to no police!" she screamed. Starting to tear up, the girl defiantly continued looking my way. Turning in the direction of the place she'd pointed out, I glanced back and mouthed a silent "thank you." Mom's anger escalated and she dragged the child away, glaring at me. I watched as they went, wanting to make sure the little girl would be okay. She was brave and took one more quick peek my way before she and her mother disappeared into one of the row houses further down the street. I just nodded.

I gathered several officers to help me search the ruined property the girl had indicated, certain we would find the running boy inside. Sure enough, with numbers on our side, he was located within a few minutes, hiding under a stinking, filthy mattress upstairs. I remember he was shaking. He was handcuffed and frisked. He was clean.

Turning him over to the officer who had initiated the foot pursuit, he was placed in an Emergency Patrol Wagon and transported to headquarters to be turned over to officers from the Juvenile Aid Division (JAD). Before catching a ride back to where I'd jumped out of my car to join the chase, I asked the initiating officer why he'd been chasing the boy.

"Radio had called me for a group of males on the corner, and that there might be drugs involved."

As far as I knew, no drugs had been found on the kid (we'll call him Robert) or in his immediate area. Once inside headquarters, investigation showed he had no record of arrests. I later learned that his mother had reported him missing. It's likely he believed the cops were coming to take him back. Which they would eventually do. The JAD officer told me that he was familiar with the family. Apparently, the young man had run away before from what the officer described as a hell-hole, one where he felt more at risk than on the streets.

Another day, another lesson relearned: running away from police did not necessarily equal being guilty of anything. I remember wondering about how Robert would fare in a juvenile facility, even if for only a day or two. At 15, I'm sure he probably felt he was old enough and street-smart enough to make his own way. I'm sure if was returned home, he'd escape again. Then what? What lessons would he be learning?

Before I closed my eyes that night, I thought again about the best part of my day: meeting, albeit briefly, the cute little girl with the braided hair who took me for a friend. She was still truly an innocent. I would've liked to go back and thank my young friend, maybe get her an ice cream or something, but I never saw her again. I want to believe that at least one cop had done (or would do) something to help that little girl at some point in her young life, maybe even before we met on that fall evening. Or at least that he was nice to her, smiled, said hello. Just because. And I hope that the cops who worked—still work—in her neighborhood and neighborhoods like hers, really *see* her when they ride by. Like she's not invisible. Not just a cute little girl with big eyes and a sad face. Like she's really there.

And while I am constantly reminded of how where you live and how you look means so much in how you may try and are permitted to manage your way in this world, I truly hope that Robert and my little braided-hair friend found the best life they could.

The Lovers

The Philly PD has lots of rules. One is that officers have assigned eating times. Although it sometimes pissed me off that I didn't get to decide when to eat, I got it. If every cop picked his or her eating time, it could leave a huge gap in the response force if a bunch of us decided to go out of service at the same time. Today, my time was six o'clock, which was now. Good thing, because I was hungry.

I called it in and parked my patrol car down the street from the Dew Inn, one of only two decent eating places in the district. I walked in, giving the place my usual once-over, checking things out. The diner was packed, as it was every Friday night, filled with neighborhood families out for a restaurant meal on payday. Making my way through the crowd, past the looks every cop in uniform gets, I sat down hard in my regular spot—the booth in the back, the one the waitresses kept for themselves. I faced the front so I could watch the door, the way most cops did.

I didn't have much time for dinner, which was called *lunch*, no matter what time or which shift. Carol, my favorite evening waitress, saw me and gave me a quick wave. I was glad she was on; she would get my order quickly so I could get back out there. Carol had worked there since the place opened and she was one of the best.

The way the lunch break worked was like this: you had exactly twenty minutes to finish your meal. The police bosses didn't care how crowded the place was or how much you wanted to relax with a cup of coffee. Exactly twenty minutes after the dispatcher put you out of service for lunch, the electronic dispatch system automatically returned you to service; which meant that if you got a call, you were expected to answer it. In fairness to the dispatchers, they were managing calls for about fifty or sixty units so we couldn't expect them to keep track of all of us, especially on a hectic

Friday night on the four to midnight shift in the always-busy East Division. They did their best to cover for any of us that missed a call.

We would all listen out for each other and if somebody didn't answer right away, another unit would pick it up—that is, unless they were on another call and unavailable. Years later, each cop would have a hand-held radio, so if the meal was running over, he could listen for his number and respond on the walkie-talkie if he got called, even if he was out of the car. But this was still the 70s and the only radio I had was bolted to the hump between the front seats in the red and white police car sitting out at the curb.

"Hey Carol, how you been? What's good today?" I asked as she hurried over, order pad and pen ready. Carol, petite and full of energy, was beaming her usual smile.

"Hi, sweetie, how're you doin'? Haven't seen you in a while. What can I getcha?"

"What do you recommend?"

"The chopped steak looks good. Comes with mushroom gravy and mashed."

"Great," I said. "And an iced tea, okay?"

"You got it, hon. Be right back with your tea."

Minutes later, after wolfing down a meal I was pretty sure would soon feel like a brick in my stomach, I left my money on the table and started for the door. I almost made it outside, just a few feet from a clean getaway, when John, the owner, stopped me. "Hallo, officer, how are you?" Then, whispering in his thick Greek accent, "Why you leave the money onna table? I tol' you before, you don' pay." This was our regular routine, every time I came in here. That's why I had stopped taking the money to the register where John was stationed.

'I know, John; I appreciate it, but you work hard here and you don't work for nothin'. Tell you what, if I get a few minutes later, I'll come back and we'll have a cup of coffee, okay?"

He smiled and nodded. "Good. I see you later," he said, patting me hard on the back as I opened the door to leave. I looked at my watch; I was about a minute over my twenty, so I jogged to the car, got in and turned the radio on, hoping I hadn't blown a call.

I didn't know it then, but I wouldn't be joining John for evening coffee. By the time I finished my shift, it'd almost be time for breakfast.

Patrolling, I knew it would probably get busy soon. So, for the next few hours, I drove around my area, looking for trouble. Two of my priorities were the two drugstores in my sector. Powell's at 6th and Girard was still open and the owner was outside smoking when I pulled up. There had been a few robberies along this part of Girard in the past couple of weeks. Maybe seeing a marked car stopping by would make any would-be bad guy reconsider. "How's it going, Allen?" I asked, looking past him into the store. "Everything okay?"

"Hi, Officer Skouf. Yeah, we're kind of slow. How're *you* doin'?"

"Good. I'll be better when midnight comes. Got a feeling it's gonna be one of those nights." We waved at each other as I pulled away, on my way to check my other pharmacy at Germantown and Master. I never got there.

"2603, 918 Lawrence Street, disturbance house."

2603, an EPW, had received the assignment because "disturbances" required a two-man response. Although the radio was usually pretty busy in the 26th, like most cops, I had eventually learned how to filter the police radio "noise" (calls and announcements that didn't pertain to me) and to listen for just my car number and any calls on or near my sector. The address was only a few blocks away, so I headed that way. Didn't matter that I hadn't been called to respond, I liked to know what was going on in my territory.

"2610, put me in on Lawrence Street," I said into the radio mic.

"Okay 10, I'll hold you out [of service]," said the dispatcher.

Driving a little faster than patrol speed, I tried to think if I'd ever been at that address before; couldn't remember. A couple of minutes later, turning onto Lawrence, I was now about a block away from 918. I started focusing, preparing for my arrival. Looking as far ahead as I could toward the location, I was trying to see if there was anything going on: a crowd, cars in the street, any unusual activity or hubbub. From where I was, everything looked okay. Car windows down, I listened for any sound that would give me a clue about what I was heading into, like raised voices, glass breaking, gunshots, or tires screeching. So far, so good. I wasn't rushing into this call; no reason to. Even so, I got there ahead of the wagon and parked a few houses down from 918. I grabbed my Maglite and baton and got out of the car.

There was nobody around. That didn't necessarily mean anything; the disturbance could be inside—most of them were. As I walked up the worn white marble steps of the three-story row house, I saw the multiple mailboxes and doorbells by the front door. I walked back to the car and called dispatch. "2610, I'm on location at 918 Lawrence. Do you have a floor or a name? The place looks like an apartment building."

"No, 10, just the address. Also be advised that the caller wouldn't leave his name or address. Use caution." Then, "2603, did you receive that? 10 is on location."

"0-3, we got it, we're a few blocks away."

Walking up the front steps again, I turned the knob and pushed open the unlocked door. I went in and stopped in the tiny vestibule to listen. Other than the muted sound of a TV somewhere, I heard nothing. I clicked on my flashlight, swinging it down the unlit hallway, then shone it on the steps to the second floor. There was an old bike chained to the banister leading upstairs; otherwise, the corridor was deserted. Everything looked okay. It was still light outside, but not here in this old place. I had learned the hard way that it can get very dark inside buildings in a hurry, even when it was bright and sunny outside. Playing my light ahead, I moved into the ground floor hall. It felt like I was entering a cave. Good thing I remembered my big, powerful flashlight.

My knock on the first-floor apartments, front and rear, got no response. With no answer and no sounds from inside like a TV, radio, or voices, I moved to the second floor. The old guy in the front unit opened his door and told me he hadn't called and that he hadn't seen or heard anything unusual. I guessed that he was hard of hearing since he leaned in close when I was talking and I still had to repeat everything. With the volume of his TV, I figured he might not hear much of anything short of a large explosion. I thanked him and moved to the rear apartment. As I got closer, I saw that the door was open a little, just enough to see lights inside. I wasn't even sure this was the place, but it felt like it might be.

Something in my head was telling me to take it easy, to not rush in. The hair on my neck, now at full attention like it always was in these kinds of situations, made me stop. *Maybe I should wait for the wagon,* I said to myself. Even as I had the thought, I knew I wouldn't. I knocked.

"Police. Hello. Anybody home?" No answer. After knocking and calling again, a little louder and with the same result, I pushed the door open just enough to see in. There was a short hallway leading to what looked like a living room. The lights were on back there. I stood there for a minute, listening and looking around, even sniffing to see if some smell would give me more information than I had. There *was* a familiar smell—burning candles. I tried to get a sense of how the place was laid out. Unsnapping my holster, I pocketed my flashlight and moved my baton to my left hand. This felt like something, I just didn't know what. The only sound I heard (more like *felt*) was the thumping of my heart. Good. I was tuned in. Slow and quiet, I moved into the apartment.

The first door on my left was a small bathroom. I shone my light in—nobody there. Next, on the right, the kitchen. It was lit up and empty. I made it through to the living room, checked it and found nothing. It looked like nobody was home. Nothing was disturbed, so it probably wasn't a burglary. I had checked the apartment door lock on the way in and it seemed fine. Was it possible the occupants had gone out and forgotten to lock their door? Maybe, but probably not. Not in this neighborhood. And this had come out as a disturbance, right? Right. So I moved on to where I figured the bedrooms had to be, further back in the place. The door to the first one was open, and I could see a light in there.

Staying close to the door frame, I peeked into the room and saw them both on the bed. I stepped into the room and saw a young man and a young woman—they looked like teenagers—lying there, very still. *Are they sleeping? Are they passed out, drunk or from drugs?* I wondered. On the dresser, near the left side of the bed, there were two lighted candles, flickering. It was the only light in the room, so I turned on the ceiling light. Then, I saw the blood.

The girl's white nightgown was splotched with so much red—blood, I figured—that I didn't believe she could still be alive. She was very still and her skin was gray. From the rips in her clothing, it looked like she'd been stabbed a number of times in her chest and abdomen. I checked her pulse. Nothing. She was dead. While looking her over, I had been keeping an eye on the male lying next to her. He, too, was dressed all in white and was lying there motionless. The guy had very little blood on him.

Walking around to the other side of the bed and reaching over to check the young man, I thought I saw his chest rising and falling. Just a little, barely noticeable. Not sure I had seen right, I put two fingers on the side of his neck to see if he had a pulse. He did. Then his eyelids fluttered. I jumped back and almost knocked the candles over. *What the hell is this?* I wondered. *Where is the goddamn wagon crew?* I went back to the guy and quick-checked him for injuries; there were none I could see. He was just fine, breathing and everything.

I heard the guys from 2603 yelling to me from the front of the apartment. I called them back to where I was. I watched the guy lying there, still not moving, but blinking his eyes. *What's up with this guy, what's he doing?* I thought, still watching him closely. As I went for the phone on the nightstand to let dispatch know what was going on and to request a supervisor, my foot came down on something hard. Stepping back, I shone my light and saw a bloody knife that had been thrown or placed on the floor, between the bed and the nightstand.

As I was talking with the dispatch supervisor, my backup ran into the room. Carlos Colon, one of the wagon cops, just stood there, looking at the bizarre scene. He shook his head. I quickly briefed him and his partner, Gary Jeffers. These guys were veterans—they both had a lot more time on the job than I had. But I could tell by their faces that they had never seen anything like this.

Like me, Colon had noticed that the male appeared to be unhurt while the girl was obviously dead. He shook the guy and shouted for him to get up. No movement, no eyes opening, nothing. Then, Colon, thinking the guy might be Hispanic, shouted the same commands in Spanish. That worked. The guy opened his eyes and slowly sat up, like he'd been raised from the dead. He stared at Colon, rubbing his eyes. Then, looking over, he saw the young girl next to him. He grabbed her and started crying. "Ana, Ana, mI amor!" he screamed over and over. Jeffers and I pulled him off and stood him up.

In Spanish, Colon asked the kid what had happened. "No se." *I don't know,* came the reply. I remembered enough of my high school Spanish to get that, but I couldn't get that this guy, whatever or whoever he was, expected us to believe that a young girl lay brutally murdered on the bed next to him, and he didn't know what had happened.

Within minutes, our sergeant arrived and assigned Officer Jeffers to protect and document the crime scene. Since the whole place was a crime scene, we took the male and moved out into the hallway. As Colon questioned the guy, who said his name was Jesus, it became pretty clear that he was involved in the girl's death. So, the questions stopped and he was cuffed. Homicide detectives would talk to him later, after they advised him of his rights.

Before taking him downtown to Homicide, we checked him over again. He was unhurt, except for three superficial scratches on his neck, so minor that we hadn't noticed them at first. They didn't even require any treatment by the fire department paramedics who'd been called in.

We found a note in Spanish on the kitchen table. Without touching it, Colon translated and the gist of it was: since their parents wouldn't let them get married (he was seventeen, she was fifteen), they had decided to kill themselves. That was the plan. The apartment belonged to a friend who later told detectives he thought the couple was planning to have a romantic evening together, not acting out a twisted, screwed-up version of Romeo and Juliet.

Once I was done at the scene, I took the long way downtown to talk with the detectives. I wasn't in a rush. Being a Friday night, I knew the unit would be jumping. It was. So, after writing my preliminary report, I sat in the Homicide Unit's lobby and waited.

I paged through an ancient, coffee-stained National Geographic, filled with photos of places I'd never been. But I wasn't really paying attention. My mind was back in that apartment bedroom. I kept seeing 15-year-old Ana, lying dead with candlelight flickering on her pale skin and bloody clothing. As I tried to imagine the terror she must have felt, I knew it wasn't my job to understand the *why's* or the *how's* of these incidents, but this one bothered me a lot. I wondered how things had gotten to that point for these two kids.

The detective, who interviewed me many hours later, told me that Jesus had admitted to killing the girl. The plan had been for them each to stab themselves so they could finally be together in death. They had decided she would go first. When the time came, Ana had told him she was too scared to do it. So she asked him to help her. Jesus agreed, promising her he'd soon be joining her. She must have suffered a terrible death: I learned later that only a couple of her many stab wounds were fatal. But Jesus persisted and finished the job, as he'd promised. When the detective asked what had happened after he'd stabbed her, he said that when he saw what she had gone through, he couldn't do it to himself. So he decided to superficially scratch his neck a few times to make it look like he'd *tried* to commit suicide, but had been unsuccessful. Really. That was his story. If I hadn't shown up, he probably would have left her there and walked away.

———•●•———

The court case was a few months later. I found out that Jesus' attorney had worked out a deal: Jesus would plead to second degree murder and they wouldn't pursue first degree. And, as a juvenile with no previous record, he would only do a short time in prison, and in a juvenile facility at that.

I wondered if the detectives ever tracked down the person who had called 911. Could he have been a relative of Ana or Jesus who'd had a feeling that something was up? Or maybe it was a classmate or somebody one of them had confided in? Or was it the friend who had let them use his apartment? I don't know. I never heard. It didn't matter.

One Man's Trash

"All cars stand by. 2611 and 2617, take 2012 North Front Street, at the Hotstuff Food Company, for a robbery in progress. Two males, armed with guns, early 20's, average height and weight, wearing dark clothing. Both were wearing dark skI masks. No further description. Cars responding use caution. We're getting multiple calls."

The dispatcher's voice broke the quiet of the Friday morning in the 26th District—an area that touched parts of North Philadelphia, Kensington, and Fishtown. I had been driving with the window down on my new Plymouth Gran Fury, enjoying the weather and paying attention. It was one of those nice fall days, halfway between Labor Day and Halloween—sunny, with a cool, sharp breeze and a cloudless sky, bright blue like a Maxfield Parrish painting.

I'd been patrolling the north end of my sector and was pretty close to the location of the call.

"2611, I got it." Then, Ed Barnes, in 2617 car, acknowledged the call, too.

Picking up speed, I realized that I knew the place. It was a small food delivery business that had been there for decades. Hotstuff's ancient brick building was so plain that it melted into the other row-type store fronts lining that section of North Front Street. The only thing different about the place in my 11 years in the district was the presence of new heavy steel bars on Hotstuff's windows and doors—recently added to keep burglars out when they were closed. But they were open now.

Driving from bright sun into the semi-light of the shadowy overhead structure of the elevated train, I threw off my sunglasses and sped past the old buildings that had once housed businesses that had been part of the landscape. One by one, they'd gone away, until only a scattered few were left.

Man, this brings back memories, I thought. This was my old neighborhood, the streets where I'd grown up. It had once been a thriving business center, bustling and active, filled with lots of sellers and buyers. Back then, lively activity had made it exciting for me and my brothers and our friends to just walk down the street and check out the windows of the stores and what they were selling: shoes, clothes, toys, sporting goods, hardware and a few good eating spots like Four Sons Pizza and the Majestic Restaurant. Now this worn-out strip was dark and as dingy like the steel El pillars that zipped by as I drove.

"2621, I'm on location. It's a founded robbery. Description same as you gave. Direction taken was North on Front and West on Norris." Since 21 car was already there, no need for me to go to the scene, so I started looking for the bad guys.

About a block away, I slowed the car to barely moving, looking for anybody that fit the description: walking, sitting, or running, even in doorways or hunched down between cars. I guessed these guys would split up and take off in different directions. I would. Other cars flooded the area and I listened for any information they might give.

I had gotten to the area within a minute of the call and the first car on the scene reported that the owner had said that the guys had left less than two minutes before. I made some swings through the narrow, littered streets. Nothing. It didn't make sense. These guys couldn't have gotten far. Too many cops had responded too quickly. It didn't happen very often, but when it did, the bad guys were usually still in the area. And they were usually nabbed.

Heading south on Mascher Street and the wrong way on Diamond, I crept along, hunting. At Palethorpe, I turned in. The street was no more than a cobblestone alley, and I could imagine the horse-drawn carriages and wagons that had used these streets so many decades ago. I was trying to be careful with the new car—its tires almost touched the curbs on either side of the narrow street. I didn't want to scuff them or worse, like scraping one of the ancient steel utility poles that sprouted from the sidewalk, just inches from the curb line.

Some people say that cops develop an extra sense, one that helps them do their work and keeps them safe. Following my hunch on that day, I pulled over and picked up the mic to tell dispatch that I would be out of the car looking for these two guys. Years later, this notification might not be as necessary, as then we would be equipped with hand-held radios. But not that day. I had heard of too many cops getting out of the car without letting the dispatcher know, usually for something as innocuous as talking with a citizen, and getting into a bad situation. The trouble was made worse because no one knew where they were, let alone out of the car. So, my rule was to always use the police radio (like I was supposed to) whenever I left the vehicle, even just to get a cup of coffee or check something out.

"2611, I'll be out of the car in the 1900 block of Palethorpe, checking the area."

"Okay 11, use caution," said Corporal Dave Smythe, the dispatch supervisor who had taken over the call and was directing personnel and managing the incident.

A minute after I got out of the car, I saw 2617 pull into the street, a little too fast. But that was Ed. He never took his time when there was somebody to back up. And we were friends. We both took the job seriously, believing that our sectors were our own little town of which we were the sheriff. I watched as he unfolded his 6'4" frame out of the car, grabbing his baton and flashlight as he hurried my way. Smart. Sometimes these things led from the bright sunshine to the basement of an abandoned house or factory. I was glad that Ed had responded. He was a great cop, one of the best I'd ever known. He was also tough and could handle himself when his usual charm wasn't enough. With catcher's-mitt-sized hands and piercing blue eyes, he commanded respect. He knew his people and how to communicate with them. The law-abiding citizens loved him and the rest were both cautious and respectful.

"What do you got, Strati?" he asked as I walked to meet him halfway down the block.

"I don't know Ed," I said, looking around. "These guys couldn't have gotten far. We got here too quick."

"Yeah. Most of the vacant houses have been checked. Nothin'."

"I know. But I still feel they're close."

We were standing on the narrow sidewalk at the edge of a huge vacant lot where five or six row homes had once stood. Because this street was rarely traveled, the lot had become a popular dumping site for construction debris and a graveyard for discarded tires, televisions, kitchen appliances and God knows what else. I made a mental note to call the sanitation department when I got the chance.

Not yet ready to give up the search, I looked around and tried to think of what to do next. Scanning the houses beyond the lot, looking for alleys and other hiding places, I caught movement off to my right, above me. I looked up and saw a guy standing on the flat roof of a two-story house about 50 yards away. He was wildly waving his arms, but not saying anything. I couldn't have heard him, anyway; he was too far away. I waved back.

Ed and I looked over the area some more and decided to move on. As we were leaving, a second guy appeared on the roof. Now, they were both waving and jumping up and down. It occurred to me then that they might not be just a couple of friendly roofers. I stopped and watched them and, tapping Ed on the arm, I pointed in their direction. Sure that they now had our attention, both of them started pointing down and stamping their feet. I thought I was pretty good at charades, so I squinted at them and tried to get what they were telling us. Nothing registered. I looked over at Ed and got the impression that he was puzzled, too. We started toward our cars. As we did, one of the roofers jumped up and down and motioned for us to walk forward, toward them.

It finally hit me that they were guiding us to the middle of the lot, toward a large pile of discarded drywall and other trash. As we got closer, they both pointed down toward their feet.

We both got it at the same time. Looking at the mound of rubble, we split left and right and moved as quietly as we could. The roof guys were watching and as we got to the middle, one gave a thumbs up. Guns drawn, I shouted, "You, under the trash, police! Come out of there. Let's see your hands." No response. No movement. Were these guys on the roof fooling with us? It didn't feel that way. Silently motioning to Ed, we moved toward a large piece of sheetrock that topped the pile and quickly shoved it forward. I saw a boot, then a leg. Ed repeated the command to surrender, but whoever was down there was either dead, scared, or ignoring us.

We moved more debris and exposed a male lying face down in the dirt. His hands were tucked under his body and he wasn't moving. He fit the description, down to the navy skI mask sticking out of his back pocket. Ed quickly bent down and cuffed him, pulling him to his feet. The guy apparently still couldn't believe his bad luck. He said nothing. Dust from the debris of his hiding place powdered him from head to foot. Shaking his head, he just looked at us.

Once he was secured, we found a gun and a pile of money where he'd been. We advised Corporal Smythe and called for a patrol wagon to transport our prisoner to East Division detectives. As we got to our cars, I looked up for our helpers, but they were gone. I don't know if they knew it, but they were my heroes. For weeks after, I tried, but never found them.

Detectives later arrested the second male who, along with our guy, was positively identified by the business owner. We recovered over $5000 from the robbery. The gun we found in the pile of trash was fully loaded and had been stolen in an earlier residential burglary.

Like many small neighborhood businesses in those days, Hotstuff's management paid their employees in cash every Friday. Investigators had learned that one of the robbers was friendly with a former employee who had told him about the payday schedule and when the cash would be in the building. Detectives advised the owner of this information and strongly suggested they change their system.

The Dark Road

What a night! Call after call with no letup. The evening shift is usually busy, but today was a record-setter. And not just simple calls: burglary reports with long lists of stolen property; auto accidents involving cars versus buildings and trucks versus buses; a report of missing twins with marginally cooperative parents. On top of it all, the unrelenting rain made getting anywhere tough, even with lights and siren. On the plus side: the night went by super-quick and now it was time to report off duty, time to relax a little.

I grabbed my jacket from my locker, pulled it on over my uniform and took the steps two at a time up from the basement squad locker room. My watch said 11:40. I could hardly wait to get out to my car and drive the mile and a half to Episcopal Hospital where my wife, Monica, would be waiting after her shift in the Emergency Room.

We were glad to work the same hours for one week each month, and took full advantage of the opportunity. Monica's steady shift was three to eleven, so on those days I dropped her off and picked her up. I worked rotating shifts (days, nights, and evenings) for six days straight, then two days off.

She was standing under the small overhang outside the double doors to the ER and smiled as I pulled up. She got in, gave me a kiss and settled back. "Let's go to the Hollywood, let's get breakfast," she said, turning my way. It was the last day of the work week for us both and this would be a small celebration and was a sort of tradition.

"Sounds good," I said. "I'm in the mood for one of their toasted cinnamon buns, with lots of butter." I pulled around a Fire Rescue truck that was urgently unloading a patient covered with a sheet but was still getting soaked in the rain.

Heading up Roosevelt Boulevard, we took turns sharing our work days. I learned that hers had been pretty hectic, too: a drug overdose and two shootings, along with a battle in the ER between the two factions involved in one of shootings.

I turned right on Grant as Monica went through her ideas for our weekend: a craft fair tomorrow morning at Tyler Park, then dinner with friends on Sunday at a hot new downtown bistro. *Good plan.* I nodded my head in agreement as I turned onto Academy Road, now just a couple of miles from the diner.

I knew this part of Academy Road well. The overhead street lights were permanently turned off for about a mile and a half because it was part of the flight path for the small Northeast Philadelphia Airport. It was *really* **dark**. Hard to see. No streetlights and no houses or other buildings to provide ambient light. All I had was my headlights. I stopped talking and concentrated on the road, the limited visibility made worse by the steady drizzle. Monica could sense my focus and sat quietly.

Driving slowly, I saw the brake lights right in front of us. They were still far enough away so I was able to slow down in plenty of time. The car ahead was fully stopped in the driving lane. As I pulled up right behind it and put on my flashers, I noticed a figure, off to my right. It looked like a male and was running around and gesturing with his arms in the air. Then he'd stop and crouch holding his hands to his head. Seeing him, Monica rolled down her window and, without turning, said to me, "Looks like there are two or three people out there. And there's another car half in the road and half on the grass on the right."

"I see them. What're they doing? Can you tell?" Before she could answer me, one of them, a young male, ran up to her side of the car.

"Please help us! Oh, my God!" he screamed. He looked to be a teenager about sixteen or seventeen and he was very upset—out of control upset. My eyes adjusting to the darkness, I could make out that the other two were also teenage boys, also extremely distressed.

As we got out of the car, I looked around, getting the big picture. Monica walked toward the group of kids and I walked up to the driver's side of the car I'd stopped behind. It was running and I noticed someone behind the wheel, slumped over.

"Strati, get me the blanket out of the trunk." Monica's voice was calm but I heard the urgency. I grabbed the blanket and took it to where she was now kneeling by the right front side of the car we'd stopped behind.

What I saw there, I'll never forget.

The young man, whom we had not seen when we pulled up, was half-lying on the ground and half-leaning against (more like pinned to) the front bumper of the car that had apparently struck him and the back of the other car. He was conscious, but barely. I could tell he was badly hurt—there was blood—I just wasn't sure how bad it was. And there was something very wrong with his left arm.

Monica, now in full ER nurse mode, kneeled down next to him, taking charge. "What's your name, hon?" she calmly asked. He looked up at her with the glazed eyes of someone who looked like he was very close to fading into shock. She laid the blanket around him to cover him without moving him, then reached into her uniform pocket and pulled out the tourniquet she kept there.

"Frankie," he said softly.

"Okay, Frankie, I'm Monica and I'm going to help you. Can you tell me where it hurts?"

"My arm…it really hurts."

"Anywhere else?"

"I don't think so. I don't know."

My gut told me that I should be doing something else besides watching her; she had it pretty much under control. I quickly went around to the driver's side of the car I was stopped behind and looked in. The middle-aged man behind the wheel had his head on the steering wheel and didn't respond to my shouting and shaking. Then as I leaned in to try to rouse him, I got a full whiff of alcohol all around. Now I was getting pissed off.

Before I could do anything else, I realized that not only was the car still running, *it was still in Drive!* I grabbed the gear shifter and rammed it into Park, turned off the ignition and pocketed the key. Inside, I was freaking out—this guy, apparently drunk, had hit a kid, then passed out. Then, all this time, Monica and the kid had been there in front of the car with the car still in gear and running! It was a miracle that his foot hadn't slipped off the brake. Yanking him back off the steering wheel, I dragged him out of the car, cuffed him, and sat him in the backseat of his vehicle. He was so out of it, he didn't resist or acknowledge my actions.

This was the 80s, long before almost everybody had a cell phone in their pockets, so I started looking around for other cars. I needed the cavalry. I took off my jacket to make my uniform more visible, and walked back to where Monica was working on Frankie. It looked like she had managed to stop the bleeding and was assessing him for any other injuries. I could tell by her tight-lipped glance at me that it wasn't good. The boy's arm looked seriously mangled and was barely attached.

I moved the other three kids out of the road to the grassy sidewalk, talking with them and trying to get them calm enough to tell me what had happened. At the same time, I kept an eye on the drunk driver, who was still out of it. Finally, I saw headlights and waved down a car whose driver slowed and stopped.

"I'm an off-duty cop," I said. "I need you to drive to the 8th district. Tell them I need some cops and paramedics here. Tell them it's an emergency."

"Okay, officer. Where is it?"

"About three blocks back the way you came from," I said, pointing. I guided him over the grassy median, and turned him around.

I went back to where Monica was helping the injured kid to see if there was anything I could do.

"No, we need Rescue." I heard the concern and frustration in her voice as I told her they were coming. Blood streaked her white uniform and she sat there holding the injured Frankie in her arms.

Walking back over to other three young men, I determined they weren't injured, just freaked out and worried about Frankie. While we waited, I got out my notebook and started taking notes: the make, model, license and registration numbers of the striking vehicle; names, addresses, phone numbers, and dates of birth of the kids; anything I could get about Frankie.

As I jotted down the information, I heard the welcome scream of sirens. I could tell that the higher-pitched, more urgent one, belonged to a Fire Rescue Squad.

When the paramedics ran up with their medical bag, Monica gave them a low-key briefing. After they had checked and stabilized Frankie's arm, they quickly and carefully placed him on the wheeled gurney and rolled him into the rear of the squad.

By then, I had given the story to the two police officers who had arrived. They hauled the handcuffed man out of his car and put him in the back of their truck. Other police cars arrived and set up traffic control with their blue and red strobes lighting the scene.

"I'll head over to Northeast Detectives to give my statement," I told one of the cops as they got ready to take the prisoner for DUI testing. Then I walked over to the officers who were investigating the crash scene and talking with the other three kids. After asking the cops to make sure the kids got to the Detectives, I gave them my name, badge number, phone number, and my district of assignment and told them to contact me if they needed anything else.

Monica was sitting in our car waiting for me. I got in and explained that I had to go talk to the detectives. "I think they might want to talk to you, too," I told her.

She looked at me and nodded her head. "Okay."

I had seen her in action before. More than once, I'd been there when she had taken charge of a seriously sick or injured patient in the ER. Automatic. Professional. Just like tonight. But I could see by the sadness on her face that this was really bothering her a lot. Me too.

Lost in our thoughts, we drove the fifteen minutes to Harbison Avenue where the Northeast Detective Division was located.

"I think he's going to lose his arm," she said quietly as we got out of the car. I said nothing and just put my arm around her.

We were there for about two hours, giving statements and answering detectives' questions. I learned what happened from the detective who had interviewed Frankie's companions.

They were on their way home when the driver of the car, Frankie's best friend, said he heard a funny noise from under the rear of the car. So, they stopped to check it out. Tragically, it was the wrong place and the wrong time. They didn't count on a drunk driver zooming by as Frankie was bent over looking under the car. They didn't expect the guy to plow into their car, pinning Frankie's arm between the two cars. I was pretty sure that none of them would ever forget this and all the "what ifs." Their only good luck was that Monica and I arrived on the scene so soon after the crash.

<hr>

About a year later, on a sunny September morning, I reported to City Hall. I was there for the trial of the guy from that horrible, rainy night—the drunk driver. As I looked around the crowded courtroom, I almost didn't recognize him. He was cleaned up and dressed nicely. He was standing with a high-dollar defense attorney, well-known for his work on DUI cases. They just stood there, chatting. It all started coming back and I was getting pissed off all over again. I turned away and found a seat near the front of the room, with the other cops.

I had reviewed my notes and gone over the case with the DA. I was ready. I took a seat and waited for my case to be called by the judge.

"HI Skouf. How have you been?" I tried to place the tall dark-haired man who sat down next to me. He was well-dressed, suit, tie, the works. At first, I thought he might be an attorney. But then I focused in on the guy. *The voice is familiar. Not a lawyer. Pretty sure he's a cop.*

"Hi. I'm good," I said, still trying to think of the guy's name whose face, by now, was starting to look familiar.

"Can we talk somewhere private?"

"Sure," I said. Just then, it came to me: This was Inspector Andy Jenkins. He was a good guy, but I hadn't seen him in years. As we walked toward a small conference room just outside the courtroom, I thought back to the first time we had ever spoken. Early 70s. He was a lieutenant in East Detectives, running One Squad. I was a rookie.

Back then, an old-time detective was grumbling to me about everything that was wrong with the robbery arrest memorandum I'd given him. The guy was textbook, right out of Barney Miller: feet up on the desk, shirt too tight to close the top button, necktie crisscrossed, not tied, bulging belly, cigarette dangling from his lips as he talked, not even looking at my report. Every few minutes, he'd stop to take a slurp of coffee from a filthy white mug that would soon be completely coffee brown, and probably hadn't been washed in years. It was also clear to me that many years had passed since this guy had been in uniform. Anyway, I knew that the arrest was good and so was my memo. So, I said nothing. I figured this was just a grizzled veteran detective giving the rookie a hard time. And he was having fun doing it.

I didn't know that then-Lieutenant Jenkins, the squad commanding officer, had been standing behind us until I heard him speak. The detective didn't know he was there, either. The lieutenant had been listening, taking it all in. After more than a few minutes of the detective berating me, Jenkins appeared and quietly said: "Detective, if you're having a problem with the officer's memo, maybe I can help you figure it out."

Feet hitting the floor as he suddenly sat up straight, the investigator said, "Oh no, lieutenant, it's fine. I was just messing with him."

The intense, dark-eyed lieutenant glared at the old-timer. This look is what I would later describe as the "Jenkins glare."

The detective, all-business now, said, "Okay Officer, let's finish up with your interview and get you on your way."

A man of few words, his point made, the lieutenant stood there for a few seconds longer. Then he gave me a slight nod and said, "Good job, Officer," and slowly walked away.

I don't know why he did it; I had never met or spoken to him before. And although I'd see him around from time to time after that, we never talked about what had happened that day with the crusty old detective, but from then on, he was okay with me.

• ● •

Now, all these years later, I followed the inspector out of the courtroom, down the hallway into a small empty room normally used for attorney-witness conferences. He closed the door, we sat down, and he turned to face me.

"Skouf, I want to thank you for what you did."

I looked at him, trying to get a clue. I had nothing, so I just sat there, waiting, not saying anything.

"Frankie," he said. He stopped, waiting for me to say something. When I didn't, he went on. "Frankie is my nephew, my sister's boy. And please thank your wife, too."

I was glad I was sitting down. There was no way I was expecting this. Suddenly, it was that rainy night again and I was back there on that dark road.

"How is he?" I asked, in barely a whisper, fearing the worst.

"He's coming along," he sighed. "He's getting there." I wasn't sure he believed his own words.

We sat there for a few minutes, both of us quiet.

The inspector looked at me and said, "He lost his arm, you know. He's been having a tough time with that and adjusting to everything…" He shook his head, looking away. "Frankie's been going through hell, poor kid," he said. "Still is. Pure hell."

My head down, I nodded, not knowing what else to say or do.

He gave me a synopsis of the horrific personal journey the kid had been on since that awful night: multiple surgeries, endless pain, depression, counseling. His whole life now terribly different, Frankie was struggling every day to deal with his new reality.

Looking at Inspector Jenkins, I saw how hard it was for him, too. In the police business, the accumulation of the tragic and senseless incidents an officer is involved with over a career is an almost unbearable weight that cops carry for a long time. This was worse. This, he couldn't get away from, ever.

"Inspector, Monica and I haven't forgotten. I don't think we'll ever forget." I searched his face, hoping to see a little softening in his eyes, hearing that we shared his pain.

He looked at me, nodded his head and got up. I stood and we grabbed each other's shoulders and held there for a long minute. Then without another word, he left.

———————————•❂•———————————

The court case against the drunk driver who struck Frankie was adjudicated as a result of a plea-bargain—an agreement between the prosecutor and defense attorney which is ultimately approved or rejected by the judge. I wasn't part of that discussion nor, to my knowledge, was Frankie. In such cases, there is no trial, per se, just a proceeding where the defendant pleads guilty (usually to a lesser offense than the most serious one he had been charged with). In this case, my recollection is that he was sentenced to a term of probation.

After that day in court, I regularly checked in on Frankie through his uncle. While he slowly got better, I know that he went through many terrible and painful periods. Eventually, he was well enough to be fitted with a prosthetic arm.

I also learned that, on the night of his injury, Frankie and his friends had been returning from a practice for their rock band. Frankie was the drummer.

"Routine"

As I waited, I thought: *What do I know that's important? Must be some things. Things that I learned just by doing them. Sometimes the hard way. How do I share this stuff with other guys and do it right?* I sat in the classroom, in a wood and metal desk-chair that had been rooted here for decades. More guys came in and scattered in seats all around the room. Looking at them I could tell that, like me, they hadn't been back here in a while. I wondered if they were thinking what I was.

When the big clock on the wall above the chalkboard hit exactly 8:00 a.m., a tall, gray-haired man in uniform strode in and stood at the front of the room, hands on hips, saying nothing. Just looking at us. Every crease in his uniform shirt and trousers was sharp enough to cut. His silver and gold badge gleamed as it caught the bright fluorescent lights. Even at 60 plus, he could have been an advertisement for how a cop in uniform should look. This was Captain James Snead, in charge of recruit training. He'd been here back in the summer of 1971 when I was brand new, going through with the rest of the guys in Class 222.

"Good morning, gentlemen, welcome back to the Academy. You all know why you're here." He paused, sweeping the room with his keen blue eyes, stopping to look at each of us. *Making sure we measure up? Maybe.* He gestured with both hands, wordlessly telling those in the back of the room to move forward. "The Department has been authorized to add several hundred officers over the next 18 months, so we need more instructors to help get them through. That's you guys. You've all been recommended by your commanding officers." As Captain Snead spoke, I glanced around at the other officers I'd be working with. All of us were fresh from the street, all experienced cops. I recognized a couple of them as guys I'd worked with either in East Division or on special details around the city. Everyone was sharp-looking, uniforms perfect, shoes shining, hair short and trimmed.

This is neat, I thought. *Back at the Academy! Seems like a hundred years ago.* Becoming an instructor had been a distant, back-of-my-mind idea, something I thought I'd like to do someday, but it was happening *now!* I had spent years on the street—just over 10 to be exact. And I loved it; it was exciting and fun, so different than any job I'd ever worked. Yeah, sometimes it was scary and sad. But what a ride!

I thought back to last Friday when my district captain, Roy Carney, had called me in and given me the news that I was being detailed to the Academy. A pleasant, unexpected surprise. Like the others sitting here, I had requested the assignment, but I never thought they'd pick me. Along with patrol experience, the assignment required a college degree. I was glad that I'd stuck it out through seven years of night classes. That had been brutal, working rotating shifts and going to school. But I'd done it and it had been worth it.

Over the weekend, considering the assignment, I began getting some conflicting thoughts: *Really think you're good enough to do this? What makes you such an authority?* And, *I'm really going to miss the street.* The last one kept repeating, making me go back and forth. Finally, I decided to take the job. Hell, if I didn't like it, I could always go back to the street. Probably not back to the 26th District, where I'd been the whole time; I loved it there. *Not going to worry about that now. I'm really into this.*

I snapped myself back and heard the captain saying, "…and later this morning, you'll meet with the platoon commanders, the three lieutenants who are in charge of the recruit classes." He described the structure of the unit and how we'd be reporting to Will Anderson, the Administrative Lieutenant, who'd be coordinating our training in lesson plan development and classroom techniques. *I wonder what I'll be teaching?*

My classes turned out to be "Report Writing" and "Vehicle and Pedestrian Investigations." I was pretty good with all of it. For years, I'd been the unofficial report-writing trainer for new cops who came to my squad. I would help new officers get used to the accepted format and show them how to write a proper report using the right words. As for the other topics, thanks to some great veterans, I'd learned how to investigate cars and pedestrians the right way. I could complete the Report Writing lesson plans pretty quickly, but the plans for the Investigations classes wouldn't be as easy. Doing it right would take a lot of thought, research, and time.

After lunch that first day, I decided to take a walk past the K9 kennels and training fields, then down to the pistol range to say hI to the instructors. Some of them had been teaching cops to shoot for decades. I also needed time to think about how to approach my new assignment. It was a lot of responsibility, providing instruction to new recruits. So I walked around the campus, enjoying the beautiful fall day, trying to come up with a way to get started.

My mind went back to my early days: *What had I wished I'd known before hitting the street? How about some of my close calls with car and ped stops? What do the incoming recruits think about all of this? Hey, they're really just civilians getting ready to put on the uniform. Can I get them past what they* think *they know?* I wandered around as my brain's rolodex was flipping through the past ten years, scanning, remembering. There was a lot. I knew I wanted to do more than just regurgitate what the books said and what I'd done and what I'd learned over time. I had to find a punch, a common denominator, something to get their attention, something to make it real for the rookies. *What*?

"Hi, Skoufalos; welcome back!" Officer Mark Lowe was standing outside his office (also the Academy library) as I walked through the lobby to leave the main Academy building at the end of my first day. I was impressed that he remembered my name.

"Mark, how are you?" I said. "Still here, huh? What's up with you?"

"Yup, still here doin' the same old same old. Hey, if you need a place to sit and do your lesson plans, I got just the spot. There's a table I ain't using and it's all yours."

"Well, thanks, Mark, I'll take you up on that," I said as we shook hands.

The next morning, I walked into the Academy Library—really just a tiny room with a lot of police-related books—and looked over the stack that "librarian" Mark Lowe had pulled for me, based on the list of the instructors' teaching assignments he'd received from the captain. I looked at Mark. He was a veteran officer ten years ago, yet here he was. Guess he liked his job. His hair had turned gray since I last saw him, but for a guy fast-approaching retirement age, Lowe was still in good shape. He was an energetic, soft-spoken guy who always smiled. And he liked to use big words. Guess that was a product of him being the "librarian"; maybe he felt he needed to sound scholarly. Or it could be that his over-achieving vocabulary is what pegged him for the library duty…not sure which came first.

Today he seemed grateful to have me for company. I guessed that the only time any of the veteran instructors came in here was to pick through his dated books to do research for their classes. I didn't know Mark's story or how he'd gotten to be at the Academy. Didn't matter, he'd always been friendly and willing to talk with me when I'd been a recruit.

For most of the morning, I sat there browsing, taking notes, still trying to hit on the *driver* I was looking for, something to hammer the lessons home. Then, without a word, Mark walked over and put a pile of magazine-sized publications in front of me. I looked over the stack which was about ten years' worth of annual booklets published by the Federal Bureau of Investigation, called "Law Enforcement Officers Killed in the Line of Duty." I started reading.

In true FBI style, there were lots of statistics—cop deaths year-to-year; regionally; by type of death; time of day and day of week, etc. But what got my attention was what I found at the back of the books: a synopsis of every incident, detailing the circumstances that led to each officer's death. There were gunshots, stabbings, auto accidents and drownings. The killers were typically desperate career criminals, usually male. But the stories also included killers who were senior citizens who'd never been in trouble, females, and even kids, some very young. And so many involved officers making car and pedestrian stops. There it was: Safety. Officer safety would be my focus. But it had to be more than that. Then, it hit me. I knew what I was going to do.

Once I had my direction, the lesson plans practically wrote themselves. I could easily relate many of the FBI incidents to my experiences and to those of other cops I'd worked with. *I can make this real.* But there was something else to consider: these recruits were a decade behind me. The social environment had changed since I sat in these classrooms, especially the way cops were portrayed in the media—TV shows, movies, newspapers. Everywhere, things were either "super-cop" stuff or they were "routine." And I knew that either approach could be a killer.

Every time I'd hear the word "routine" in a discussion of police work, my jaw would tighten and I would want to have a serious one-on-one conversation with whomever was saying it. I wanted people, especially cops, to understand that "routine" has no place in any discussion of the work that police officers do.

So I decided to include the definition of "routine" —*the regular way something's done*—in my lessons. Now, one needn't be a police officer to understand that, because people and situations are all different, there cannot and should not be "standard" or "regular" way to make car and pedestrian stops. Still, there've been so many incidents, sometimes ending tragically, where the officer's work is reported as "routine." Such as: "The officer was responding to a routine domestic disturbance when…." or, "the police were conducting a routine car stop…." So we spent a lot of class time talking about "routine." I wanted the recruits to really believe there were dangers in doing *any* part of their job in a routine way.

Once I felt that they had the concept, we spent hours discussing vehicle and pedestrian stops, including those involving felony suspects. Every time I stood before a class, I considered every word, every scenario, doing my best to get and keep their attention. They were watching and they were listening. I had to get it right.

And so it went for weeks and weeks.

After the class work was done, we'd be outdoors, gathered on a small, dusty (or muddy, depending on the weather) rarely-traveled access road between the Academy and the adjacent city Water Department property. We were there to practice what we'd been talking about. I had one of the Academy's marked police cars for the recruits to use in our exercise, and I'd borrowed an old beat-up unmarked cop car to serve both as the civilian car in our traffic stops and the suspect's car in our "felony" car stop simulations.

The latter required a much different approach from start to finish than a traffic violation stop. Felony car stops had to be conducted following specific, ordered steps necessary to establish and maintain control of high-risk individuals—drivers and passengers whom officers believed to be dangerous criminals.

I had a couple of other instructors along, dressed in old clothes and sneakers, who played my "bad guys." They sometimes carried a concealed pistol loaded with blank cartridges and, if the recruits got sloppy or lazy or forgetful, these guys would "shoot" the recruits with blanks, if given the opportunity. (Actually, they were instructed to shoot at the ground, but just the sound was quite a jolt.)

We'd walk the first couple of two-recruit officer teams through the scenario, constantly reminding them (and the others) of the proper approach—to watch the occupants' movements, their hands, their body language, and to have only one officer giving commands to the driver and passenger to eliminate confusion and better ensure their compliance. After safely getting the "bad guys" out of the car and down on the ground, the recruits would practice the step-by-step procedures for cuffing and frisking them for weapons. The rules were that if the recruit officers were doing things right, pretty much as they'd been taught, the cops playing "bad guys" would cooperate. But, if a trainee made a significant safety-related mistake, all bets were off.

The situations were often based on real-life incidents—some of them from the FBI books, and some of them from the experiences of the instructors. And they *felt* real. We varied them to get the greatest number and variety of scenarios and so the exercises didn't become predictable. We wanted the new officers to feel like this was the real deal. One day very soon it would be.

The exercises could be intense, especially when recruit officers let their guard down and found themselves getting "shot." I believe it felt very real to them; they looked shocked and scared. A few actually backed up and looked down, checking themselves as if they actually *had* been shot. Exactly our intended outcome. No question, any recruits that thought this was going to be just an out-of-the- classroom skate, soon started paying attention after a couple of their classmates experienced the rude awakening of being "shot,", vowing to not make the same mistakes.

One memorable scenario involved a felony stop with two of the Physical Training (PT) instructors as the bad guys. One of them, Officer Jack Henry, was the closest to an actual giant I'd ever seen. At six-six, more than 250 solid pounds, his soft-spoken, friendly demeanor belied his power and quickness. He was the driver in this case and the passenger, Officer Jeff Martin, whose muscular, wiry, normal-sized frame was deceptive, especially next to Henry's. In the exercise, the two recruits had been told that the car the bad guys were in fit the description of a vehicle that was being sought for a bank robbery. It started out well.

"Occupants of the black car, put your hands on the dashboard, so I can see them. Do it now!" said the recruit officer giving the commands. They did. Then, "Driver, with your left hand, turn off the ignition and throw the keys out your window. Do it now." Henry, the driver, complied. The recruits continued with a near-perfect, textbook implementation of commands and moves, getting both bad guys out of the car and down, carefully watching them. As the recruits moved up to cuff him, Henry, who was face-down on the ground, and apparently tired of lying in a mud puddle, turned over and protested about his situation. The recruits, not expecting this, hesitated for a few seconds, not sure what to do.

Henry saw his chance. "Why the hell are you pigs making me lay in this shit? How would you like it, huh?" Then he started to get up, slowly moving his huge frame. Both recruits started shouting at him to get down, then moved together to get the big guy under control. Totally ignoring Jeff Martin, now out of their view, who quickly got up, walked up behind both recruits and banged two blanks into the ground behind each one, simulating their being shot. Neither one saw him coming and both jumped several inches off the ground as they heard the gun go off. Both stood there shaken and embarrassed.

The scenario was over. After a short break I called veterans Jack Henry and Jeff Martin over and we were all circled around for a recap. "Bill, talk to me. What happened here?" I asked the recruit who had been the lead officer in the stop

"We started out okay, then I guess we relaxed a little. Then when Officer Henry started getting up, we only focused on getting him controlled."

"Okay. Marlene, what were you thinking when I started getting up?" Officer Henry asked the other recruit.

"We had to get you cuffed. You looked dangerous, so we saw you as the biggest threat."

"What about Officer Martin?" I asked.

"He was totally cooperative and did what we told him to," explained Bill. "We took our attention off him when Officer Henry started his shit." I said nothing. Nobody else did either. We all just stood there, replaying the scene in our minds and thinking about it.

"We should have been more decisive, moved to cuff him faster. Then this probably wouldn't have gone bad," said Bill quietly, head down.

Marlene nodded, then said, "We should have frisked both of them first, especially since we knew they could be armed".

"Right," I said, then asked, "Jack, Jeff, did you guys have a plan?"

"No," Jeff said. "Our plan is always to watch the cops and if we can, we just try to overpower them. We saw them both hesitate, so we made our move. Once they both focused on Jack, I just got up and pulled my gun." Jack nodded his agreement.

It was an important day; a powerful lesson for the whole class. While I knew the exercise had been invaluable, part of me felt sorry for the two recruits, but I couldn't let it show. It had to remain a hard lesson, one that every recruit there would remember for a career. That was our last—and best—lesson that day. I remember thinking later: *THIS was where a scenario like this should play out. In a safe, controlled setting, not out there some night on a dark, deserted street.*

Over the next days and weeks, I made it a point to engage both Bill and Marlene frequently. I wanted them to feel okay, to *be* okay, and to realize that every cop makes mistakes. Training exercise mistakes are the best ones, because you get a do-over. And I wanted them to take the lesson to heart and remember it forever, although I was sure that part was already cemented in for both of them.

Word got around. Sometimes we'd get other instructors stopping by on their breaks to watch our exercises. Even some of the veteran officers, on campus for their annual range training, would walk over during their lunch hour to observe. Then there were recruits from newer classes who'd heard about what we were doing, some of them sneaking down to get a clue, trying to get ahead of the game. They'd be chased back to the main building. It was important for us to keep the classwork fresh and unexpected for each new group.

Much of the credit for the success of this program went to the "bad guys," the instructors who shared my enthusiasm and commitment to educating our newest cops in one of the most unpredictable and potentially dangerous activities they would ever do on the job. Also, a lot of credit to the bosses, the senior Academy administration, who supported and encouraged us as we conducted our training using such an unorthodox approach.

After each exercise, back in the classroom, we reviewed every incident. In detail. These were always very focused, no-nonsense sessions. The "bad guy" instructors were there too; their observations and comments were critical to the learning process—for all of us. No blame was ever placed, no recruit officer's effort diminished. Believe me, those that made mistakes, especially the major ones, had learned their lessons the hard way;

they didn't need us to remind them. Just a replay of the action, followed by a review of procedures and a strong reinforcement of what was always the-same-lesson: nothing's routine. It was serious business and, looking back, I don't remember a single recruit who didn't agree. To me, a lot of them seemed profoundly changed after those scenario exercises. They became more thoughtful, more serious. Like a switch had been turned on, lighting up a new part of their brain, helping them to see the world in a very different way.

The "Pedestrian Investigation" classes were conducted in coordination with the PT instructors, who played "the pedestrians'" and also taught self-defense technique. The exercises combined how to safely approach and interact with individuals stopped by police, and how to apply self-defense techniques, if necessary. Although not usually as powerful as the felony car stop exercises, there were some dramatic and sobering (and sometimes even funny) occasions when the instructors, all physically imposing guys, showed how unwilling they were to "give a break" to the poor recruit who got too close or didn't conduct a thorough frisk. Good stuff, all of it.

In preparation for the Report Writing course, I had written about two dozen sample 75-48's—the department's Incident Report form used to document everything a police officer does. The samples represented the most common kinds of incidents new officers respond to. I wanted to make it easier for cops to know what to write in their reports. And *how* to write it. Most new cops tend to write more than they need to, maybe afraid to leave out something important. Law enforcement writing is way different from any other type. I emphasized that a police report is a legal document that must be complete and accurate, yet concise and factual, with no personal opinions or speculation.

The samples were used in class and also were my graduation gift to the recruits. Some officers, when we'd met years later, mentioned that the sample reports had been very helpful as they made the shift from civilian "creative" writing to police writing Some even showed me the photo-copied packet I'd given them, still stapled and dog-eared and apparently well-used. Great!

And so it went, for well over a year. Class after class, with hundreds of eager men and women who gradually made the transition from civilian to police officer.

Graduation day was a very proud time for the new officers and their families. And for me and the other instructors.

I loved my time as an academy instructor. I felt honored to have been given the opportunity to have a part in preparing the new officers for their careers as Philly cops. It was gratifying and rewarding, one of the high-points of my career. I was also proud when some of "my" recruit officers accomplished notable achievements. And doubly proud when they were promoted, as a good number of them were.

—————————•●•—————————

After about a year, the hiring push over, I returned to my assignment in the 26th. I had missed the street. Even though I was back in a familiar environment after only a short time away, it felt different. I was a little rusty. I found myself having to refresh myself on some of the same basics I'd been giving the recruits. There were some new faces, but most of the guys who'd been there before were still there. And some of the recruits I'd worked with were now 26th District cops. The circle of life, cop style.

A couple of years later, I was permanently transferred to the Academy and given the same course instruction assignments, plus another "Patrol Procedures." Picking up where I left off, my new students got the same training and even more, to accommodate the new expanded state-mandated curriculum.

When I eventually returned to street patrol, it *was* to the 26th, this time as a sergeant. I was lucky. My time away as an Academy instructor had taught me a lot. It was there that I got to meet and work with some of "Philadelphia's Finest" veterans. And I got to be part of training and developing the next generation of Philly cops. It was all interesting and important and meaningful. None of it was routine.

A Funny Thing Happened

Some people think that cops are serious all the time, that they have little or no sense of humor. That's not true. In fact, some of the greatest jokers I've known wear a uniform and a badge. Sure, a lot of police officers think that they must always be "on," ready for the serious business of law enforcement. They think that if they smile or joke around it takes away from their image. Whatever. This isn't about those cops.

The guys I'm talking about are those that never miss an opportunity to lighten things up and make the other cops, and even citizens, laugh. They have a certain way of thinking, of acting, and of *being* that helps the rest of the guys get by. It's just natural for them. They are the class clowns of a district or unit, the ones that sometimes get themselves into trouble with the bosses, but do their funny stuff anyway. Maybe they can't help themselves. Anyway, this is one of my favorites.

About halfway through my career, when I was a police officer assigned to the police academy as an instructor, I met the king of jokers—Lieutenant Bob Michaels. He was in charge of all the recruit classes and was a first-rate prankster. Bob was excellent at organizing the activities of the recruit classes, sometimes two or three at the same time. He commanded the respect of the rookies and the police staff. Although Bob did his complicated job of managing the recruit training process with the requisite seriousness, he never missed a chance to play a joke. And nobody was exempt: from a recruit officer to the instructors, even the captain—everybody was a potential target.

I could fill a book with "Bob stories," but I'll limit it here to one incident that shows his genius for coming up with a prank and his ability to make the victims believe that the whole thing was legitimate. It had to do with another instructor, Tom Earnest, and used a young male recruit officer, who we'll call Roberto Sosa, as a foil for the gag. Tom Earnest was a nice guy and a good instructor. The new officers under his supervision loved his easy-going manner and that he always looked out for them. The recruit, Roberto, was soft-spoken, polite, and worked hard to do well in the classroom. And he always followed the rules. Two good guys, just doing their jobs, minding their business.

For some reason, the lieutenant clued me in on many of his gags and asked me to be there when this one went down. It all started one afternoon when he called in Tom Earnest to discuss an issue involving one of Earnest's recruits.

By the way, this was about the time the police department was hiring female officers in increasing numbers. Obviously, there were many things (rules and accommodations) to be considered when women first joined the Philly PD. Any time there's change, there are wrinkles to iron out. One of the issues was the hair of the females. Unlike the men, the women usually had longer hair and donning the uniform police hat was not automatically simple. It was a challenge for women to figure out ways to style their longer hair, wear the hat, and satisfy the rules. Rather than cut their hair super short, they'd try a tight-fitting short wig or a cap to hold down their hair so that it would fit properly under the hat. You can't blame them for trying to figure out how to have it both ways.

It wasn't long before the bosses nixed that idea. They came up with a new regulation prohibiting the wearing of hairpieces *of any kind* while in uniform. In doing so, they forced the women to cut their hair into styles that met the regulations without artificial help. Since most of the women were *really* into becoming police officers, the matter was moot.

But back to Bob Michaels and Tom Earnest. As Officer Earnest walked in to the lieutenant's office, I pretended to be looking over a class schedule as Michaels told him to sit down. "Tom, you're familiar with the latest policy about hairpieces, right?"

"Yes sir," said Tom, looking a little nervous. As much as Lieutenant Michaels would joke around, his serious side (real or faked), with his large, glaring eyes drilling into a subordinate, could be scary.

"Well, I was walking around before roll calls this morning, and I noticed that one of your recruits is violating that rule."

I could see Earnest quickly rolling through the list of recruits in his head, trying to pinpoint who Michaels was talking about. He shook his head. "I don't know who you mean, lieutenant."

Michaels, more serious now, building it up, said, "Tom, I don't know how you *couldn't* notice this. I mean, it's so obvious, I'm surprised the captain hasn't said something about it."

"I'm sorry, lieutenant, who is it?"

Jokester Bob Michaels was now ready to set the hook. Glancing down at a paper on his desk, he said, "C'mon, really?" When all he got from Earnest was a blank stare, he said, "It's recruit officer Sosa, Roberto Sosa. You *really* didn't know this?"

"Sosa? Lieutenant, are you sure?"

Michaels glared at Officer Earnest, the look intended to melt away any doubt.

"Lieutenant, Sosa is bald!" said Earnest. "Completely bald."

"Really? I saw him standing around without his uniform hat and it looks to me like he's wearing a *bald cap*." Lieutenant Michaels said this with such seriousness and authority that the allegation made Earnest step back. I'd been listening to the conversation and when I heard Michaels say that, I quickly turned away, turning my unexpected chuckle into a cough.

Michaels went on, taking advantage of the clearly stunned Earnest. "He's got til four tomorrow afternoon to get rid of it. Got it?"

Tom Earnest didn't know what to say. "B-but, lieutenant, I'm sure that kid's not wearing a…"

Michaels interrupted him. "Tom, are you sure enough to take a chance on getting disciplined and transferred out of here, back to a district? If the captain gets involved, we'll both be in trouble."

Now Earnest just looked at the lieutenant. No, he didn't want any of that. Being an academy instructor was a great assignment and he didn't want to lose it. "Okay, lieutenant, I'll take care of it."

"Okay, Tom, remember, talk to Sosa and get him to take off that damn bald cap. And get him to write you a memorandum agreeing not to wear it again while he's at the academy. Okay?"

"Yes, sir," said Tom Earnest, looking a little pale and confused.

When Tom was gone, Bob Michaels closed his office door and laughed so hard he had me rolling right along with him. It was one of those times when one of us would stop laughing and then, looking at the other, would start all over again. We laughed until we cried, bent over with sore stomachs. No doubt, this was the lieutenant's best ever. The game was on. *But*, I thought, *now what? How would Tom handle this?*

For the next day and a half, I watched and listened as Tom Earnest spent his time divided between up-close peeks at Roberto Sosa's head, and asking other instructors their opinions of the kid's hairless appearance. By then, the lieutenant made sure the rest of the teaching staff had been brought up to speed on the prank.

Given my presence when Michaels sprang this on him, and thinking I might have been in on it, I was one of the first guys Tom approached. "Skouf," he said hopefully, "the lieutenant's just messing with me, right? I mean, anybody can see that Sosa isn't wearing a bald cap, right? You can see that, can't you?"

I just looked at him. I've always been terrible at keeping a secret and even worse at keeping a straight face with stuff like this. Still, I had learned that anybody who interfered with Bob Michaels' jokes would, without fail, be the next target. And based on previous experience, I sure didn't want that. So I said, "Tom, I hear ya, but have you taken a really close look at that kid's head? It's really smooth, to me it looks *too* smooth."

"He's just got smooth skin, that's all. How the hell am I supposed to do what the lieutenant wants? It's embarrassing!"

It was true; Sosa's skin was very smooth; so smooth that I could see the basis for the lieutenant's gag. "Hey, man," I said, hoping to get out of the line of questioning before I cracked up, "just get the kid to write the memo that he understands the 'no hairpiece' rule and give it to the LT."

"That won't work. Michaels told me that he'd be checking Sosa out personally to make sure he took the cap off. *But he isn't wearing a cap!*"

Through it all, the instructors would check in with each other to make sure everybody knew the latest developments, especially how the victim, Tom, was faring. We all agreed it was a brilliant practical joke. We also agreed we wouldn't say anything to Tom, although we knew he'd be pissed at us afterward. Oh well, he'd get over it. Besides, we'd all been in his situation—or would be eventually.

As the deadline approached, Tom Earnest walked around campus, deep in thought—trying to resolve his dilemma, I supposed. I felt a little sorry for him. An hour before he was due in the lieutenant's office, he came to me again. "Hey Skouf, this ain't funny anymore. Please tell me that Michaels is messing with me. Right?"

It wasn't easy, but I said, "Tom, you know how he is when he gets something in his head. I'd hate to see you get sent back to the street. Just do what he wants." Tom looked at me for a while, trying to see something in my eyes, some hint of *You got me* Now, I'm not saying I was proud of myself, but somehow I managed to pull it off.

Resigned and with his head down, Tom slowly walked over to where the unsuspecting Recruit Officer Roberto Sosa was standing with a couple of his classmates out front of the main building, taking a break between classes.

As Tom got within a few feet of Sosa, I saw Lieutenant Michaels call Earnest over to a bench where he'd been sitting, observing the action. Out of earshot, I watched as Earnest approached the now hysterical Michaels, who was just sitting there, convulsing with laughter. The conversation wasn't long, probably not even needed, given the lieutenant's out-of-control state.

Tom Earnest turned toward me and shot a dagger or two my way. I thought that Michaels had somehow implicated me in the thing. *Thanks, Bob.* I just stood there, grinning, and gave him a thumbs-up. Then, Michaels waved me over and we both grabbed Earnest in a giant bear hug. As we held on so he couldn't get away, Tom (both relieved and pissed off) showered us with all sorts of juicy names, some of which called our heritage into question. But soon, he was laughing along with us. He was a good sport.

To my knowledge, Recruit Officer Sosa never learned of the matter.

There were plenty of antics during my several years at the Academy, most of them dreamed up by one Lieutenant Bob Michaels. I was not spared. Neither was my desk (stacked with paperwork, lesson plans, and notes) on the only-funny-later afternoon when Bob and his two "deputies" burst into my office and soaked everything in sight, using water cannons.

In time, the greatly-outnumbered Michaels received his fair share of paybacks from the instructors under his command, all of whom he'd taught so well. As they say, "He who laughs last…"

All I Want for Christmas

Christmas is my favorite holiday. Something happens within me and it makes everything and everybody just a little nicer, a bit more cheerful, or so it seems. Like a little magic in the air.

Growing up, my two brothers and I knew that our Christmas presents were going to be clothes, stuff that our mom and dad felt we needed. Except for one gift. A special one. It would usually be a toy, but always something we wanted. Not always exactly the thing we had pointed out and hinted about regularly since September, but close enough to make us happy. Looking back, these gifts weren't expensive; they weren't even whatever the rage was that year. I still remember the thrill of getting to that present and opening it. Mom and Dad never disappointed us.

And so, long-conditioned to this exciting expectation, the anticipation is still with me. But now, I hope and wish for things more important than toys and other gifts.

———————————•●•———————————

It was my fifth year as a Philly cop and the fifth Christmas Day I was scheduled to work. It was still a little strange for me, going to work on such a big holiday, but I was gradually getting used to the idea, the idea that this is what cops do.

Heading to work, south on I-95 at 7:00 a.m., traffic was light. It was the time of day when most folks were already at their destinations for the holiday. It was pretty cold, about 28°, with bright sun and no clouds, and I was glad that the snow predicted for this Christmas day had never happened. Hopefully, that would mean fewer auto accidents. I hated writing them up.

As usual, the sergeant had split the shift, with half of the guys coming in at the normal 8:00 a.m. and leaving at noon when the second half of the squad arrived. So it wouldn't be too bad—just four hours.

Roll call was quick, just the basics today: our assignments and coverages, none of the usual review of the yesterday's crimes and other information that was usually part of the ritual. The sergeant reminded us that we were working short and to back each other up. Then we (the eight other guys and I) headed out back to the district parking lot. After I checked and gassed my car, I headed out to the north end of the district, stopping along the way for a cup of 7-Eleven coffee. After a quick run-through of the sector, I parked at Germantown and Lehigh and started my patrol log, sipping the coffee, not altogether trusting the quiet on the streets and on the police radio.

The normally busy intersection was practically deserted. Just a few cars trickled through as I sat and watched. I patrolled my area, slow and relaxed, stopping to talk with the few people who were out and about, and we wished each other a Merry Christmas.

There were hardly any calls. To keep busy, I drove around the empty streets some more looking for something, anything to do. I made a couple of security checks looking for broken windows or doors, then noting on my log each location and the time I was there.

A down-side to the split shifts was that we each had to cover expanded patrol areas, sometimes in sectors we didn't normally work. But that was okay, I could use the time to get familiar with this part of the district. It was a good day to do it, since it was so dead. For the next two hours, I patrolled the empty streets and backed up a couple of guys in the adjoining sectors on their calls for burglar alarms, one at a drug store and the other at a clothing warehouse, both secure.

This part of North Philly was old and mostly dilapidated; the factories which used to employ the area's factory workers and their families were long gone, either knocked down to rubbled lots or deserted, many then targeted by arsonists or owners looking for an insurance payout. Sometimes, they were one and the same. All of the two-story red brick houses were connected, except where a vacant lot interrupted the line with a yawning space overtaken by rubbish. About half of the properties were abandoned, littered inside with trash and outside with graffiti. But today, none of this bothered me; I barely noticed. It was Christmas.

The district was inhabited by a mixed bag of citizens. Blacks, whites, and Hispanics, although each of these groups typically lived in their own areas, each choosing to be gathered and living with folks like them. In my sector on this day, the majority of the residents were African-American and poor. This was the '70s and I soon learned that these folks didn't always trust the police. Even so, they knew we were the ones to call when all hell broke loose. We knew it too. I thought about how different their Christmas must be from mine.

Just before 11:30 a.m., I got my first and only radio call of the day: "2618, take 924 West Arizona for a hospital case. Rescue's enroute." I acknowledged the call and activated my lights and siren, even though traffic was non-existent. Habit, I guess. I drove, trying to focus on the quickest route, thinking about what this call might be. Could be almost anything. Maybe a kid fell off his new bike and hurt his arm. Or it could be someone who'd had too much celebration and was having chest pains and needed a ride to the hospital. Whatever, I'd find out in a minute or two.

"I believe it's Mister Hopkins, Officer. There's sumptin' wrong." The old Black guy standing by the front steps as I pulled up looked at least 80. His eyes were dark and bloodshot and he kept looking back at the house where I was headed. I figured those eyes had seen a lot in his substantial life. I caught a sense that he was upset or maybe a little scared. Though it was cold, he was wearing just a yellowed t-shirt and threadbare black pants. He was shaking, I guessed from the low temperature. He shuffled toward me in slippers that had once been black, now scuffed brown. "I heard some kinda commotion in there," he said as he came up.

The place was quiet, so I figured if there'd been a disturbance, it was all over.

"What's your name, sir?"

"John."

"John, did you hear anything? Yelling or anything else goin' on in there?"

He shook his head and I got the sense John felt that he'd already said too much.

"Well, did you see anyone enter or leave the house before I got here? A car?" Maybe there had been someone who'd left the scene, somebody that John might have recognized being from the neighborhood. Or a stranger.

"Nope."

As I tried to get something more from the old gent, I could hear the wail of the Fire Department's Rescue Squad, breaking the silence of the day, screaming my way, still blocks away. I wrote down the old guy's name and address and told him to go home, which he seemed glad to do. As he walked away, I slowly approached the house, antenna up. Experience had taught me to be cautious on these kind of calls, and the old man's demeanor made me take a few seconds to check things out before I walked into the house. Shading my eyes, I looked through the streaky window into the front room of 924.

Damn! This wasn't a falling-off-a-bike injury and it wasn't chest pains. I called for backup and a supervisor.

Bill Karper, who was the closest in 17 car and two sectors over, picked up the call. It would be a few minutes before he got here—an eternity in this kind of deal. I quickly grabbed my Maglite and baton from the car and moved to the front door; it wasn't locked, so, using the flashlight, I slowly pushed it open. I waited a few seconds, listening and adjusting my eyes to the darkness. Inside, the house was deathly quiet. What I'd seen from the window was someone down on the floor of the front room. As I crept past the small vestibule into the main part of the house, I realized that my adrenaline was rocking and rolling. *Breathe. Just breathe and calm down,* I told myself.

It was pretty dark in there so I clicked on my flashlight, swinging it over to the guy lying there; he wasn't moving. He looked between 50 and 60, wearing gray sweat pants and a light blue checked flannel shirt, which had some dark stains just above his waist. No shoes. No weapons I could see. As my eyes adjusted, I saw that his shirt had some tears where the stains were. Now, just a couple of feet away from him, I could smell the booze and the blood.

Cop's dilemma: there were two things I had to do first: check on this guy's condition and give him first aid; also determine if whoever did this was still here.

Rushing to mind were words my mother had instilled in me: '*Ta matia sou ekato*'. My folks hated that I was a cop. They worried all the time and told me to be careful. Whenever we talked about the job, Mom would always tell me in her native Greek: '*Ta matia sou ekato:* ' "Watch everything around you as if you had a hundred eyes."

I slowly bent over the man, two fingers on his neck, trying for a carotid pulse, then leaned over to check for breathing. Nothing. He was dead, already starting to cool. I looked at his face and saw a middle-aged Black man, thin, with a dark stubbly beard. His eyes were half open, looking at me, seeing nothing. *Some Merry Christmas.*

I saw no person or weapons in the area. From the time I went in, I was watching the hallway and the stairs to the second floor, listening. I switched off the flashlight and stood up. Still no Rescue and no backup. In those days, we didn't have handheld radios, so I went back to the car and let the dispatcher know what was going on, telling them to expedite the backup.

I'm sure it had only been about two minutes since I'd first entered the house, but it seemed a lot longer. I knew I had to do something. Common sense told me to wait for Karper outside. But I knew I couldn't wait. I had to go back in.

I quietly reentered the small house, kneeling to keep a low profile. Looking around, my eyes now used to the semi-darkness, I noticed a dim light from the back of the house, where the kitchen would be. And it sounded like somebody was back there. I stood up and unsnapped my holster.

"Police. Come to the living room with your hands where I can see them," I shouted. Silence. I repeated the command, louder, more insistent. No response.

Revolver in hand, I crept along the short hallway leading to the kitchen. I tried for quiet, but the old house's creaking floor boards gave me away. I hoped this wasn't an ambush. I inched closer, a step at a time. Then, just a few feet from the doorway, I heard mumbling, almost ranting, but soft. I tried, but I couldn't understand a single word. Whoever was there continued like they didn't know I was coming their way; that was good. When I was close enough, I moved deliberately into the room and saw a Black woman sitting at the table, a glass next to a half-empty bottle of what the label said was gin on her right, and a large, bloody kitchen knife on the left. The knife was lying on the yellow-and-blue-checkered vinyl tablecloth where the drying blood had it stuck there. Quiet as I was trying to be, the creaking of my leather jacket and gear brought her back just before I announced myself.

She turned to look at me. No surprise in her eyes. Just some tears drying. She turned away and just sat there. I quickly and carefully grabbed the knife by the very tip of the handle to secure it. It made a soft, sticky, slurpy sound when I picked it up from the table and moved it out of the woman's reach. She just sat there, watching me, then picked up her glass and took a drink. I noticed that her pink and white housedress had some spots on the front that looked like blood.

The immediate threat gone for now, I holstered and moved to the other side of the table, into her line of sight. I asked her name. She appeared calm as she regarded me. It seemed to me that, at some level, the mind behind her bleary eyes was trying to compute who I was and what I wanted. I asked her a second time before she answered so softly I almost couldn't hear her, "Sheila."

"Sheila? Okay, Sheila, are you hurt?" I asked, pointing to the spatter on her dress. She looked down and touched the spots, then shook her head.

"Nah, but I think he is," she said cocking her head toward the front room. Her voice was flat. No anger, no grief, just the words.

Watching her, I asked, "Who is he?"

"James, James Hopkins, he's my old man. It's gonna be four years pretty soon."

As we talked, I did another quick scan of our immediate area and saw no other weapons within reach. I learned that Sheila was Sheila Jones and she was 47. She'd lived there with James for about two-and-a half years.

Since I was pretty sure she was responsible for the dead guy in the next room, I advised her of her Miranda rights, and she acknowledged that she understood. It wasn't typical for street cops to give suspects their Miranda warnings, but then it wasn't normal for the suspect to want to talk so much. I normally wouldn't have an extended conversation with the perpetrator of such a serious crime—that's the work of the detectives, Homicide in this case—but Police Radio had directed me to remain with Sheila at the scene till the detectives arrived. They were on their way. And Sheila wanted to talk

At some point, the sergeant and Officer Karper got there. I sat with Sheila while they checked the rest of the house, with negative results. As the sarge was leaving, he said he'd notify the Medical Examiner. Karper guarded the crime scene while Sheila talked and I listened. The paramedics arrived soon after and confirmed that Mr. James Hopkins, 52, was indeed dead.

While we waited for the Medical Examiner and detectives, Sheila and I continued our conversation. It was mostly Sheila talking and me listening. Even when I would interrupt her and try the Miranda warnings again, she'd just wave me off. She clearly wanted—needed—to talk. So I started taking notes.

She said she was a high school graduate, first in her family. As she said this, she sat up straighter, like she was proud of that. She had a grown daughter who had a couple of kids and was living in New York; they didn't keep in touch.

She and James had met at a bar and they got along pretty good. Sheila had lost her job at a neighborhood grocery store about a year earlier when they closed and she couldn't find another one. She told me that James was a working man, but lately, was drinking more and working less. "He's pretty much a good man," she said. "I just wish he would listen to me like he used to. I wish he was nice to me like before." Her references to James in the present tense meant that she didn't know he was gone, or she was blocking that information from her consciousness.

"When we first got together, James would take me club dancing on Saturday nights. Sometimes we'd go to Atlantic City." She smiled at the memory, shook her head, then took a long drink from her glass. "Then, he changed, you know mister? He started drinkin' a lot, gettin' *mean*." She told me that she thought about leaving, but where would she go? She had nothing; no money, no job, and no family that could help. I wondered when we might get to today's events, but knew she had to do this her own way and I let her roll on.

Sheila seemed like a woman who'd had some bad times and was fed up with how her life was going. But she was still trying. She had some picture of how a better life could look, and she was especially disappointed with James. Seems *she* had supported *him* their first few months together, since he hadn't been working at the time. I got the sense that he had started resenting that she wasn't working while he was.

She told me that after Thanksgiving, she had signed up for a job training program so she could get some help finding a new job. The program was geared toward women just like Sheila who were struggling to get into the job market, but needed a little assistance. She was supposed to start the first of the year and she seemed excited about it. Sheila believed she'd soon be working again and helping with the bills. And maybe, she hoped, that would make James happier with her…nicer.

To get ready for a new job, she'd borrowed some clothes from friends. She really needed a new pair of shoes, but had no money. So she had asked James if he would buy them for her as a Christmas present. He had said yes.

Fast-forward to today, Christmas morning. She waited and waited for her "surprise" present from James. Morning rolled on and still no gift. When she reminded him that he had promised, all she got was a drunken James who screamed at her that if she wanted new shoes she should "go out and get the damn things" herself. If it had ended there, things might have been different. But, on that Christmas morning, he had begun drinking extra early and often and, being the nasty drunk he was, kept after her, insulting her, berating her, smacking her around.

"After 'while, I had enough of his shit, you know?" she said in a voice so calm it was eerie. "He wouldn't leave me alone, so I decided to leave, to get away from him awhile. But he was chasin' me around the house, cussin' at me and hittin' on me. I was getting scared, so I got the knife for protection and when I passed him, he grabbed at me again, tryin' to hit me. I was tryin' to get away, but he kept on comin'. Next thing I know, I just waved the knife at him to get him to let me be… I didn't want to hurt him, mister. I didn't. All I wanted was…. "

…the shoes he promised me for Christmas, I thought, finishing her sentence. With that, she put her head down, sobbing.

By then, the M.E. was through and the homicide detective in the next room caught my eye and nodded. It was time to take Sheila downtown. I left the house and stood by while the detective walked her outside. I'll never forget the hopeless, helpless look on her face as she sat hunched over, handcuffed in the back of the patrol wagon.

I don't think she remembered me when we saw each other in court many months later. Didn't matter.

The story the defense gave was essentially the same Sheila had given me. Sheila was not convicted of any crime. She'd had a pretty good public defender and some of her neighbors testified about the abuse she'd endured.

Throughout my police career, I usually got pissed off when people I arrested didn't get convicted. Especially for serious crimes. Not this time.

———————————•●•———————————

In the more than forty Christmases since then, not one has passed without something reminding me of that day and Sheila. I remember that woman was so determined to make her life better. She really tried, but all too often even strong determination is not enough. I really hope Sheila got her new job and new life.

Sunday Drive

Routine. There's that word again—a word I'd never thought much about before the job of being a cop. I had learned that what cops do can never be categorized that way. I've tried to convince others—cops and civilians—that the word really has no place in police work. Disturbances (on the streets and in residences) are common calls for services (we call them "disturbance highway" or "disturbance house"). Vehicle investigations ("car stops") are among the most repeated assignments to which police respond. Frequent, yes; routine, no.

In the context of describing police work, "routine" is used constantly and it's wrong. The news says, "The officer was on routine patrol when she…" or, "The police were conducting a routine vehicle investigation and…" or, "Two officers were shot while responding to a routine call for a domestic dispute." A "routine approach" is typically defined as: "the regular way something is done." But I'll say here what I've been saying for decades: No two assignments of the same category are **ever** precisely the same. The only constant is that the citizens with whom the police are interacting know a lot more than the cops.

Specifically, the person or persons the police are dealing with know that a) the police have tremendous power and authority up to and including the ability to arrest anyone; and b) more critically, the cops can use force as they deem necessary, including deadly force. That's what mister and missus citizen know for sure. The cops? They know that this guy ran through a red light and the cop is pissed that he would do that right in front of him. They can't know that the driver is wanted for a felony that just occurred. Or, that this is the third call this week to this couple's apartment and it's what happens every time one or both of them have had too much to drink. They're not aware that she told him she's going to tell the responding cop that he punched her before they arrived. Or that he has a gun. That's what cops *don't* know. The citizens involved in such incidents are more prepared than the cop because the cop usually believes that this will *not* be an exceptional event. That kind of thinking, that this is just a typical, routine assignment, holds such potential danger if people (citizens as well as officers) start believing it. Still, *routine* is how we regularly hear many of these activities described. So, what happens when *routine* meets *reality*? Let's see.

●●●

Like any typical Sunday day work, it's pretty quiet; nothing's going on. It's been like that all day. Dull and boring. I liked getting lots of calls, something to do. Not today, though. It was just after one and I still had about three hours until my shift's end. I liked day work. It was the closest to a regular schedule: working during the day, sleeping at night. So, I was good.

Traffic on Girard Avenue, a four-lane main artery, was so thick that it felt like a Friday rush hour, not a Sunday afternoon. I'm thinking many folks had cabin fever. The long, Philly winter was finally easing and people were using the sunny, warm afternoon to shake off the doldrums that northern winters bring; this one had been especially brutal, with tons of snow and ice.

Everybody was behaving—no honking or yelling out windows with raised middle fingers, and no cutting other drivers off. Maybe me driving along in a blue and white cop car had something to do with it. Whatever. My road companions were just people out for a Sunday drive. Maybe some of them were coming from the zoo, about three miles west. Or maybe, a family picnic in Fairmount Park. It had to be the nice weather. I guessed some of the cars were driving *to* Fairmount Park for a spring picnic. The bouncing, laughing kids in the back seats gave me that clue. Maybe some of them were headed to one of the Schuylkill River Drives for a stroll along the grassy walks along the river. *Maybe they're going for ice cream; I could go for some!* Wishful thinking.

Time for a break. I stopped at the Dew Inn restaurant for a coffee and was met at the door by John, one of the owners, outside sneaking a smoke. "Yasou, Strati," he said as I stepped in. "How are you?" His heavy Greek accent reminded me of so many of my relatives who'd been in the US for years, but still held onto their unique Greekish dialect.

"HI John, how are *you*? How's Coz?" John and his brother Coz had opened the restaurant shortly after arriving from Greece. Their English was much better than it was when I first landed in the 26th District ten years before. Like my mother, they were still afraid to make a mistake, say the wrong thing, so they were careful when responding to people. Like Mom, many of their responses involved a lot of nodding, smiling, and the word, "Yeah."

I took the blue-and-white cardboard cup of super-hot coffee and left my usual one-dollar tip for the waitress. (John and Coz wouldn't let cops pay for their coffee. Like most business people, they appreciated the police stopping by.)

Back in the car, I pulled into traffic, heading west on Girard, and stopping at the red light at 6th Street. I was looking forward to sipping that good coffee in a quiet, out-of-the-way place.

The car in front of me, a two-year-old brown Chevy, made me think of the production problem GM cars had been having the past few years: it was a manufacturing defect that allowed anyone to start the car after cracking open the steering wheel collar (easily done with a screwdriver) and then pushing a lever to start the car. I'd lost count of how many of these stolen cars I and other cops had recovered in the same condition. Out of habit, I grabbed the list of stolen vehicles from between the rubber bands on the sun visor. Every 24 hours, a new "hot sheet" was printed and distributed to every cop at each roll call. The stolen cars were listed in alpha-numerical order and gave us a quick way to determine if a car we were investigating was stolen. As I waited for the green light, I scanned the sheet. It was something I did, just muscle memory.

There it was! The tag of the car right in front of me was there. The light changed and the car started moving. The still-full coffee cup went out the window. I was driving to keep up and double-checking the sheet. *Couldn't be.* But it was.

I kept an eye on the driver and any other occupants. Couldn't really see them because of the headrests. I wanted to see if the driver was watching me in the rearview mirror or if any of the occupants were turning to see if I was paying attention to them. Nothing. No movement. No changes in speed or direction. Just driving normally. I had to call it in and I had to do it quickly, because my district's border ended in a few blocks. I pressed the call bar on the receiver and gave the dispatcher my car number. "2610 to Radio."

"Go ahead 2610."

I gave him the description and tag number of the Chevy and my location and direction. In less than 30 seconds, the dispatcher was back on the air. "In the 26th District, any car in the vicinity of 7th and Girard available to back up 2610 on a car stop. 2610 and any car responding, be aware that this vehicle has been reported stolen and was used in an armed robbery."

At least five other cars responded, overriding each other as they tried to acknowledge the call. I could hear sirens coming from all over.

Show time. I flipped on my overhead blue and red strobes and chirped the siren to get the driver's attention. As often happens, when the driver realized that a police car was behind him, he jammed on the brakes. I had expected this, so I had increased the distance between us just before the lights and siren.

Now the driver *was* watching in the rearview mirror, so I waved him forward and, as he continued watching and driving very slowly, I gave him hand signals directing him to turn off Girard Avenue onto Franklin Street, a block that had no residential homes, just across from Giuffre Hospital. After stopping the car, I got on the air. "Radio, I have the vehicle stopped in the 1200 block of Franklin Street."

"2610, number and description of occupants."

Then I saw what I *really* had. "Radio, it looks like one white male driver, one white female front passenger." But something wasn't right. Because as I stared through my windshield into the back window of that car, I was stunned to see the faces of a little boy and a little girl pop up, their huge eyes staring back at me through the back window of the car. I hadn't seen them before the stop. "Radio, have all cars use caution. I also have two small children in the back seat of the car."

Silence. Then, the dispatcher: "In the 26th District, all cars responding to 2610's location use caution. There are children in the rear of the vehicle."

The kids were no older than seven or eight. They looked terrified. I'll never forget the scene: little hands holding on to the top of the rear seat. I could only imagine they were kneeling on the back seat, looking at a police car with all the strobe lights flashing in their eyes. They were hearing a whole lot of sirens screaming in from all directions. Eyes as wide as they could be. I wanted to be able to go up there and tell them everything was going to be alright. But I couldn't do that. I wasn't sure if it was true.

Now, the fact that this car had been involved in a robbery made this more than a typcial vehicle investigation, not a usual car stop. It was classified as a "felony car stop," which assumed that the occupants were very likely armed. The procedure required that, once the vehicle was stopped, the initiating officer would use the patrol car's public address system to direct the occupants of the suspect vehicle to methodically exit the vehicle, one by one, then walk backwards toward the waiting police, hands raised. They would then be handcuffed. This would be repeated until all occupants had been secured. As I sat there, I thought, *The kids… what about the kids?*

Several backup cars arrived and took positions to the left and right of my vehicle. They waited.

Over my years on the street, I had been involved in a number of felony car stops, both as initiator and backup. *This is different*, I said to myself. Something didn't make sense. I had to figure this out. Still, I had to make sure that everything we did here was done carefully, for everyone's safety.

I turned on the PA system and directed the driver to turn off the car and toss the car keys out the driver's window. He did. Then I ordered the driver and front passenger to place their hands on the dashboard where they could be seen by the other officers. They complied. Then, taking a big risk, I changed it up. Back on the police radio, I requested information on the owner of the vehicle: name, address, date of birth, physical description shown on license. I also wanted to know where and when the car had been reported stolen, and for any descriptive information about the perpetrators of the robbery.

I ran through my experience with these kinds of stops, then considered what my training told me. Then, I wondered, *what are my options? Do I even have options?* I knew what the book said in this case. I also knew what I was seeing. I weighed what should happen versus what could happen. But I also had discretion. What if, in this case, I modified the usual procedure for felony car stops based on my observations? I hoped I was doing the right thing.

I used the PA system to order the driver out of the car, keeping his hands raised. He was directed to walk backwards to an officer who was waiting to cuff him. The officer walked him back to my location and I was not surprised to see this 30-something guy literally shaking so hard, the handcuffs were clanking together. He was scared. Good. I retrieved his wallet and, comparing his license and registration to my notes, confirmed that he was the owner of the vehicle and his address was the location of the reported theft of the vehicle. So far…

"Sir, is this your car?"

"Yes, Officer, it's my car."

"Did you report this car stolen to the police?"

"Yes."

"Okay, and did the officer to whom you gave the report give you any further information or instructions regarding the recovery of your car?"

"Uh, yes, he did. He said that if the police found the car, the police would notify me." The man stopped and looked away. Now he was figuring it out.

"Anything else?" I asked.

In a very quiet voice he said, "He told me that if I found the car on my own, that I should notify the police."

"I see. And did you?"

"No, sir."

"Why not?" I asked. His answer stunned me.

"I didn't think it was important."

"How about *now*? Do you think it's important?" His hanging head was the answer.

Now, I'm not usually the preacher type, not one to go on and on with folks informing them of the wrongs and consequences of their actions. But this time, given this scenario, and especially the faces of his kids, I felt the need to provide a little lecture.

"Where are you coming from?" I asked.

"We went to the zoo. The kids have been asking to go all winter."

"Did you have a good time?"

Head still down, he nodded.

"Well, I guess this'll top any excitement you all had at the zoo, especially your kids. What are their names? And you wife?"

He told me.

But I still wasn't sure if he got it, whether he knew the whole story. No, how could he possibly know?

"Sir, we usually don't conduct vehicle investigations in this way, you know that, right?"

"I guess not, I'm not a cop."

I thought, *so, you're going to be a wise ass now*. I looked at him and said nothing.

"I'm sorry," he said meekly.

"Let me fill you in."

I gave him the short version of his car's adventures while in the possession of the individuals who had taken it. Now it was his turn to display saucer-sized eyes. He said nothing; I said "Yeah."

Seems that my new acquaintance—we'll call him Mr. Smith—had gone out on his own looking for his stolen car and, quite unexpectedly, found it in a vacant lot about six blocks from where the robbery had occurred, and a few miles from where he lived. He assumed that it was just kids out for a joyride. I didn't have the heart to give him the old "…you know what happens when we assume, don't you?" It was so shockingly clear and ugly to him right then.

We talked a bit more, gathered the information I needed for my report and then, Mr. Smith and his family rode off into the sunset.

Driving to headquarters to finish the paperwork, I was suddenly exhausted. A couple of hours later, as I left for home, I knew the faces of those kids would stay with me for a while.

Still see them.

Breakfast, Interrupted

Last Out, twelve to eight: the night shift. I hated it. I doubted I would ever get used to it. Daywork was okay, lots of people out and about, and it's like a normal job, like regular people: work during the day, home in the evening, and sleep at night. Normal. But day work is filled with lots of bullshit: auto accidents, burglary and theft reports and the worst—school crossings. Four to twelve is the best of the three shifts as far as being busy fighting crime. But though often action-packed, it's not a good schedule for life outside of work—you can't fit in much before or after that shift. All in all, four to twelve was my favorite, I guess. But on this night, I was about to join the other Last Out cops for the night shift.

Parking my personal car on Montgomery Avenue just up the street from the 26th Police District, I glanced at my watch and saw that I had about 20 minutes before my shift would start. Plenty of time to change into my uniform, gather my equipment, and check what's been going on for the last two days I was off.

Roll call was scant, just 10 guys. As the sergeant completed his inspection of our uniforms and equipment, he ambled back to the podium to read assignments and orders of the day.

"…Skoufalos, Duncan, 2603." *That's odd, I usually work alone—2611 car, and Art Duncan has 2610.* Whatever. Must be a good reason for old Sergeant McCabe to pair us up, I figured. Anyway, I was kind of glad. The first day of the working-in-the-dark shift was always the most challenging due to the body and mind adjustments required.

It was a welcome change to be working an Emergency Patrol Wagon (often busier than most of the cars), transporting hospital cases and prisoners, handling disturbances. Another plus was that I would have someone to talk to during those hours when my body started telling me *it's nighttime; sleep...sleep...sleep.*

Out in the parking lot, Art took his three-foot-long Maglite and checked the van for any new damage. The rule was: if the damage to the vehicle had not been reported and *you* don't report it, *you* own it. Seems unfair, but we learned pretty quickly to do a thorough inspection. Nobody wants to get written up and maybe lose a couple days pay, especially when somebody else did it. I got out with my light and took a look at the front of the old Ford Econoline as I lifted the hood to check the oil. *This baby's been around the block a few times*, I thought as I noted the dented and faded hood. Just three years old, it had more than 150 thousand on the odometer. But she still ran pretty good—and who wants to walk a foot beat at night?

Art seemed to handle the night shift better than I did, so he jumped into the driver's seat, while I settled into the passenger seat or, as it's known, the recorder's seat, since the cop who isn't driving has to do all the paperwork as well as handle the police radio. I lucked out getting to work with Art, very active and a great cop. And he liked to drive. I did too, just not at night when my eyes want to close all the time.

"Coffee?" he asked, not waiting for my response as he turned onto Girard Avenue heading toward the only diner open at that hour—the Paradise. He pulled up to the corner and I jumped out. Stepping into the bright lights of the restaurant, I did a quick cop-survey and saw nothing out of the ordinary: the usual locals, drunks, and various other nighttime denizens who regarded me suspiciously as I ordered two coffees. I thought, *I'm going to write a book about these characters someday...*

The owner, chef, and cashier, John, in his whites and grease-smeared long apron, smiled and patted me on the back as he came to the register with two blue-and-white cardboard coffee cups. I knew the stuff was strong and nasty, but I was looking forward to the caffeine. John's glad when the cops stopped in and, looking around, I got it.

He shook his head when I held out my money. "That's okay, officer," he said with a heavy Greek accent, "you don't pay." In the few years I'd been coming there, his English had gotten better. I could usually understand him.

"Thanks, John," I said with a smile, and tossed the bills on the counter anyway as I left.

Art drove us to Front and Girard and parked where we could keep an eye on passengers exiting The El train stop and the seedy Station bar across the street that advertises "sTOPLESS dancers." Most nights, there was at least one battle between drunken macho types who were prepared to fight to the death for the privilege of taking one of the ladies home. Sitting there also put us close to the middle of our coverage area, so we could be ready for a quick response. We could still watch the passing show of travelers and characters while we sat back and enjoyed our muddy coffee.

Despite the near-freezing temperature, we both had our windows all the way down so we could hear what's going on. Over the years, I learned to listen and hear differently. Sounds that I used to take as "normal" and easily ignored (or didn't hear at all) occurred very differently to me. It's like I grew specialized antennae. When my cop ears hear such things as screeching tires, yelling, or glass breaking, these are meaningful, not just noise. So, the windows were down as Art and I talked about mundane stuff—family, sports, what we had done on our days off. The pounding music from the Station bar blared on.

The radio and the streets were really quiet. I guessed that the biting cold was keeping normal people inside, so I settled in for a long night. I knew I'd be going back for more of that delicious coffee soon. Art drove us around for a while and we made our first round of security checks: the hardware store and bank on Girard and the Stetson hat factory on Germantown.

About 2:30, we backed up Joe Ginelli in 263 as he made a car stop, down near the river. The driver, a kid of about 17, told Joe that he was lost and that's why he had ended up in an industrial complex of winding, dead-end streets. When Joe spotted him, he thought the kid might be a burglar, so he had stopped to check him out. The kid's story seemed legit, so he was given directions to I-95 northbound and sent on his way.

Then we heard, "2602, we need a supervisor at second and Fairmount." The call was the first radio traffic for at least half an hour. We weren't far away, so we took off to see if we could help. When we arrived, Sergeant John McCabe and a couple of other cars were already there. The cops working EPW 2602 (Ron Lassiter and George Cooper) both looked worried and pissed off at the same time. They each had almost 20 years on the job, so I figured this must be something. We listened as they told the sergeant that their prisoner had escaped. This was a big deal.

"She's a skinny thing," George was saying, shaking his head. "We picked her up at East Detectives to take her downtown. We could hardly get the cuffs to stay on her wrists. We cuffed her in the back, double-locked the back doors, and headed to the Roundhouse." He meant the nearby police headquarters, so named because of the design of the building: two big, side-by-side round sections that, when viewed from above, looked like a giant pair of handcuffs.

I looked at the back doors of their van and saw that they were still locked, but both doors had been pushed out, creating about an eight-inch space at the bottom. It was hard to believe that someone could squeeze out through such a small opening, but she'd apparently done it.

George said that they didn't know that she had gotten out until a motorist pulled alongside them and told George that their prisoner was running away from them, northbound on Second Street, while they were headed southbound.

There are some things that a police officer hopes never happens to him during his career and losing a prisoner is one of them. All the excuses in the world—good and otherwise—are not enough to make it any better. The only thing that comes close is recapturing him or her. This female prisoner was being charged with shoplifting, a very minor crime, but now they'd be charging her with Escape, much more serious.

The sergeant told Cooper and Lassiter to go to the Roundhouse and get copies of the escapee's mug shot, since we knew from the detectives she'd been locked up before. Then they were to pass out copies to the cops in the area and to the detectives who would be going to her home to find her. (I know it sounds low-tech, but then, passing around paper copies of mug shots got results.)

Armed with a description, Art and I headed to the area where she was last seen and started looking. I felt bad for the guys in 2602, but I was glad to have something to do. It was getting near the witching hour of 4:00 a.m., when my I'd always get so tired that my head would involuntarily drift downward and I'd be doing the drop-and-jerk, sitting up.

When we got our copy, I saw the face of a woman in her twenties who appeared much older and with much more mileage than would be normal. She looked thin, but it was hard to tell from an arrest photo. Her rap sheet was long, listing about a dozen arrests for drug possession, prostitution, and shoplifting. Now it made sense: she was likely a drug addict, hence the shoplifting pinch; and she *needed* her drugs, so the consequences of her escape were not her top priority, not even on her radar.

For hours we looked everywhere: in vacant houses, gas stations, alleys, bus stops, and apartment house vestibules. No luck. She was gone. I guessed she was inside somewhere, laying low.

At about 6:00 a.m., as it was getting light out, we started up toward the Paradise to get some breakfast. As we pulled up, I put us out of service with the dispatcher and we found a table in the back. I ordered us coffee and Art went to the men's room. The night's activities had worn me out—I couldn't wait to get home to my warm bed.

As I looked over the menu, a woman sitting a few tables away began shouting for the waitress, who was super busy. The woman kept it up, impatiently tapping on the table. I noticed that she had hardly touched her food, but told the waitress who finally showed up that she wanted her meal packed to go. She was also watching me. I just figured she didn't want me to get involved in the disturbance she was causing. *Not me, lady,* I thought. *I just want some eggs and lots of coffee.*

Wait….there was something about this chick. *What?* I didn't know. Then the fatigue made room for the cop-brain. Nah, couldn't be, could it? I looked some more. The body type and age fit. *No way, Jose. It can't be her.* Different hair, different clothes, and that makeup…it looked like she was going onstage. *Where the hell was Art?* I didn't want to spook her, but I wanted him to go call for George and Ron to come over and take a peek at this little lady. But she was already getting up to leave. I had to do *something.*

I sat there while she moved toward the cash register and the exit. Once she was in line, I took the side door out and met her as she left the diner. She hurried past me and, in my most charming tone, I said, "Good morning, young lady, how are you today?" She said nothing, didn't even look my way. I moved to cut her off and stood blocking her way as she waited for the red light to change. We were very close. Now I was almost positive this was our missing prisoner. But I wanted to talk to her a while to make sure. *Art, where are you?!*

She didn't want to talk to me, so I forced the issue: "I need to ask you something, Miss. It'll only be a minute."

"I don't want to talk to you, Mister, leave me alone."

"What's the rush?"

"Uh… I have a job interview and I don't want to be late."

It was about 6:15 a.m. and couldn't imagine where this interview might be at this hour, so I asked.

"At the church. Second and Jefferson," she said, avoiding eye contact.

"Okay. Who're you meeting?" I think I'm doing a marvelous job, keeping a bullshit conversation going and keeping her here. *Where is my partner?* By now, she was getting antsy so she pushed past me and started running across Girard Avenue, a four-lane highway, complete with trucks and trolley cars. I grabbed her arm and said, "You can't go until I'm done talking with you." She clearly disagreed with that and swung her bony fist into the side of my head. Now it was on.

I grabbed her arms so then she head-butted me. I reached for her hair and her wig came off in my hand as she again tried to escape. Next, she tried to knee me, which really woke me up. *That's not nice, young lady!* By that time, we had drawn a crowd and I'm not sure they were cheering for me. Think about it: a grown man, a uniformed cop no less, wrestling with a skinny little woman. Now we were rolling off the hood of a parked car, landing in the street just a few yards from an oncoming trolley. I was intentionally holding back, not wanting to hurt her, but this wasn't going well. This chick was kicking my ass!

The battle had now been going on for about five minutes, an eternity for these kinds of deals. Finally, Art was there, grabbing her and cuffing her quickly. She was cursing and spitting at us and kicking as we each grabbed an arm, lifted her off the ground, and locked her in the back of our wagon. As Art called for 2602, I guarded the back doors. Inside the van, she did a great imitation of the demon in *The Exorcist*, ranting and raving and throwing herself against the sides of the truck. Exhausted, I doubled over as I tried to catch my breath.

I felt good about getting this prisoner back where she belonged, but this had been a real battle. *I'll never again complain that Last Out is too slow. Ever!*

Art came back and stood with me as we waited for the other guys. I was still trying to catch my breath and promised myself I'd exercise more. "Are you alright?" he asked me over and over. I kept saying "yeah," but he didn't seem so sure. I wasn't either.

Ten minutes later, Sgt. McCabe showed up just ahead of 2602. The sarge looked at me and at Art and back at me. He didn't say anything, but there was a little smile there as he patted me on the back. George and Ron exited their truck and ran over to the rear of 2603. "Hey Strati, you okay?"

"Yeah. Take a look at your prisoner." With that, my partner unlocked the rear doors of the wagon, expecting her to rush us. But she just sat there, clothes and wig askew. Her heavy makeup was now streaking down her face as she stared at us like an angry and beaten caged animal.

Art closed and locked the doors again as George turned to me and said, "That's not her."

That's not funny, I thought. *Oh, I get it: cop humor. Let one of your brothers get his butt kicked by a girl half his size and age and you tell him he got the wrong person.* Getting the joke, I chuckled. Then I looked at Ron and George and their faces were dead serious.

"Look, nothing about her is the same," said George. "The clothes, the hair, all of it… it's not her."

"Very funny, guys." But I was getting a bad vibe. If this wasn't her, what the hell did I just do? Go round and round with some citizen whose only crime was getting her breakfast to go? Not good. Hearing this, Sergeant McCabe came over and told us to drive her to the Roundhouse and get her fingerprinted, to find out for sure.

All the way, I was thinking about the trouble I could be in: civil suit, departmental discipline, ridicule. *I really hate Last Out!*

At the Identification Unit, we had to wait—change of shift. Great. More delays, more stress. Our little lady was secured in an interview room while a technician took her prints and went to his office to check them, manually. This was before the days of computers and automated criminal photo and fingerprint databases. After what seemed like forever, the tech came and found us and gave us a slip of paper with the results: The fingerprints matched!

My relief was palpable. I was not the brutal cop I thought I might be. I couldn't stop smiling. I must have looked like a simpleton, shaking my head and grinning, but I didn't care. Last Out had been changed forever, and in a good way.

I called the sergeant and gave him the good news. He chuckled and said, "I thought so." On our way back to the 26th, we drove past the Paradise and Art looked over at me, like, "Do you want breakfast?" I just shook my tired and aching head and motioned for him to keep going.

The adrenaline was quickly subsiding. I just wanted to finish out the shift and get home to sleep. There would be plenty of time to sort out all of the day's intense emotions and events during my mind's replay later. But from then on, I knew that shift could be a real roller coaster where you just had to hang on and ride it out.

Front Street Ladies

On the lower end of the 26th District, Front Street was dark and lonely. It felt sad, too. From Poplar all the way up to York (about a mile and a half), the roadway and the buildings alongside were shadowed by the aging, steel-and-concrete, elevated train structure. The "El." Creating a giant overhead tunnel the whole way, it was like the buildings and the street never saw sunlight.

There were a few clumped remnants of homes—red brick row houses—some two-story, and some three. Scattered in along the way were a school, a church, and some small businesses: machine shops, corner groceries, bars, warehouses. Places where hopeful entrepreneurs toiled every day, ignoring the cold, uninviting feel of the area. The place was so desolate that a driver could go for many blocks without seeing another car.

After dark, the place was a different story. There were plenty of cars. A lot of them were there looking for the attraction that brought Front Street to life: the "ladies of the night."

Some of the ladies were homeless; others also worked at other, more traditional jobs. Many were drug-addicted and usually looked pretty sick. I knew that a few weren't junkies—though it was hard to tell sometimes, but at least that's what they'd said—they were just girls and single moms without enough money to take care of themselves and their kids.

I didn't know them by name, but I knew who they were and the unofficial boundaries of their staked-out territory. As far as I could tell, they all got along. No turf squabbles; nothing like that.

They kept away from the occupied residences, mostly lurking on sidewalks in front of vacant houses or vacant lots, in the shadows of the El train pillars, where their customers knew to look for them. Out of the shadows, one would emerge when she'd hear or see a car approaching.

Even in the coldest weather, the die-hard ladies were out there, marching up and down. I guessed part of that was to keep warm.

They were street-wise and knew which cops were which. I knew that some of the officers chased them away, moving them along with a blast of their sirens and threats of arrest yelled out their car windows. Like their lives weren't miserable enough without badge-heavy cops messing with them. Anyway, I didn't do that. Besides, chasing them off never worked; as soon as the police car left, they'd be right back out there.

I never understood some cops' tough-guy approach with the ladies. They weren't really bothering anyone. Sure, their business was illegal, but it was one of those so-called "victimless" crimes, although that characterization wasn't something I believed. I'm pretty sure the Front Street ladies would agree. And, unlike the occurrences of violent crime, there weren't any loud, persistent complaints from the neighborhood citizens. And then there were the times when the ladies themselves were victims of crimes.

Also, as I'd learned from a street-smart veteran, years earlier, the ladies' presence from dusk until dawn gave police a lot of extra eyes on the streets. He had called them "our sad little helpers."

Many of the women wouldn't talk to *any* cops, *ever*; they had learned that the hard way. But a few of us who were assigned to the Front Street sectors had a pretty good live-and-let-live rapport. Whenever they saw a squad car approaching, their usual reaction was a hasty exit from the area, but a short beep would let them know we only wanted to talk. Or that we were just passing through. And those who knew who was who would sometimes wait to find out what was up.

I discovered that it could be startling to see these women up close. They had tired and wary eyes and were typically dressed in worn-out and dirty clothes. The addicted ones always did what I called the "junkie dance" when we talked, unable to stand still even for a few seconds. Some looked like they were in their twenties—maybe teenagers—a few much older, and many in between. Regardless of their years, those who'd been out there, for even a short time, were street-aged. It was understandable. Always out in the weather, they led marginalized lives and many endured addiction, mental health issues, and deep poverty. Some even with kids to take care of. None of it was pretty.

Late on a slow 4:00 p.m. to midnight shift, an hour or so before quitting time, I had an idea. I turned south on Front and, spotting one of the regulars, I slowly pulled over and stopped at Jefferson. We had an understanding:

I didn't bother her and she would move on when she saw me. Stopping wasn't a usual part of the understanding, so I waited to see if she would figure out that I wanted to talk with her. I didn't want to spook her. She'd seen me pull over and halted her normal march up the sidewalk. Unsure, she stood there for a minute, then started walking my way. When she was about twenty feet away, she bent down to look into the windshield. Seeing it was me, she strolled over.

"Hi," I said. "How you doin'?" Names were never part of the conversation. When she was close enough, I handed her a cardboard cup of hot coffee through the window. She paused for just a second, then grabbed it with a pale, gloveless hand she'd pulled out of her pocket.

"Okay," she said, fidgeting, her voice shaking. It was January and she was shivering in her thin cotton jacket and short skirt.

"Everything alright?" I asked, watching her. I supposed her manic movement was both drug- and weather-related.

"I'm okay." Her whole body was shaking as she sipped the steaming coffee, her eyes looking everywhere: across the street, left and right down the block; every once in a while, she'd turn and take a quick look behind her.

I said, "Listen, we've been getting our asses kicked with stolen cars. It could be kids, but it looks like it's organized, you know, like a chop-shop gang." I waited.

Looking down at me, she said, "I ain't seen nothin'." It was the answer I expected and I understood. We didn't really know one another. And there wasn't anything in it for her.

I nodded and waited a few beats in case she found she had something else to say. She didn't. I asked her to keep an eye out, thanked her, and left. I remembered that this young lady had given other cops good information before, so I thought it was worth a try. Turned out it was.

In those days, GM cars—Chevys, Buicks, Oldsmobiles, Pontiacs, even Caddys—were being stolen in huge numbers thanks to a factory defect. It worked like this: a car thief would crack the collar on the steering column, exposing a lever that, when pushed, started the car. It was so simple that the car would be gone in seconds. For the thieves, it was a bonanza. Cars with smashed steering columns were showing up all over the district, littering vacant lots and sidewalks in sparsely-populated neighborhoods. I had recovered plenty of them on my sector, sometimes two or three in a single day. Another factor was that the cars, sold in parts, were worth many times what the whole car was. So the bad guys would teach the local kids how to get the car started and tell them where to drop it off. For each car delivered, they'd give the kid a hundred bucks. Some of these kids were stealing three and four cars a day, making a lot of money. It was big business for everybody involved. I really wanted to catch these guys.

For the next few weeks and months, the beat went on. The stolen cars kept showing up. It was getting old. Talking with the other cops, nobody had a lead. Maybe some of them didn't care like I did. Part of it was personal; I'd always had a thing for cars and couldn't imagine somebody taking mine to destroy and scrap for parts. We scoured our sectors, hunting for the guys and the chop-shops. They were invisible. Some of us had even called the Major Crimes Unit (MCU), who would typically handle such crimes but, because they were city-wide, they were getting slammed and didn't have enough manpower. "We'll put you on the list," they'd said.

Figuring that the MCU would eventually grab these guys and put them out of business, I backed off a bit. I still wanted the thieves and still looked for them but I wasn't as obsessed as I had been.

On another 4 to 12 in mid-March, just before dusk became full dark, I turned onto Front Street from Girard and headed north. A couple blocks up, I spotted my would-be informant as she trudged southward. We passed each other and it looked like she gave me a slight nod. Then she gave me a "come here" signal with a curled index finger. I made a U-turn at Thompson and sat there. She had turned around and was coming my way.

"Hi," I said as she walked up.

"Uh," she said, pausing. Looked like she had something to say, but not sure she should. I waited. Then, she said, "I heard about some guys with stolen cars." She was looking around, making sure nobody else was close by.

"Where?"

Leaning down, she was whispering now. I had to lean out of the window to hear. "It's at um, Mascher, near Jefferson, I think. It's an old garage. It's vacant, and there's three or four cars in there."

I knew the block. The 1500 block. It was a tiny street, barely wide enough for a single car. And it was on my sector. There were just a few occupied houses on the south side and some old garages on the north. Some of the garages used to be auto-repair shops and others were used as storage for nearby businesses. But now, most were abandoned and filled with trash. It was a perfect spot for a chop-shop.

"I'll check it out." Then I asked the logical cop question: "How'd you find out about it?"

She looked at me, not sure what else she should say. She opted for silence.

I waited, then realized she probably thought she'd already told me too much. I said, "Look, it doesn't matter. Thanks, I really appreciate you telling me."

"Listen, you can't tell nobody I told you." She was suddenly scared and nervous.

"No, I won't," I promised. "I'll go see what's up with the place." I was charged up and wanted to drive over there right then. But that wouldn't be a good idea, in case somebody had seen us talking and put two and two together. Traffic on Front Street was picking up so it was time for me to go. I thanked her again, and pulled away.

For the rest of the shift, I resisted the urge to drive over to Mascher Street. It wasn't easy.

After roll call the next day, I grabbed my coffee from the Dew Inn at 5th and Girard and took a spin around my sector. Just like I always did. Nice and easy, looking for anything different, anything that stood out. When I passed Jefferson and Mascher, I slowed down and peeked down the block. It was deserted. I continued west on Jefferson and took a leisurely drive in a big circle, my mind still back there.

Then I got busy for a while, getting call after call. I handled them, thinking about Mascher Street the whole time. It was a of couple hours later, just after dark, when I finally got back there. This was when I thought they'd come back to work on the cars. But I was wrong. I turned in and drove slowly, like I was just checking things out. Couldn't be sure if anybody was watching. Marked police cars are kind of obvious.

There were two or three spots on the block that might be the place I was looking for. My spotlight lit up the old wood-slatted garage fronts as I went. The first two were locked, heavy silver chains and serious padlocks shining as my light hit them. When I reached the third one, I hit the chrome jackpot. My helper had been right.

The old wooden double doors of the triple-wide garage were partially open. No chain and no lock. As I slowly rolled by, my light reflected off chrome and I could see the front end of a late-model Pontiac. I drove past, checking to see if anybody was around. Nobody. I continued up the street and made a right on Oxford, pulling over to finish my coffee and watched the street in my mirror. No people and no cars. Time to move.

I returned to the block and sat there, a few yards from the garage. I listened for voices and other sounds: nothing. I looked around and saw nothing. I used my car spotlight to brighten up the opening, then got out and looked inside. Shining my Maglight all around the small space, I could see three cars—the Pontiac and two Chevys. They were squeezed in tight. I unsnapped my holster and walked into the place, playing my flashlight all over. Nobody home. All three cars had cracked steering columns, but looked otherwise intact. Recently stolen. I looked some more and saw a bunch of tools stashed in a back corner—wrenches, drills and other things used to work on (or disassemble) a car. Then, from outside, I heard the dispatcher calling my number.

Taking another quick look around as I left the garage, I walked back to my car and took the call. It turned out to be an old woman reporting loud music from an upstairs apartment. I arrived in six minutes and, at my request, the people upstairs apologized and lowered the volume.

"2610 put me back. The matter has been adjudicated. Can you ask 26BD1 to meet me at American and Master, if they're available?"

"Okay 2610."

Before the dispatcher could call them, 26BD1, our Burglary Detail, got on the radio and said they'd meet me. The two officers working that assignment—Jim Brous and Lou O'Hara—wore plainclothes and drove around in an old piece-of-junk Toyota, something that blended right in. Unlike uniformed cops, they didn't normally respond to calls unless they were crimes in progress or other hot jobs. And they were pretty good at making drug arrests. The team was happy to help out uniform guys, who often knew about stuff but couldn't just sit someplace in a marked car watching for the bad guys. Without mentioning my source, I told them about the garage and they said they'd stake it out. "Call me if you get anything," I said. They said they would.

A couple hours after midnight, after I'd gone home, the thieves returned to their storage place and started working on dismantling the stolen cars. BD1, whose shift didn't end till 3:00 a.m., was there and nabbed them. Caught them in the act. After the three guys were cuffed and sent to East Detectives for processing, Brous and O'Hara called all three grateful owners, and stood by till they showed up and took back their cars, which had each just survived a near-death experience.

I heard about it when I got to work the next day. Ultimately, the bad guys fessed up: there was a total of 18 cars recovered from five other locations around the district. It was a big deal. These guys had been busy.

"Thanks, fellas. I owe you guys lunch," I said to O'Hara and Brous later that evening.

"Thank *you*, Skouf," said Lou O'Hara. "Hey, you don't owe us nothin'. With all those stolen cars, these guys're gonna keep us in court for months. Lots of overtime."

The next day, I grabbed a couple of coffees and found my friend strutting up Front Street, just north of Girard. I handed her a cup and filled her in. She gave me a gap-toothed grin. I smiled back.

With the arrests of these guys and the other district cops tuned in, the numbers of stolen cars in the 26th slowed down and eventually moved to other areas in other districts, where the same game was played with different cops and different assistant thieves.

I and the other cops continued doing what we could to lock up the bad guys and keep the residents of our district safe. The Front Street ladies kept walking up and down, doing their thing. And, every once in a while, they'd be our "sad little helpers."

—————•●•—————

Later that year, a few neighbors, feeling that the neighborhood was going downhill, filed several complaints about the Front Street ladies (not the term they used) with the 26th District Commanding Officer, who assured the citizens swift action. The captain attended all roll calls for several days and, like a preacher from the pulpit, stood up there and railed on about the sins of the world, especially "…those terrible women who sell their bodies." He ordered us to arrest them whenever we saw them. We were a captive audience, so we listened. But we all knew his impassioned message wouldn't change much. After all, walking down the street and occasionally talking to guys in cars isn't exactly illegal. If the captain wanted to have these women arrested, he'd have to bring in the Vice Squad—that's their job, it's what they did. But we all knew that wasn't going to happen. Like the MCU, Vice was too busy and short-staffed.

Weeks went by and the whole thing settled down. I had completely forgotten about it. There were real crimes and calls for service that kept us busy every day. Apparently, the captain hadn't forgotten about the issue because he kept bringing it up at roll calls. Then something very strange and unexpected happened.

Since there had been zero arrests for prostitution in the 26th District, despite his strong message to us, the captain did what any good leader would do: he decided he'd show us how it's done. And so he did.

It was on an early morning when our illustrious leader took an alternate route to work. Instead of his normal I-95 commute, he decided he would cruise down Front Street and make an example of one of the Front Street ladies. Boy, did he ever.

Somewhere along Front Street at about 6:30 in the morning, he pulled up next to a woman who was standing on the corner. He exited his car and, in full uniform, began screaming at her, telling her and anyone else within earshot that he was the District Captain and he wasn't going to allow whores like her to disgrace the neighborhood. Stunned and hysterical, she hurried to a nearby house, entering quickly, getting away from him. A few seconds later, she came out again, this time with a big guy. We later learned that the guy was her husband and who might've smacked our captain right there, but he'd already left the scene of the crime. No problem, they knew where he worked.

And so, the husband and wife came into the 26th to file a complaint of their own, a complaint with some teeth, which eventually made it all the way to the office of the Divisional Inspector, the captain's boss.

Turned out that the woman was a secretary and was waiting for a bus to go to work when our boss spotted her. Observing her on the corner, Dudley Do-Right made a terribly incorrect assumption about the lady and her occupation. I don't know if it was her clothing or her makeup or just that she was a woman standing on the corner. Whatever it was, he screwed up royally.

Needless to say, there were no more fire-and-brimstone roll-call speeches about hookers. The Front Street ladies remained on Front Street and the captain stayed in his office, leaving street work to the street cops.

And, whenever I patrolled Front Street during the hours of darkness, I kept a protective eye on our sad little helpers.

Nightfire

"Can't believe it," I said. "It's been a whole ten minutes without a call! Hey, Frank, let's go to lunch. If we don't go now, we're not gonna get to eat." It'd been a hell of a tour of duty. Saturday night in the big city. We needed a break.

"Okay," said Frank, squealing a U-turn and heading west on Girard Avenue. Frank Monroe and I usually worked solo, but tonight we'd been teamed up on Emergency Patrol Wagon 2603 because both guys normally assigned to it were off. A busy night, but a good one.

Frank was great to work with. He was a natural comedian and really knew the job. I preferred having a partner on the twelve-to-eight, the dreaded overnight shift. Besides, the wagons were usually a lot busier than cars and got most of the calls needing a two-officer response. "Len and Fred sure picked a good night to take off," said Frank, looking tired as he pulled up to the Dew Inn, slamming the truck into park.

"You got that right." I said, grabbing the mic to call it in. It felt like a record night—one job after another from the minute we'd climbed into the truck just after midnight. "2603, put us out at five and Girard for lunch." Lunch was the accepted term for our 20-minute meal break, regardless of shift or time of day.

"Okay, 2603, enjoy."

"Thank you, sir," I said. It was 5:00 a.m. and the place had just opened. I couldn't wait to sit somewhere other than this worn-out, sagging van seat, to relax with a cup of coffee and eat something. As we got out of the wagon, the air was finally cooling, but still pretty warm, even for late July. I pulled my sweat-stuck shirt off my back. Yeah, the truck had a/c, but when you're driving slow with open windows, it doesn't help much. Anyway, this was an old truck—about 175 thousand miles on it—so the air that pushed out of the vents was not much better than barely cool.

We took a booth in the back, by the kitchen. My favorite waitress Marie arrived with our coffees in about a minute. The waitresses here really *got* cops. They knew we had to eat fast and got us in and out like clockwork. Marie was the best of the bunch. She could run this place by herself. She put the two cups down, and before she could ask, Frank ordered scrambled eggs and scrapple, white toast. "And what'll it be for you, hon?" she asked, looking over at me. "Your regular?" I always got the same thing: eggs over, crisp bacon, wheat toast.

"Yes, ma'am. How you doin', Marie?" I asked.

"I'm always great, hon. You guys workin' together tonight or is one of you sneaking in for breakfast off your regular time?" Boy, she really knew the routine. Each unit had an assigned eating time so we wouldn't all be out of service at once. Of course, if you were tied up when you were scheduled to eat, you'd get another lunch time. The only other exception was a wagon crew; they always ate together.

"We're a wagon," said Frank. "The Bobbsey twins are off."

"Who?" asked Marie.

"You know, Len and Fred—the Bobbsey twins." Pretty sure it was Frank who came up with the nickname because the two cops had been teamed up for more than five years. And because their families did a lot of off-duty stuff together.

"Oh, *those* two," she said, rolling her eyes as she left to put in our order. Five minutes later she served up our breakfasts, hot and steaming, smelling great. Five minutes after wolfing that down, we were finished. Marie came over, collected the plates and poured us a fresh cup. I checked my watch and we had about seven minutes until the automated dispatch system put us back in service, available for calls.

I'd been out of the academy for just about three years. Frank had been on for almost seven. We hadn't worked together much, but I'd seen him in action enough to know the guy was a good cop. I figured that if I listened, I'd learn. "You know, Strati," he said in a low voice, putting down his coffee and looking around. "It's been a while since I locked somebody up for mopery."

Now, Frank was a prime-time joker, so naturally I thought this was another one of his gags. Even so, just in case he was serious, I ran "mopery" through my brain. *Did I learn about this in the academy? Is he talking about some kinda sexual perversion?* I had nothing. So, knowing him, I figured he was joking and decided to play along. "Yeah, me too, Frank. I've only had one mopery arrest in three years. *That'll hold him. Now, he'll give us that big, out-loud laugh and say,* "You got me."

He didn't. Instead, he looked over at me, bent closer, all serious, and whispered, "You don't know what mopery is, do ya?"

Trapped, I spun my wheels. *What do I say? This guy's an experienced cop. I don't want to look like a dope.* I figured I'd cut my losses. "You're right," I said, looking down. "Never heard of it."

"Well," he said, sitting up straight and taking a long sip of ice water, "you'll know it when you see it." He stopped, making sure I was paying attention. "I remember my first time…" Then, he looked at his watch and said, "Hey, we better get out there before they call us."

Our time was up. We laid our money on the table and headed out the door. *Wonder when he's gonna finish his story? Bet it's a good one.* Soon after he'd been transferred to the 26th, I'd talked to some cops who'd worked with Frank in the 39th District and they told me about some great arrests he'd made.

We climbed back into the hot truck and drove east on Girard, then north on Germantown. We'd been rolling for about twenty minutes, just looking around, waiting for the last two hours of our shift to go by.

"I don't want to jinx us, Frank, but looks like things have finally settled down."

"Yeah. Don't jinx us."

We cruised up Germantown, made a right on Diamond, creeping along. It was just getting light out and like most Sunday mornings, the area was like a ghost town, no drivers, no walkers—I mean nobody was out, not even the late-arriving-home partiers. I leaned back, trying to relax. After a couple minutes, I remembered his mopery story. "So Frank," I began. But before I could finish, I caught a whiff. I leaned over and put my head out of the van window. "You smell that?"

"Yeah," he said, speeding up. The smell got stronger. Then we could see the smoke a few blocks east. I listened for fire engines. Nothing.

"2603, we're eastbound on Diamond at sixth," I reported. "We're seein' a lot of smoke ahead. We'll give you more when we get closer. Notify Fire Board. Radio, this looks like more than a trash fire."

"Okay '03, use caution."

As we sped along, I could see heavy smoke billowing out of the second story of a building right at the corner of 3rd and Diamond. We pulled up and I could see fire glowing behind the thick smoke. Looked like the whole second floor was involved. I updated Radio as Frank climbed the van onto the sidewalk. We jumped out and I knew what we had to do. I wasn't crazy about the idea.

•●•

About six months earlier, again on the 12:00 a.m. to 8:00 a.m. shift, I was driving solo along Girard Ave, headed east. Just before Aramingo Avenue and the entrance to northbound I-95, there were two single porch-front houses, set back from the sidewalk. They were kind of secluded, hard to see, especially at night. I always made it a point to check them out when I went by.

It was around 4:00 a.m. As I drove by, I slowed down and clicked on the spotlight. I glanced over at the two houses and screeched to a stop. Smoke was pouring out of the first-floor window of the house on the right. The place was dark. I called it in. After chirping my siren and waving my spotlight into the upstairs windows, I jumped out of the car. I couldn't see any movement inside. I ran to the front door and pounded and yelled. No response. I forced open a first-floor window and climbed in. Zero visibility. Hot, heavy smoke hit me hard in the face.

All right. You got this. Stay close to the floor where the air is better. Use your light. Remember how far it is from where you came in so you can get back out. All this going on in my head as I quick-crawled toward where I guessed I'd find the steps to the upstairs. The smoke, thick and choking, was burning my eyes. I couldn't go more than a few yards before I had to turn back. I'd stick my head out the window, gulp a couple deep breaths, then go back to crawling on the floor. It wasn't working.

I couldn't hear anything from upstairs, and I wasn't going to make it up there to check it out. After a few tries, I made it back to the open window and fell out onto the porch. I knelt and coughed and coughed. *When would the firefighters get here? Think, Strati, think! There're people in there!*

144

I looked around for something—a ladder, a rope, anything. I got it! The drainpipe. I started climbing; not easy; slippery. I scrabbled my way, inch by inch. *Boy, I'm out of shape!* I made it to the little porch roof and pulled myself up. On hands and knees, I worked my way over and shattered one of the windows with my flashlight. Now I heard sirens behind me. *Finally!*

As I leaned in, I could hear coughing inside the house. I waved my light around and yelled, "This way! Follow my light! Come to the window!" They did. The man and woman climbed out and we stood on the porch roof, waiting for the firefighters to set up a ladder to get us down.

"Anybody else in there?" I asked, short-breathed. "Kids, pets?"

"No. Just my wife and me." I don't know how that fire started. I *do* know that I thought I was going to die in there that night. And I remember that it took me a few days before I could breathe okay again.

⎯⎯⎯⎯⎯⎯⎯●◉●⎯⎯⎯⎯⎯⎯⎯

That's what I was thinking about as Frank and I ran through the front door of 300 West Diamond Street. "It's apartments, Strati." Frank yelled as we ran down the hallway. "I've been in here before. There's lots of kids."

We made it as far as the stairs to the second floor. The heat and the black smoke were like a wall. We couldn't get up. No way. I heard people up there yelling in Spanish and I could hear kids screaming and crying. We could barely see them. And they had no way out. By now, Rich Newton in 2621 car was there with us. In Spanish, Frank yelled up for them to go to the front windows, waving his arms in the direction he wanted them to go.

Then, Frank was running back out the door; Rich and I followed him. He drove the van on the sidewalk to the east side of the building, getting it as close as he could. He got on the wagon's PA system and shouted something in Spanish. I didn't understand what he said, but it worked.

People came to the windows above us and broke them out. Frank and I climbed on top of the wagon and reached up as they starting handing the kids down to us. We could barely reach them, but we stretched up and grabbed hands, feet, legs, whatever, till they were down. Then the adults. One by one, they hung out the window and dropped onto the roof of the truck. We passed them down to Rich. After they stopped coming, we wanted to be sure that was all of them. Using our combined Spanish and

145

with the limited English of the residents, we were pretty sure everybody was accounted for. When we were through, eleven people had made it out.

The roof of the wagon was pretty caved in, but we didn't care. Wasn't important. The firefighters got there and, in just a few minutes, put out the fire and checked the apartments. Thankfully, there were no others inside. Other than some minor smoke inhalation, everybody was okay.

After the fire trucks left, I sat in the smoky smelling truck and wrote the report. Then we headed to the district to report off.

A few blocks later I remembered. "So, Frank, tell me about mopery," I asked.

"What?"

"You know, you were saying, in the restaurant? Been a while since you made a mopery pinch? Remember?"

"Oh, yeah. Well…," he said, nodding. "Mopery is tricky, you know?" I *didn't* know so I sat there, saying nothing. "See," he continued, "Mopery is a lot like carrigering and banana-poaching, only it's more serious. Especially if the guy's also doing dopery." He paused for effect. "Mopery and dopery criminals can be real bad asses!"

We were both exhausted, but I looked over and saw that famous Frank Monroe smile starting, then the big laugh. *Got me again,* I thought. *When am I gonna learn with this guy?* I laughed hard and kept it up until the smoke in my lungs turned my laugh into a cough.

———•●•———

A few weeks later, I stopped by the 4th and Girard firehouse; the guys were watching the Phillies, who were actually winning. Some of the firefighters on duty had been at the Diamond Street fire. From the back, somebody yelled, "Hey Strati, how's it going? All better from the smoke you ate back there?" That was Joe Francis, the resident wise guy.

"I'm okay, Joe, thanks for asking."

"If you guys are going to keep doing that shit, we'll get you a couple Scott Packs." (The breathing apparatus firefighters use.)

"Great. I'll take 'em." Serious now, I said, "You know, Joe, I don't know how you guys do that every day. You're nuts. I mean, you run into burning buildings when everybody else is runnin' out. That's crazy!"

"Yeah, well we think *you* guys are crazy," said Joe. He wasn't joking.

"Yeah, why's that?"

"You and your brother cops rush into places where there's guys with guns."

I thought about it, shrugged. "Yeah, I guess you're right."

This was the age-old enigma of cops and firefighters: both did dangerous work, but each thought the other's job was far more risky. *I guess it's a draw. Guess we're all crazy.*

I left, heading to my car. I had to get back out there. Hey, I didn't want somebody accusing *me* of mopery.

Friday at the Starlight

I rolled up to Franklin and Master and saw that the two Highway cops had a guy against the wall, frisking him. Their black Plymouth Gran Fury sat running at the curb, both front doors wide open, indicating a sudden exit. Didn't look like they needed my help, but I stopped anyway. I walked over, standing back, and watched them work. Their movements were practiced and efficient. No wasted effort, everything done for a reason, probably done a thousand times.

I knew this Highway team—Jackson and O'Hara. They'd been working in East Division for a while and had been partners for at least the six years I'd been in the 26th District. They were good cops. I knew they'd seen me as I pulled up and got out, but they stayed doing what they were doing; all business.

Highway Patrol was an elite unit within the Philly PD. Unlike district cops, these uniformed officers were assigned to high-crime areas city-wide and went where the trouble was. They responded only to priority calls: robberies, burglaries, shootings, and other crimes in progress. Always working in two-man teams, they were very effective, partly because they often drove unmarked squad cars and also because every Highway cop had proven himself as an eager and aggressive patrol officer in a district assignment for years before being transferred to Highway.

"Hey, Skouf, how're you?" said Mike Jackson, without turning toward me. He kept his eyes on the guy his partner was checking. All business.

"Good, Mike. Whaddya got?"

"Not sure, but I saw this guy throw something under that silver Caddy behind you when we drove up. We'll check it out as soon as we get him secured here. I remember seeing him in the area of a gang shooting a couple weeks ago." Jackson's partner, Lou O'Hara, finished the frisk and, keeping his hand on the male's belt, nodded to his partner who walked over to the beat-up old Cadillac at the curb. Moving his big flashlight around, he lit up the car's interior, then scanned the gutter near the curb. He knelt down and shone his light under the car, front to back, searching. I went over to take his place near his partner, who kept the male in the proper control position. The suspect, no older than sixteen, stood silent and still. He was angry, steaming, staring at the brick wall of the abandoned row house.

"Here it is," said Jackson, standing up, holding a plastic baggie. Inside, there were small cellophane packets of a white powder, probably heroin.

"Hey, man, that ain't mine," said the kid without turning. His protests were half-hearted.

"Really, chief? I saw you toss it there as soon as you spotted us," said Jackson. Knowing the drill, the kid shut up.

O'Hara quickly cuffed the male; I called for an EPW to transport him to the Narcotics Unit, and stood by until the wagon arrived and loaded the prisoner.

I resumed patrolling my sector, just five square blocks on the southwest end of the 26th. It was a small area, but, like many such sectors in the city, a busy place for cops on the 4:00 p.m. to midnight shift. I was grateful things were slow, at least for now.

My watch and my stomach told me it was time to eat, so I made a left on Columbia from 10th and headed to Girard Avenue and the Dew Inn. I had skipped lunch, so I was pretty hungry. *I could go for one of their Salisbury steaks,* I thought. *And some of that great rice pudding they make. Yeah!* The thought of the meal made me speed up. I almost made it.

"2610, take six and Thompson, at the Starlight Bar, report of a disturbance. Use caution, we had a 'man with a gun' call there earlier. Car to back 2610?"

A couple seconds later, Ed Barnes got on. "2617, I got it." The dispatcher got back on and gave us the description of the person supposedly causing the problem: Black male, 20s, white shirt, blue jeans, black jacket, brown hat with a white band. Most of these calls were false alarms, for whatever reason. You never knew. But this was pretty specific information, so heads up.

I'd been to the Starlight before—lots of times—mostly for fights. But I remembered that there'd been a couple robberies and some shootings, one of them a homicide. So this could be real.

I was about seven blocks away; Barnes, probably a few more. I didn't want him getting there and going in before I got there, so I switched on the strobes and hit the gas. I pulled up, grabbing my Maglite and baton as I got out. Ed was just pulling up and parked halfway on the sidewalk. I was glad Ed Barnes was backing me. He had an imposing way about him that made people pay attention. And he had great cop instincts.

"I'll take the front, you take the side entrance, okay?" Ed said as I walked up.

"Got it," I said, and headed that way, telling myself again that this could be founded, trying to make a plan. I cleared my mind and unsnapped my holster as I stepped through the faded red door marked "Ladies Entrance," into the dark, smoky bar. I stood there, my eyes adjusting. The crowded space was long and narrow, with neon blinking and flashing all around, giving it a carnival feel. Old beer and fried food smells hung in the air, sour and greasy. People were everywhere, laughing and talking in extra-loud voices, competing with the blaring music. Folks having a good time. But we weren't there for the party.

I was at the back end of the place, which was just one long room. There were about five or six tables for those who wanted more than just liquid nourishment. They were all filled. I looked at the patrons who were sitting there, enjoying food along with their drinks. Didn't look like our guy was there. My presence and serious look quieted their animated conversations. Now they glared at me—an unwelcome guest.

Further back, beyond the tables, sounds from the kitchen added to the clatter with orders being shouted and the sounds of pots and dishes banging. Turning toward the main bar area, I squinted in the semi-light, looking for Ed. He was up front, leaning over, talking to the bartender, probably asking him if he had called. I saw the man shake his head 'no.' As Ed stood and talked, his eyes, like mine, were everywhere, looking things over, trying to find our subject. The place was packed. It was Friday night. Payday. The small bar was standing room only, people two- and three-deep up and down the long bar, drinking or waiting for drinks. The jukebox was blasting Motown, loud and brassy.

On my left, I checked out two young men who were engaged in a slow-motion game of shuffleboard. Their sluggish, unsteady movements and slurred conversation suggested they'd been there awhile. Neither one looked like the person we were looking for. Anyway, a bad guy would have paid attention to cops coming in. Expecting us. Probably would've seen us before we saw him. He'd have been alert, not like these two.

So far, I hadn't seen anybody sitting or standing who looked like the guy we were here for. We kept going, kept looking. I moved toward the front as Ed moved back my way, working toward the middle.

We both saw him at the same time.

Our guy *knew* it too, because he put his drink down on the bar. He'd been watching us in the mirror behind the bar. He was sitting on a stool about halfway between Ed and me. And he fit the description perfectly, right down to his hat. I stopped and looked at Ed, who gave me a little nod. Then we walked to where the man was sitting.

Like a well-rehearsed scene, the people on either side of him and in the general area grabbed their drinks and moved away. Like it was routine, what you did in this situation. Like a scene from an old Western movie where there was going to be trouble in the barroom and everybody around the target guy just wanted to get out of the way. A few seconds later, we stood right behind the male.

I was watching him, especially his hands as he sat there looking straight ahead. I slowly drew my revolver and held it down by my side. Ed did the same. Pretty sure the guy saw that. His eyes were in the mirror. He was watching as hard as we were. I stood behind and to the right of the guy, not too close, just close enough. Standing off to the man's left, Ed said, "Hey, pal, we need you to stand up, okay?" I watched the guy's reflected face as he looked at us, first Ed then me. He didn't say anything and he didn't move. Maybe he didn't hear Ed over the crowd. I doubted that. I figured he'd been watching us the whole time and probably could figure out we wanted to talk with him. Now, he had a not-so-nice smirk on his face as he sat there with his hands on the bar, not moving. Guess he's not a big fan of the cops. His non-responsiveness had me on high alert.

I forced myself to take a breath. I could feel the tightness in my arms, my shoulders, and especially in my right hand that tightly gripped the gun I hoped I wouldn't have to use.

"Keep your hands where we can see 'em," said Ed Barnes in his strong voice, his free hand making slight contact with the man's left shoulder. The guy stiffened, but still didn't move. He was silent, still watching us in the mirror. "Stand up," commanded Ed. No response.

Then, as Ed reached over to grab him, the man threw his arms out to the side, like a baseball umpire signaling a runner *safe*, like we were playing charades, like he was telling us he posed no danger to us. I still wasn't sure.

I leaned close to the guy's right ear. "Mister, we got a call for a man with a gun in here. You fit the description. We need to check it out." I said in a too-loud voice. Then he did something stupid and very dangerous.

Without a word or warning, he suddenly reached his right hand back under his jacket, toward his rear pants pocket—*or his waistband?* I backed up a couple steps and tightened my grip on the Smith & Wesson, bringing it up. Finger off the trigger, but close.

"Relax, officers, just my wallet, see?" he said, smirking as he turned toward us, wallet in hand. The wise-ass grin vanished as he looked down at the two revolvers pointed at his chest. "Whoa, whoa! Hey man, put that shit down!" he said, scared now, looking back and forth between Ed and me, dropping his wallet and throwing both hands up as far as they could go.

What an asshole! We both holstered and reached for him. Ed grabbed him first, stood him up and, holding him tight by the collar of his jacket, pushed him against the blaring jukebox and proceeded to whisper—more like growl—his assessment of the guy's stupidity and lousy judgment. I walked over and added my two cents.

We didn't conduct a frisk. What we did was a goddamn search: jacket off, pockets turned out, work boots off, all his stuff thrown on the floor, the whole deal. We needed to be sure. In front of the whole bar.

There was no gun. Still, we ran him for wants and warrants. There were none. He was just a guy out having a drink at the corner bar on a Friday evening. A guy somebody wanted the police to hassle. That's all there was to it. Except his attitude and actions could have caused a bad outcome and ruined everybody's Friday night.

The whole thing, start to finish, took less than five minutes. Felt more like an hour.

As we were leaving the bar, I noticed that, for the most part, our intense interaction with the man in the brown hat hadn't changed the dynamic of the room. Though some of the younger male patrons were quietly watching us, nobody came over. There were no protests or raised voices. It was business as usual. Like this was normal, an expected part of the evening's activities.

There could have been so much more to it. It could have been so bad. Scary bad. Ed and I stood outside the Starlight, just looking at each other. I wondered if he was thinking what I was. Maybe. Probably. Neither one of us said anything. Just nodded and went to our vehicles.

Ed got in his car and drove north back to his sector and I sat in mine. I told the dispatcher the outcome of our investigation, holding myself out of service to complete the paperwork. I got away from there and pulled over a few blocks later to write my report. I was still tight. And a little shaky. This had been one of my closest calls.

After writing just a few words on the report, I put my pen down. *What had the guy been thinking?* I wondered. *What made him act that way?* He was close to my age, but clearly our life experiences were way different. I would never have handled an encounter with police the way he did. Ever! *Who'd made the call? Why? Was it an ex-wife or girlfriend so pissed off at him they would drop a dime and start the wheels of this dangerous thing turning? Or maybe it was a neighbor or a co-worker who was getting even for something. A buddy playing a sick joke?* I didn't know. It didn't really matter now.

Still, I couldn't stop thinking about it. The whole thing was hard to understand. It had been scary, things moving so fast, almost out of control. So much could have gone wrong.

As I sat there, my mind kept going back to the man in the bar. We didn't know enough about him, but he knew *everything* about us. If he was planning something bad, he definitely had the advantage. Bad guys usually did.

I had known from the start that being a cop required a lot of new learning, everyday on-the-job stuff. And I'd done that. *Been* doing that. But *this*? This was new, and very different.

I finished the report and filed the experience away under "lesson of the day." It had worked out—this time. Still… if I'd been by myself, with no backup, would this have gone differently? No way to know.

I told the dispatcher I was back in service. I pulled out and drove slowly toward the north end of my sector, away from the Dew Inn. I was on super-alert, looking everywhere, listening. I forgot about dinner. I wasn't hungry anymore.

Maggie

The first time I saw her was on a Sunday night, about 10 o'clock. I was driving the squad car south on Germantown Avenue. Cold, windy rain sheeted on the windshield so hard it clattered like pebbles on the glass. Even with the wipers going full speed, I could barely see. I was slowing down, pulling over. Good thing. The woman came out suddenly, from between two parked cars right before Thompson, just a few feet from my front bumper, right into the middle of the street. Her small stature and dark clothing made her appear like a phantom in the misty light. She didn't see me and didn't slow down. Her mind was made up: she was crossing then and there, cars or no cars.

I flicked on my spotlight, and followed her as she slowly made her way, lighting her up. She looked like a moving ball of rags. As she went sloshing through the downpour, I heard her muttering loudly, almost shouting, words I couldn't make out. Maybe cursing me for almost whacking her with the car. It was dark and pouring, but I could see that she wasn't dressed for the rain or for the November night. Then she was gone. I'm not sure she even knew I was there. It didn't seem like she cared one way or the other.

This was the early 70s. The number of "street"' or homeless people that were now out and about, wandering the city, had ballooned since the recent closing of many mental health facilities in Philadelphia. I was pretty sure the story was the same everywhere. After years of complaints from a small but persistent group of concerned citizens citing cruelty against the mentally ill, the government people in charge had decided to release most of the folks living in state-managed mental health facilities.

In Philly, the Philadelphia State Hospital was a place called "Byberry," so-called for its location on Byberry Road at the Roosevelt Boulevard. It was a massive complex of tall, brown brick buildings, once filled to capacity, now mostly deserted. Its only occupants now were those who were so sick they couldn't be released—patients so disabled and so heavily medicated that they could barely talk, let alone walk and function on their own. They had to stay.

The issue of "warehoused" mentally ill patients had, for years, been a hot topic for politicians and social activists. It had finally led to the mass release of people, many who hadn't been on their own for years, even decades. But I don't think the decision-makers thought the whole thing through. Most of the newly-released folks, used to a highly-structured environment, found themselves having to make their own life decisions, good or bad. Many were unable or unwilling to maintain their medication levels—or the fundamental discipline necessary to function in daily life outside the facility. And they wouldn't be required to attend the structured and supportive therapy sessions, as when they were hospitalized. Most would go live with families or in marginally managed group homes. Many would adapt. But in time, those who didn't take their meds and refused to get professional help became unmanageable. A large number of those were either put out or just walked away. The streets became their new homes.

I wanted to follow the woman, to make sure she was okay, but as I U-turned, the radio called my number for an auto accident half a sector away. My fourth or fifth tonight. *Why the hell don't people slow down when it rains or just stay home?* I answered the dispatcher, then headed to the three-car crash.

I forgot about the woman in the rain, but once in a while, something would remind me and I'd think about her. *She looked homeless, but who was this woman? Where does she live?* How *does she live?* Then I saw her again.

This time, she was sitting on the tumbled-down white marble steps of an abandoned row house near Howard and Master. Trash spilled out of the destroyed front door, but it didn't seem to bother her. She was rooting through her two beat up vinyl shopping bags—first one, then the other— looking for who knows what. She heard my car and looked up, startled. She started to gather what she'd laid on the steps, trying to throw it all in and get up and leave at the same time. Some stuff fell to the ground and she bent down and grabbed it, watching me like I was a threat. As I sat there watching her in her mild panic, I thought it made sense: how many times had cops moved her along from someplace where she'd been resting or just sitting, not bothering a soul; or forced her to go to one of the half-dozen "shelters" in the area?

I stayed back, just watching her. Keeping an eye on me, she finished packing her things and shuffled off. I let her go. This was the second time in three weeks I'd seen her. I was pretty sure I knew all the homeless people in my area. She was new. *Wish I knew her name,* I thought. For some reason, she looked like a "Maggie" to me, so that's how I thought of her.

I figured Maggie was around. I didn't know where she slept, but from time to time, I'd run into her. She'd see me and move on before I got very close. Then, one early summer evening, driving west on Oxford, I saw her sitting, leaning against the wall of the Moffet Elementary School, which was closed for the summer. Her chin was down, buried in the layers of clothing she had on. I wasn't sure if she saw me rolling by. I quickly drove to the Dew Inn, picked up soup, coffee, and a hamburger, then headed back. This time Maggie saw me coming, and struggled herself up, grabbing her two overstuffed bags as she went hurrying away. I imagined all her stuff was in those bags. I called for her to stop—not my best idea—and she just shuffled faster. I could hear her talking to herself.

I let her get about half a block away. Then I got out, walked up and laid the bag of food where Maggie had been sitting. I backed out of the street so she wouldn't see me drive past her, and left. Then, the radio got busy and I was bouncing around answering calls and doing what cops do. A few hours later, when radio the calls had slowed down, I went by the school. Maggie and the food were gone. Good deal.

And so it went for months. We'd see each other here and there and she always made the assumption that I wanted her to move on, so she left. I felt bad, like I was chasing her. I would sometimes bring her something to eat and leave it a safe distance away. It felt almost like I was leaving food for a feral animal.

One day Maggie didn't walk away when I got out of the car with the bag. I didn't get too close, though. Pretty sure she wouldn't like that. After a minute or so of staring at each other, I put the food down and left.

A week or so later, when I saw her sitting on a pile of trash on the sidewalk by a factory, I took a chance and got out of the squad car, just close enough for her to see me. I just stood there. Like I was part of the scenery. I tried to look less like a cop, leaving my hat and jacket in the car, radio turned down. It worked. She didn't leave. But she was watching me.

After a few minutes, I got back in the car, waved to her and drove away. It was a start.

One busy day, on my way to back up another car on a disturbance, I flew by the Moffet School, glancing over like I always did, to see if Maggie was there. She was, but she wasn't alone; there was something going on. Two good-sized boys—they looked like teenagers—had her backed up against the wall and were hassling her. She just stood there, small and helpless. "Get away from that lady, or you're both locked up!" I called from my car's PA speaker. They jumped back, turned and looked my way, starting to run. I couldn't stay there, had to go to my call, but I couldn't leave her like this. So I got out, which made them run faster. She was looking over, so I gave her a quick nod. Then I was off. After the call, I came back, but Maggie was gone. No sign of the bullies, either.

The cat and mouse, getting-to-know-you game went on between Maggie and me for a while. Eventually, I hoped she would see me like just a harmless guy, nobody to worry about. Once in a while, I'd see her lift her non-bag-carrying arm in a little *hello* wave. On and on we went, each doing our own thing.

Finally, months after that first rainy night, we had our first conversation, sort of. I was parked, finishing up a burglary report, when I saw her heading my way. I watched her in my mirror as she came up the street. Maggie was looking too, maybe trying to see which cop was in the car. I gave a little wave, then went back to writing. Then she was right there, a few feet away from me.

When I looked over and nodded, her mouth turned up in what I thought was a little smile. She seemed friendly and not too afraid. I looked at her: *younger, but old-looking—about 45 or so*, I thought. Everything about her was a mess; dirt was the common denominator on her skin and clothes, but it didn't seem to bother her. I knew that there were places where she could go to bathe and get a change of clothing. But it didn't look like Maggie had done that in a while.

I put my pen down and looked at her. "Hi, how are you?" I said quietly. *What a stupid thing to say.*

"Mmm-hmm," she murmured, standing there, looking past me, shifting her bags from one hand to the other, still not sure if it was safe.

"I haven't seen you around. How've you been?" *What a dopey thing to say. Look at her; how do you* think *she's been?*

She shrugged and said something that could've been "Okay."

I wasn't prepared for a protracted Maggie conversation, so I didn't know what else to say. Guess she didn't either. So, we just looked at each other. Glad to finally meet Maggie, I sat there, nodding my head up and down, like that would make sense to her. She was probably trying to figure out why I was doing that.

"What's your name?" I asked and got the Maggie stare. That was about it. After a couple more minutes of silence, she adjusted her shopping bags, then turned and walked away.

"Bye. Take care," I called after her. *Strati, you're a bonehead!*

It looked like her head nodded "goodbye" without turning. Maybe I imagined it. Back to her own private world.

For a few months after that, I didn't see Maggie. Worried, I checked with some of the other cops working the area. One of them, Harry Clifton, said he'd seen her but that she'd looked terrible. I didn't know what that meant. Glad that she was still around, I continued stopping by her usual hangouts. She wasn't there. Then, one day, I spotted her as I was out of the car, walking around the Moffet School checking doors and windows. She came out of the shadow of one of the out-buildings in the schoolyard, an area separate from the children's play area. She was shuffling toward me. Hurrying. I stood still and waited.

Clutching her bags, she came closer and closer then stopped. Now pretty close, I could hear her mumbling something I couldn't make out. It was like she was doing both sides of a conversation with herself. I wondered if she was trying to convince herself to talk to me. Did she even remember me? Looking at me, her tired eyes warily moving up and down, she was considering the risk. I waited.

Maggie shuffled a little closer. Then, she shrieked, "Those boys did it!" spitting the words out. She shook her head wildly back and forth in angry frustration, her unwashed hair matted to her face and falling over her eyes.

I didn't know what to say, so I said nothing, waiting for her.

"They beat me, mister," she said, slurring the words. A little sob. Then, she surprised me: placing a weathered and scabbed hand on my arm for balance, she put her bags down and lifted her long raggedy skirt to her knees to show me her swollen legs. I saw old and new bruises and cuts up and down both legs. Nasty cuts too, and some of them looked infected. She watched as I looked, saying nothing, just mumbling low. *She needs to go to the hospital,* I thought. When I told her, she freaked out. Then she backed away, putting both hands up, warding me off.

"No, no, no, no, no!" she cried. "Please no!"

"Okay, okay, no hospital," I said, trying to calm her. "No hospital." I almost called her Maggie. Then I asked, "What's your name?"

No answer. She was instantly suspicious, maybe thinking that giving me her name was the first step to the hospital. She quickly turned to go.

"No, no," I said. "No hospital." Then I said, "My name is Nick," using my middle name, something I did when "Stratis" might be confusing.

She stopped and looked at me, still leery. Like a half-tame being, wanting to trust but remembering other times, other humans… "Boys hit me," she said.

"Which boys?"

Thinking for a bit, she then mumbled, "Schoolyard boys."

After a few seconds, I remembered. They instantly became a priority. "Okay," I said. "Don't worry, I'll find them." Then, changing the subject, I asked "Are you hungry?"

All I got was a cautious look through her narrowed eyes.

"Okay, just wait here. I'll be right back," I said, pointing to the hiding place she'd come from. I got some food and returned. Of course, she was gone. But the well-used cardboard and dirty plastic sheets suggested this is where she camped. I hid the sandwiches and drinks in there and left.

Now that I knew where Maggie spent her nights—at least some of them—I'd stop by once in a while. She wasn't there. I learned that other cops had seen her. So where was she? Maybe she was avoiding me. Maybe she'd forgotten we'd ever met.

Then I had a bright idea. I tried to find someone in the city's Department of Human Services who could get Maggie help beyond the local shelters and soup kitchens, but every phone call gave me another department, another number and eventually a dead-end. After a while, frustrated, I got off that city-run carousel.

I eventually caught up with the two tough-guy kids who'd assaulted Maggie. I brought them and their parents in, after explaining everything to the adults. What followed was a *come-to-Jesus* meeting with Ken Hartwell, a soft-spoken, yet intense Juvenile Aid officer, assigned to the district. Ken sat them down and gave them the real, hard facts of criminal life. The ones about boys their age being charged as adults and spending time in Graterford State Prison with *real* bad guys. By the end, they were listening. Scared now and not so tough, with tears starting, they apologized and promised to be good. Their parents, having heard everything, saw this as an opportunity and promised us they'd hold them to it. I would, too. But I never saw them again. That was a good thing.

I never saw Maggie again, either. And I never learned her real name—or her story.

There were hundreds, maybe thousands of Maggies in the 26th District and all around Philadelphia back then. Sick, homeless, and alone in the big city. Since then, there've been too many more and, even today, as this is written, they're still out there. Even more of them, I think. And now, there are plenty of military veterans joining the scene of street life, trading one hell for another. Their problems and their lives are like Maggie's. Only different. And more complicated. It doesn't seem like anybody's doing much to help. Just the same old, same old.

Overnight Drive

As we wrapped up roll call at 12:15 a.m., and I was walking out to my squad car in the district parking lot, I thought, *I'm already tired; I'll never get used to Last Out. How the hell am I supposed to stay awake in the middle of the night? It's unnatural.* The overnight shift had always been tough for me. I remembered back to the army. We MPs were the military's version of police, doing pretty much the same kind of work, and doing it all hours of the day and night. Seemed like a lot more nights than days. I hated it then, too. *What possessed me to do this for a living?*

I pulled my car onto Montgomery Avenue and turned left on Girard. As always, I had the driver's window all the way down and the other front window half open. It was what I did so I could hear what was going on and try to stay alert. Problem with open windows on a frigid night like this was that I got cold, even with the car heater blasting. I'd take the freezing air on my face as long as I could, then roll the windows back up, for just a few minutes, long enough to take the chill off. The cranked-up heater fan was great, except that in about three minutes with the windows up, the warm car made me want to put my head down and sleep—wouldn't even need a blanket or pillow.

So, I was doing my best to keep busy, especially during the hours between 3:00 and 7:00 a.m., the toughest times of all for most cops.

"265, 266, take Memphis and York, disturbance on the highway." The dispatcher's call was a jolt—there hadn't been anything on the radio for over an hour.

Ron Sawyer, in 265, and I both answered the call right away. It was about 3:30, the time the bars closed, so this could be something. Before I got there, Ron was on the radio. "265, resume the other car, there's nothing here." I guess the crowd moved on or it may have been some night-owl wise guy making a phony call just to see if we'd come.

"266, I got it." I was only a block away, so I rolled up to Ron's car, parking so our driver's windows were next to one another. As Ron wrote the unfounded report, we sat there, just talking. Both glad to have something to do for a couple minutes. But now it was over. Back to the boredom.

I rolled over to the Paradise, the only open diner, for a cup of strong coffee. As I waited for the waitress to fill the cardboard cup, I looked over the half-dozen or so patrons that were scattered around the place. A couple of young guys were nodding off at the counter, their food untouched. Others were conversing in alcohol-fueled, too-loud voices with their tablemates. Probably all coming from the local bars and clubs, getting something to eat before heading home. At the front counter I asked Maria, the owner's wife, in Greek, "Ola Kala, Maria?" ("Everything alright?")

"Malista," Nodding yes while also feigning annoyance, she pushed back the money I had put down by the register. Like all the restaurant owners I was familiar with, she was glad to see a cop stop by. They showed their appreciation and encouragement by giving us coffee from time to time. I wasn't going to get into a thing with Maria over it, so I thanked her, picked up the cash and handed it to the waitress as she passed.

Next stop: headquarters, to drop off paperwork and take a bathroom break. Before returning to my car, I went into the Operations Room, where the inside crew was just finishing up their daily chore of organizing and filing the previous shift's paperwork. We talked about how the Eagles were looking better than last year. "They're gonna make the playoffs, you'll see," said Corporal Tony Girardi. Probably just wishful thinking. Back out to the now-cold car.

On my way over to my sector again, I checked out the deserted streets and sidewalks, looking for some action. I took another slow spin through my six-by-eight-block sector, playing my spotlight over factory windows and down some of the alleys as I cruised. After a while, I pulled up narrow Sepviva Street, which led to the St. Mary Hospital Emergency Room. This was one of my regular stops—checking to make sure everything was okay and taking some time to chat with the night staff who, if they weren't busy, were in the same boat I was, trying to stay upright.

"Hey kids, how you doin'? All awake?" I asked. They were all just sitting around, looking bored. Looking up, Bill Burris gave me a tired smile.

"Officer Skoufalos, where you been? Haven't seen you in about a month."

"You're right," I said, reminding him that on my rotating schedule, I worked the night shift only about six days a month. Bill was a thirty-something nurse who had been telling me for years that he wanted to be a cop, but hadn't made the move yet. He sauntered over to where I was leaning on the counter.

"Anything good goin' on?" He always wanted to know about any exciting incidents I'd had.

"Nah. It's really quiet out there, Bill. What's happening with the Police Department thing?"

"Nothin'. My wife still ain't goin' for it, ya know?"

"Yeah," I said. "I get it." After a bit, I waved to the other two nurses, who looked as tired as I felt.

I slowly made my way back out to the car and went back to patrolling my sector. Every couple of minutes, I forced myself out of the warm cocoon of the car with my flashlight to physically check properties. First, Miller's drugstore at Memphis and Susquehanna, looking in windows, shaking doors. After that, St. Laurentius Catholic church and school at Memphis and Berks; then Holy Name, a few blocks further east. All secure. Besides making sure the places were okay, this was a good wake-up routine so I'd do each place a couple times per shift.

Then, on to one of my favorite try-to-stay-awake activities—looking for plug parkers (cars blocking fire hydrants). I knew the location of every hydrant on my sector. The Pennsylvania Motor Vehicle code was specific: 15 feet was the closest you could park to a plug. I usually gave people some leeway, especially in densely populated neighborhoods like this one where finding a parking spot near your house felt like a divine gift. But I *always* had zero tolerance for people who parked their cars completely *blocking* a fire plug. If it was daytime and I wasn't too busy, I might look for the driver and give him or her the chance to move it. But not at night. No breaks. The reason was simple: during my first year as a cop, I'd gotten called to a house fire in the middle of the night, where a couple of the occupants didn't make it out. They were both little kids. I'll never forget that. Nothing should hinder firefighters' chances to save lives—if you're too lazy to walk a little, you're getting a ticket. A few minutes later, I had made my rounds—all my hydrants were clear tonight. Good. Maybe they were getting the message.

I also liked to hunt on the overnight shift—prowling around, looking for bad guys or good guys doing bad things. Having the car windows down was critical. In the dark silence of the early morning hours, sounds like breaking glass, any kind of banging, as well as building and car alarms could be heard for blocks and blocks. Usually, it was nothing, but sometimes it turned out to be a crime in progress. So I drove, very slowly, looking and listening.

There usually weren't many people driving around between three and six in the morning, just out cruising. After a while, I got to know most of the cars and people in my sector who were going to or coming from work in the early morning. But, once in a while, there were some who didn't fit into this category. Sometimes these folks were legitimate and sometimes they were up to no good. I just kept an eye on them as they drove through. You never knew.

Rolling up to the red light at Front and Susquehanna, I stopped behind a light blue Chevy Impala, couple years old, Jersey tag. I wrote the number down. Just because. I could see the driver's eyes looking at me in the rear-view mirror. Instinctively, I reached up to the visor and grabbed the "hot sheet," the daily listing of wanted cars—most of them stolen—and checked. Not there. *Okay, my friend, guess you're okay,* I thought.

The light turned green and we both pulled out, the Chevy going west on Susquehanna, and I, north on Front. Creeping along under the elevated train trestle, spotlight on, I scoped out the store fronts on both sides as I passed through the three-block deserted business area. I looked at my wrist; my watch said 4:30. *Is that all it is? Damn watch must be stopped!* I griped to myself. *Three-and-a-half more hours?*

As I passed the Kent movie theater, I made a right onto Cumberland. I pulled over a couple blocks later, at Emerald—my parents' store with the house above. This'd been my home growing up. All dark. I got out and walked around. My flashlight told me that everything looked okay. *Remember to call Mom and Pop later*, I said to myself. *It's been about a week since you talked with them; they worry.* I worried too. They were getting up there in age and the neighborhood wasn't what it used to be.

I drove on, past Kensington High, the massive dark brown brick building hulking up, covering a whole block. It looked secure.

Still heading east on Cumberland, I caught the red light at Frankford Avenue. Sitting there, waiting and rubbing my tired eyes, I saw headlights coming from my left, southbound on Frankford. I took a peek. The left turn signal of the approaching car was on, but instead of turning, it went straight. This time of the morning was when I was as tired as I got. But something—a hunch, sixth sense, something—made me watch the car all the way through the intersection. *Looks like the Chevy I saw a few minutes ago.* As it passed, I checked the license plate. New Jersey. Couldn't make out the numbers, but pretty sure it was him. Now I was a little interested. Probably nothing, but it seemed like the guy was driving in a big circle. And, the Jersey tag factor had me curious. I turned to follow and just caught the tail end of the blue car as it made a right onto York and, by the time I got there, he was gone. "Okay," I said out loud, "Let's play." Focused now, I sat up straighter and, picking up speed, drove halfway up the block, turned right on Amber and stopped just south of Cumberland. Lights off, I sat there. I didn't have to wait long.

The car zoomed by, heading east. Heading to where he'd been going a minute ago on Frankford, then changed his mind when he saw me. Thought so. He passed where I was stopped and drove east on Cumberland. I gave him a second or two, then pulled out and got close enough to confirm the tag. Time to call it in. "266, I'm east on Cumberland from Frankford. Could you run a Jersey tag?"

"Okay 266, do you have the car stopped?"

"No, Radio, just following it." I was about half a block behind him now, and I was pretty sure the driver knew I was coming.

"Stand by." Before the dispatcher could request a backup to start rolling in, I heard a couple cops call out their car numbers and head my way. Then things started happening way too fast. Soon, the whole deal got strange.

The driver of the Chevy, seeing me closing on him, sped up. A block later, he screeched to a sideways skidding stop, just missing a couple of parked cars. He got out and took off, leaving the door open and the car running. That usually meant the runner was headed in the opposite direction of the pursuing cops. That's what *usually* happened. This guy didn't do that.

He ran up the front steps of one of the houses halfway down the block. He was trying to get in, but couldn't. As I pulled up, he looked back at me as he frantically kept working on the door. The delay gave me time to get a good look at him. *He's young*, I thought. I got on the radio, my voice up now, talking fast. "266, the driver jumped out and he's trying to enter a house on Cumberland Street." I gave Radio the guy's description.

"Okay, 266. All cars stand by." The dispatcher sounded the alert tone—a long beep to let everybody know that what followed was a priority message. Then, "All cars responding to the 2300 block of Cumberland, 266 is in pursuit of a male who bailed out of the car and is running east on Cumberland."

As I ran from my car to the house, I radioed the address. By now the guy was inside. Decision time. I tried the door; it was locked. My mind was zooming, bouncing around, trying to figure out what to do. *Does this guy live here? If he does, what should I do? Should I wait for backup?* Then, *What if he* doesn't *live here and he broke into this house where the people are in there sleeping?* I had to take a chance. I stepped back and kicked the door hard, just above the doorknob. All that did was bounce me back, off the steps. Not so easy. It sure wasn't like TV where the lock breaks right away and the door flies open. Nope. I tried again and again. It took two or three good slams but it finally gave. Then, I was in.

The vestibule door was open and in front of me, my flashlight told me that the living room and dining room beyond were dark and empty. It was quiet. This guy could be anywhere. Hardly breathing, I stood still, listening. I didn't want to go any further in, but I couldn't just stand here. I'm thinking, *This is creepy. Slow down, careful.* I felt my heart banging and my stomach was tight. I unsnapped my holster. Wide-eyed and crouched, I moved ahead slowly, following the beam of my Maglite. I was only about ten feet in when I saw lights come on upstairs. I heard muffled voices and shuffling, somebody moving to the stairs. Then there was loud barking. Like BIG-dog barking. *Oh shit!* I saw a man coming down the stairs from the second floor and he was holding a good-sized Doberman by the collar. I backed up into the vestibule, grabbing the doorknob, just in case. I pointed my flashlight toward the stairway. "Police officer!" I yelled. "Hold your dog." This was all happening way too fast. *Backup's still not here. Where the hell are they?*

The man, all the way down to the bottom of the stairs now, flicked a switch, lighting up the living room. He stood there in his pajamas with the barking dog, looking at me. I could tell the dog wanted to come over to me but not for a friendly lick *hello*. His eyes were trained on me and I could tell he was braced for action. "What the hell's going on? What are you doing in my house?" the man shouted. These were both good questions.

"I chased a young guy into your house a minute ago. I think he may have been in a stolen car; I'm not sure."

"Are you crazy? We were all sleeping, nobody came in here. Nobody here stole a car."

"Sir, do you have a young man living here…about 16 or so?" I gave him the description of the guy I'd seen.

"I have a 17-year-old son, but he's asleep upstairs." He pointed up with his head.

"Okay, can we check?" I asked.

"This is crazy," the man repeated, struggling to keep the dog under control.

"Sir, I'm Sergeant Brownlee." I turned around. My supervisor was standing right behind me. I hadn't heard him come in. "The officer saw somebody jump out of a car and then run into your house. We think the car may be stolen. We're checking it now. We'd like your permission to look around to make sure that this guy isn't in your house. And he could be dangerous."

"I can't believe this," the man with the Doberman said.

"I know," said the sergeant calmly. "It's a little strange. You can come with us and help us check, but you need to put your dog away."

The man, fully awake and muttering to himself, walked the dog through the kitchen and put him out in the backyard. "Okay, now what?" he asked.

"Skouf?" asked the sergeant.

"Where's your son's bedroom, sir?" I asked.

"On the third floor. But you're wrong, officer," said the man, calmer now. "He went to bed about ten and he never left."

"Let's take a look, okay?" I asked. With the owner leading the way, Sergeant Brownlee and I started up the stairs. Meanwhile, Brownlee told a couple other cops to check out the basement and the rest of the downstairs in case the guy I'd seen was hiding somewhere.

Standing in the 2nd-floor hallway, I asked, "Whose rooms are here on the second floor?"

"My wife's and mine and my daughter's. She's twelve." As if on cue, a girl in pink flannel pajamas shuffled out of a room down the hall, rubbing the sleep from her eyes.

"Daddy, what's goin' on?" she mumbled. "Why are the cops here?"

"Go back to bed, honey, everything's okay. Don't worry. Just go back to sleep." She stood there watching as we walked down the hallway to the stairs.

We climbed to the third floor where there were two more bedrooms. "The front one is my older son's. He's away in the Army," said the man. I acknowledged with a nod and we moved toward the back bedroom. "This one's Brad's room, the 17-year-old."

"Let us go in first," I said quietly. From the doorway, I moved my flashlight over the bed in the dark room. Sure enough, it looked like there was someone under the covers.

"See, I told you," said the man. "Right where I said he'd be."

I found the switch and turned on the ceiling light. The person in the bed didn't move.

"Brad, wake up," said Brad's father. Still no movement under the covers. "Brad!"

Brad, covers up to his chin, slowly rolled our way and opened his eyes, squinting against the light. "Whaaat?" he said in a pretty convincing I'm-sleeping-you-just-woke-me-up voice.

Uh-oh, I thought. *Did I screw up here?*

"Get up," his dad said. "The police are here and they want to talk to you."

"What for? I'm sleeping. I didn't do nothin'."

"Just get out of bed, son," said Sergeant Brownlee. The kid didn't move. Dad moved past us over to the bed and ripped the covers off his son.

There. Brad was fully dressed, shoes and all. The clothing was the same I'd called in to Radio. The boy's father backed up, stunned, speechless. He shook his head, just watching as I got Brad up and we all started downstairs. Nobody was talking.

When we got back down to the living room, one of the wagon cops who had responded told the sergeant and me that the car had been stolen earlier that night, but hadn't been reported yet. Overhearing, Brad again denied that he'd had anything to do with any stolen car. I explained to Brad and his dad that I was going have to take Brad in so we could check it all out. With that, I cuffed the boy and turned him over to the wagon crew who transported him to the Detectives for further investigation.

Turns out, the owner of the car had been visiting friends a couple blocks from where we were. When Brad went out for a walk, "'cause I couldn't sleep," he told the detective, he was really looking for an unlocked GM car—any GM car. He wanted to see if he could do what his friend, Billy, car thief extraordinaire, had shown him: how to take advantage of a manufacturing defect by cracking the steering column and starting the car by simply pushing a lever inside. Unfortunately for Brad, it worked.

As I came out of the house, getting ready to head up to the Detectives for the arrest paperwork, Sergeant Brownlee was sitting in his car, waiting for me. He flashed his lights, calling me over. In his usual calm way, he looked up at me and said, "Skouf, nice work. It makes us all look good when we get a stolen car back, especially before it's been reported."

I felt good. I *had* done a good job. Standing there, proud and all… However, the good sergeant had more to say.

Still calm, he said, "Listen, Skouf, you took a big chance goin' in there by yourself. All kinda of bad shit could've happened, ya know?" I hadn't thought about it, but, standing there then, I *did* think about it—*the homeowner could've had a gun and seen me as an intruder; the dog could've gotten to me; instead of it being Brad, the guy I was chasing might have been a* really *bad guy and he could've ambushed me.* I just looked at the sarge, said nothing.

"Look," he said, "I know you feel you had a damn good reason to bust down that door and go after him, and you *did.* But, Skouf, it was too big a risk, wasn't worth you or somebody else gettin' hurt. Hey, we all got here pretty quick, right? So I wish you woulda waited. Get what I'm sayin'?" I did, but I felt like I had to explain.

I wanted to say that I was trying to protect the occupants of the house, to get the bad guy. But I didn't. I didn't say anything. Just nodded. The wise old sergeant looked at me some more and gave me a small nod back, then drove slowly away. I knew he was right. Whatever my reasons, no matter how right I was, I should've waited. Then it hit me: *Damn, I hope I'm not in trouble.* Hadn't thought about that in the heat of the whole thing.

Hours later, paperwork done, I headed back to my district to report off—two hours past my regular time. So tired... So much for *trying* to keep busy on the night shift.

━━━━━●●●━━━━━

The detectives charged Brad with Theft, Receiving Stolen Property, and Unauthorized Use of a Motor Vehicle. Heavy charges for the young kid. Months later, the court case came up. I sat there and watched as Brad pleaded guilty to a lesser charge. It was his first offense, and the judge gave him a break—a few months probation along with some community service. Another part of the deal was that he would pay for the damage to the car. Not bad.

Citing police-community relations, the city paid for the damaged door.

Following a complaint from the homeowner, the PD investigated and considered disciplining me but nothing ever happened. Somebody told me that Sergeant Brownlee had gone to bat for me with the captain. He never said anything, but I believed it. That's how he was.

On night patrol the following spring, I drove past that house on Cumberland. I stopped and looked over at the new front door. Just like that, it all came back—the good and the bad of it, and the scary stuff that comes from thinking about it too deeply. Driving away, I thought: *Lessons learned? For me, yeah, pretty sure. For Brad? I hope so.*

Banana Poaching and Other Crimes

It was quiet and I was headed east on Girard, going to headquarters to fill my squad car with gas. I saw him stopped at the red light at 4th Street, coming the other way. Sitting in traffic in his police car. He was leaning out of the car—more like his whole upper body was out of the window—and he was looking straight up at the sky.

What's he doing? I wondered. Curious, I leaned out and looked. Nothing.

Some other drivers saw him and started looking up, a couple of them peering through the windshield, a few leaning out, straining to see what was going on.

I couldn't tell anything. *Did I miss a call about a jumper? Is there a plane in trouble?* But there hadn't been a call for a while… *What's going on?*

The light turned green and, pulling himself back into the car and sitting up straight, he slowly pulled away. As he passed me, he waved. He was smiling—that sly, mischievous grin. I waved back and shook my head. *Wow, Frank,* I thought, *that's a new one.* What a character!

Frank Monroe was new to our district and our squad. He had some years on the job and had come from one of the other North Philly districts—the 39th, I think. The talk was that he'd gotten into some kind of trouble. Nobody knew if it was true or what the trouble might have been, but now he was here, in the 26th, One Squad. In the few months since his arrival, he'd had to put up with the usual cool treatment all newbies get from the guys in the squad, waiting to make a judgment on him: Was he reliable? Trustworthy? A good cop? Time would tell.

The cool treatment didn't touch Frank.

Some of the older veterans just ignored him, wanted nothing to do with him. But they were like that with every new guy; even with me when I first got there. None of that seemed to bother him at all.

I liked the guy right away. He knew cop work and wasn't afraid to step in when he had to. He showed that his first week, when he pulled a crazy man off a cop who was trying to settle a domestic disturbance. He'd saved him, then cooled the gathered crowd. He was made for this job, a natural.

And he was funny! The few times we had worked together so far, we'd laughed a lot, especially me, and mostly because of Frank's sense of humor and his wacky take on things.

Like the first time we had lunch together. Sitting in a booth at the *Dew Inn Restaurant*, waiting for the waitress to bring our food, he was across the table from me, hands folded, all serious. He leaned in. Looked like he wanted to say something, so I looked over, listening. "Why is an orange?" he asked me.

"What?"

"Why is an orange?" he repeated, dead serious.

"What are you talking about?"

He repeated the question.

I thought about it. "I don't know. What does that even *mean*?" I said.

"Strati, why is an orange?" he asked again, patient but rolling his eyes like he was talking to an imbecile.

"I don't know. Why?" Meantime, I'm wondering if there is some deep philosophical meaning to his question I just wasn't getting.

"What other color would it be?" he chuckled, waiting for my reaction.

I shook my head and laughed out loud at the absurdity of his perspective and his humor. He was unique. I'd never met anybody like him. Even when I was in the army with guys from all over the country with lots of clowns, no one came close to Frank.

Make no mistake: doing the job, he was no nonsense. Well over six foot and athletic, sharp and confident, the guy was imposing. Polite and a good listener when he was talking with citizens about problems and answering questions, but he was tough when he had to be. His size and appearance were backed up by a deep, booming voice he used to get his point across. He was one of the guys I wanted there next to me when the shit hit the fan.

After a few months, Frank was permanently assigned to 265 car, covering the sector next to mine. We both patrolled a small section on the east side of the 26th, known as Fishtown, an area that had once been the center of the shad fishing industry on the Delaware River.

In the late 70s and early 80s, this was the busiest district in the city, call-volume-wise. Especially on weekends. On Fridays and Saturdays in the summer, on the evening tours of duty, the dispatchers would get hundreds of calls. So, for efficiency, they would usually bunch a few of them that were in the same general area and assign them to a pair of solo patrol cars. That way, the cops could respond to multiple calls at a time and do it with the backup that was usually needed.

During his first summer there, I *really* got to know Frank Monroe. It was one of those crazy-busy weekend evening shifts and we'd been teamed up most of the night. As we rolled from domestic disturbances to calls for fights on the highway, as well as reports of shootings and thefts, we got into a rhythm, taking turns at leading the contact and writing reports. We got pretty good at reading each other's vibes, each keeping the other safe while we took care of business.

Then, as the shift was winding down, we got a call for a disturbance on the corner of Thompson and York, outside *The Anchor*—a bar famous for Friday night fights. We arrived within seconds of each other. Frank was first out of the car and started walking up to a guy who was mumbling to himself, wobbling back and forth, doing the drunk man's dance. When he saw us, he tried leaning on the wall—hoping that would help keep him upright. On our side of things, if he fell and got hurt, we'd have a hospital case. Nobody wanted that. Not the drunk, not us, and certainly not the ER nurses who already had their hands full and would probably be upset with us for bringing in a bloody, pissed-off drunk.

Frank calmly walked up to the guy who was still sober enough to notice a big cop coming his way. The wobbler was apparently an experienced drunk, so he decided to leave the area before Frank got to him. But, as he tried to walk away, his feet evidently didn't get the message, and Frank had to grab his arm to keep him from taking a dive, then sat him down on the curb.

Frank and I quickly checked inside the bar and confirmed that the disturbance had been this guy causing a ruckus. We decided to check out the drunk, to figure out if he could make it home by himself or if we needed to take him in to sleep it off. This is where I saw the Frank Monroe drunk-citizen-assessment method for the first time. Unique.

"What's your name, pal?" he asked the guy.

"Hi, officer, I don't want no trouble. I just had a couple beers and I'm goin' home now," he slurred.

"Great," said Frank. "What's your name?"

"Sharlie," he slurred.

"Okay Charlie, besides having too much to drink, are you okay?" Frank asked, giving him the quick once-over for any cuts, bumps, or bruises.

"Yessir, officer, I'm fine. Just a little drunk," he said, holding his thumb and index finger about an inch apart to show us what "little" meant. "Me and the old lady just had a little fight and I came down here to get a beer and leave her alone. But I'm good now." This whole time, Charlie was swaying back and forth, each back and forth less steady than the last. He was very close to toppling. Frank mentioned this to Charlie and, somehow, the guy stood stock still. *Sobering up by cop.*

"Charlie, have you ever been locked up?" asked Frank.

"No sir officer, never!"

"Well, can we trust you to go right home and straight to bed?" I asked, joining in.

"Ab-absloot-ally," he tried, then settled for "Yeah."

"No more fighting with the old lady?" Frank asked, looking for the truth in his eyes.

"No sir."

Now Frank: "Charlie, if you go *don't* go home to bed and we have to come back, we're going to have to arrest you, understand?"

"Yeah, I do. But I ain't done nothing."

Frank again: "Really, Charlie?" Now Frank had Charlie where he wanted him: Frank stood back a little, hands on hips. "Have you ever heard of the Felton-Sibley Act?" (Felton-Sibley was a paint manufacturing company in 19th century Philadelphia.)

"No sir! Whatever that is, I never done it!" *Getting more sober by the minute.*

"Well, Charlie, it's pretty serious and I don't want to lock you up for it," said Frank, sounding a lot like a concerned big brother. I shook my head emphasizing Frank's assertion.

Looking more than a little confused, Charlie politely asked, "What is it?"

"It's a law against painting the town red," replied Frank with a straight face. I had to turn away.

Charlie, now much more alert than when we'd arrived, just shook his head, not sure if what he was hearing was real. I figured he wasn't going to challenge this big cop, especially when the cop was going to give him a break. "I got it, officer. No, none of that for me. I'm going home and straight to bed." And I guess he did, because we never heard from Charlie the rest of the night.

It was stuff like that, a little fun that lightened the mood, while helping the occasional drunk and wacky citizen that made my time with Frank quite memorable. In fact, whenever I could, I would back him up so that I could see that wonderful imagination and personality in action. My efforts paid off; I saw the show a lot. I never got tired of it. And, like a guardian angel, Frank always made sure, whenever possible, the intoxicated or otherwise impaired citizens made it home safely.

Over the next few years and in numerous encounters, mostly with the 26th District's inebriated citizens, I witnessed Frank use several variations of the "Felton-Sibley Act" approach. Such as:

Drunk guy: "I ain't done nothing. What're you stopping me for, Officer?"

Frank: "We got a call that somebody was *aardvarking* on the highway out here. And they gave us your description."

Shocked, the guy would straighten up and say, "It wasn't me, sir. I never done that."

"Are you sure? You look like somebody that likes *aardvarking*." Serious for the whole thing.

No matter how many times I'd seen this routine, I always had to turn away so the poor guy wouldn't see me laughing.

Then there was this:

Frank: "Hey buddy, come here," waving the guy over to where he was standing by his squad car.

"Why? I didn't do anything." He'd just look at them and, eventually, they'd walk over.

"Oh yeah?" Frank would say, putting his arm around the guy's shoulders. "Looks to me like you've been *cariggering*." With his most serious expression, he'd let that sink in. I could almost see the guy's wheels turning, looking at Frank and trying to figure out what this crazy cop was saying. "You're not the career *carrigerer* we've been getting calls about, are ya?"

"No!" would be the usual reply. Funny, but hardly anyone asked for a definition of the alleged crime. When someone did, the answer he got just expanded their confusion

But Frank always *had* an answer, like, "Well, cariggering is when you're walking around on your hind legs with both arms moving at the same time." This would always result in another denial.

Or this one—probably my favorite:

Frank would pull up to a drunk and ask, "Hey pal, can I talk to you for a second?"

"Sure," the poor unsuspecting guy would say, staggering over.

"How long you been out here?" Frank would ask, serious and straight-faced.

The guy would usually say, "Not too long. Why, Officer? You want me to leave? I'm goin'."

Frank, looking right in the guy's eyes: "We got a call that there was somebody out here *banana-poaching*. Have you seen him?"

"No, I haven't," the guy would say. And it never failed that the drunk would then quickly look around like he might have missed the person involved in such an activity.

Sometimes, Frank would use a combination of these violations. That special treatment was reserved for individuals who would try to give him a hard time or didn't want to talk at all. Once in a while—rarely—one of these guys would *get* that Frank was putting him on and he would call him on it. Frank would let out that deep, rolling laugh of his and shake the guy's hand saying, "Good for you, pal, you figured it out!"

That was my friend, Frank.

He left the 26th after a few years and a million laughs and joined the elite Highway Patrol, something he'd always wanted.

I miss him. I'm not sure if the drunks do. Maybe. I hope that, wherever he is now, *he's* regularly "painting the town red," in direct violation of the Felton-Sibley Act.

Friendly Fire

I didn't know them until that Friday in the spring. Not really. To me and every other cop who drove past their house on the 400 block of Carter Street, they were just *The Friendlies*. The name went way back for generations of cops, certainly way before my arrival in the 26th District. It was a term of affection, given by men not usually known for that kind of softness.

A three-story red brick house, just sixteen feet wide, was typical of the row homes in this part of Philadelphia. It looked pretty much like the other thirty plus houses on the block — unremarkable. The house, that is. The people living there, well…

Tom "Newt" Morris was one of the most respected officers in the district. He had over thirty years as a cop, joining the department right after serving with the Marines in Korea. All his years on the force had been in the 26th and he was the most senior guy there, so, a few months prior, I stopped him in the parking lot. "Tom, what's the deal with *The Friendlies*?" I asked.

Tom wasn't much of a small-talk guy, so I didn't really expect an answer. He stood by the open door of his squad car. "Know why they call them that?" he asked me, his sharp blue eyes steady on mine, his voice soft.

"Well," I offered, "they always wave when cops drive by. Is that it?"

"You got it, kid. They really like cops." I got the sense that there was more, but it didn't look like Tom was going to explain anything more to me, a rookie. Done talking, he got into his car and drove away.

That's it? I thought to myself as I walked over to my patrol car. In the back of my mind, it felt like there was more to the story—like there *should* be more—like some mysterious urban myth. Oh well, no big deal. Hey, it was good to have people like *The Friendlies*, folks that appreciated us. God knows there were plenty who didn't. And I was pretty sure, the cops appreciated them. As far as I knew, every cop always waved back. Completed the circle.

They were out there a lot, sitting on the front steps and not just in the nice weather. Sometimes they'd sit in the cold, wearing coats. Yeah. But no matter how many times in an eight-hour shift I would drive by their house—six, seven, more—if they were out, they'd all wave. All together. Like their arms were connected by an invisible string and some unseen person was pulling it, whenever a cop car passed. They never said anything or called out. Just sat there waving and smiling. I got the feeling they were a close family.

Little by little, I learned more about them from guys who'd been around awhile. I heard that, over the years, the family had had some bad luck and the cops had helped them through some of it: a house fire that a young officer had braved to get the family out; a burglary that would have pretty much wiped them out if the detectives hadn't gotten most of their stuff back. Then somebody told me they had cops in their family. I wasn't sure if there was any truth to any these stories about cops helping them out, but it was a way to make sense of it.

I just wish I hadn't met them for the first time the way it happened.

It was a Friday 4 p.m. to midnight shift, and it was kicking. It was so busy that if you didn't get the paperwork done from the assignment you were finishing up, it would have to wait because, as soon as you put yourself back in service and available for a new assignment, you were getting one. Part of it was because it was so warm—an early spring heat wave. That meant that lots of kids (of all ages), sick of winter, were out playing and raising hell. Friday nights were bad enough, being the end of the work week and all, but add the nice weather, and everybody seemed to want to celebrate something.

On this Friday, I was working Emergency Patrol Wagon 2603 with Jim Stanley. His regular partner, Larry Brady, was off so Jim had requested me. We'd worked together before and were both young, active cops. It was only a couple of hours into the shift and already we were up to about fifteen calls. The average number for Fridays on 4 to 12 was twenty to twenty-five, total, so we were moving right along.

He was driving and I was finishing up the paperwork from our last job—a call about a missing child. Turned out that the kid had been playing in the basement and fell asleep behind his fort of stacked boxes. Mom and Dad were both relieved and pissed off at their four-year-old.. I was a little worried that the kid might later get a beating for scaring the hell out of his folks, so, Jim and I spent a few minutes talking to Dad and Mom, explaining this was normal for kids his age. And we made Junior apologize and promise to never do that again.

About twenty minutes later, as we were finishing up a car stop, we got the radio call: "2603, take 457 West Carter Street, Hospital Case, Rescue enroute."

"0-3, we got it," I told the dispatcher as Jim picked up speed. As he made a quick U-turn on American Street, I turned on the lights and siren. We were pretty close—only about eight blocks. The lights and siren and Jim's borderline reckless driving would get us there pretty quick.

"You know the address?" Jim asked, slowing a little before running a red light.

"No," I said, trying to picture the location. "Don't know it."

Coming from the firehouse at 7th and Norris, we heard the screaming siren of Rescue 12, also responding. I was always glad when Rescue showed up, especially when the hospital case was serious. Most of these guys were skilled paramedics, trained to deal with all kinds of injuries, especially trauma. They were way past my basic first-aid training, that's for sure.

Rescue was already inside when we pulled up. As we got out of the truck, Jim and I both realized it was *The Friendlies'* house. One of the paramedics came out to get the rolling stretcher, and he wasn't rushing. He didn't say anything, but I could see on this face that, whatever was going on in there, it wasn't good.

"What do ya got?" I asked.

"Gunshot."

Running up to the open front door, I heard screams and sobbing from the front room. I'll never forget the scene.

The *Friendly* kids were right there, near somebody on the floor. They were hysterical, trying to get past the paramedics to get to where they were working on their dad. I recognized him from our countless waved greetings. He wasn't moving or saying anything. I made eye contact with one of the paramedics. He shook his head slightly, just enough for me to notice.

They had the medical part covered. Jim and I had to figure out who the shooter was and if he was still here. That was our number one job.

As Jim moved the kids back, I looked around and I saw the mom. She wasn't over near where her husband was lying on the floor; she wasn't pulling at the paramedics, like the kids; and she wasn't crying and yelling. She was sitting on an old worn-out green sofa, across the room, looking down at the floor. I moved closer to her and saw the gun on her lap.

I quickly walked to where she was, watching her. When I got close, she turned slightly and looked up at me with glazed-over eyes. She was gone. I carefully picked up the gun, a .22 caliber semi-automatic. I went to a corner of the room and, once I was sure it was unloaded and safe, tucked it into my gun belt. Even though it seemed like an open-and-shut situation, I had learned that things were not always as they appeared. We needed to find out what we could.

Jim, who'd seen all this, came over to me. "I gave Radio our status and they called detectives and the Medical Examiner," he said. "They're on their way. So's a supervisor. They said to hold the scene and wait for the detectives." I nodded. Experience told me it would be a while. We had time to get the story from mom and the kids. Since the family knew us, the district cops, they were more likely to talk with us than the detectives who'd be coming soon, and with whom they were unfamiliar.

Our sergeant, John Burns, showed up and we briefed him out of earshot of the others. We told him we wanted to get some basic information before the detectives got there.

"Good, go ahead," he said. "I'll get somebody to hold the scene while you do that."

"Let's go into the kitchen, Missus," Jim said to the mom. Taking her gently by the arm, he walked her slowly out of the living room. I guided the three others into the tiny dining room: the two *Friendly* kids — the brother and sister — and another young male I'd never seen before. I sat them down around the dining table, trying to figure out how to proceed. I couldn't imagine their thoughts and feelings.

Taking out my notebook, I started by asking the *Friendly* kids their names and ages. She was Jackie, a pretty, plump sixteen-year-old and was crying and shaking. Her brother, Will, told me he was fourteen. He looked like a miniature version of his dad. He was just sitting there, looking down. The other kid, the one I didn't know, was a seventeen- year-old, who said his name was Jose Cruz (not his real name). Jose was a tall, good-looking kid who seemed nervous and wouldn't look at me. He had his arm tightly around Jackie, who looked pretty close to going down.

"Jackie, tell me what happened," I asked, using my softest voice. "I know you're upset, but I need you to tell me. It's important."

She let out a heaving sob. "Daddy got shot and it's my faaauuult!" she wailed.

I gave her a minute. Leaning in, I said "Okay, Jackie, go on, tell me what happened. Why do you think it's your fault?" The story that followed couldn't have been scripted to be more bizarre and tragic.

She let out a deep, sorrowful moan, hitched a couple of deep breaths and looked over at Jose, then turned my way. "Jose is my boyfriend. We've been going out for a couple weeks."

"Okay."

She was calming a little, trying hard to get the words out. "My dad didn't like Jose, so I wanted him to come over to spend time with us, and then Daddy would see he was a nice guy, you know?"

I waited for her to go on. She was crying again. I needed to direct the conversation.

"Jackie, what time did Jose get here?"

"About five-thirty," she sobbed. "We were going to get pizza. Jose just got a new job at the box factory, and he was going to buy us dinner."

"What else? I asked, never expecting what came next and the rest of it.

"Jose brought a gun with him that he carries for protection. He lives in a really bad neighborhood so, you know, he told me he needs it 'cause of the gangs and all."

Jose started to say something. I cut him off, my hand up like a stop sign. "Hold on, Jose, you'll get your chance. Just let Jackie talk now, okay?" He nodded and sat back, crossing his arms.

"Do you know why he brought it here, tonight?" I asked Jackie, watching Jose for his reaction.

She shrugged, and then said, "He thought Daddy would be impressed. My dad was in the Army and he knows about guns. Jose just wanted Daddy to like him." Jose nodded.

I wasn't following. I put my pen down and looked over at Jackie and Jose. I didn't think the boyfriend was the shooter. *What had happened here?* I waited.

Jackie went on. "Daddy was watching the news, you know, sitting in his chair, having a beer. He did that every day after work. He was real tired. He wasn't bothering nobody or nothin', not ever paying attention." Jackie was getting upset all over again.

"Did your dad and Jose have a fight? Were they arguing?" I asked, trying to get her back on track.

"No!" she said, shaking her head emphatically. "Daddy was ignoring all of us. That's how he always was. After work, he just wanted to sit there and watch TV and drink his beer."

"Go on, Jackie, you're doing fine."

"Me and Jose were sitting on the couch with my mom, talking. Then, Jose took out the gun and showed it to my mom. She looked at it and said she'd never seen one before, so Jose took out the thing in the bottom, you know, where the bullets are, and handed the gun to her. I told her to be careful, *I did!* Jose said not to worry because it wasn't loaded. *"*

I was starting to get a clearer picture. I didn't like it.

"Then what happened?" I asked, watching Jackie and Jose as I scribbled some notes.

"My mom never had a gun in her hands before; she didn't know nothing about guns, so I guess she didn't know what she was doing. I kept telling her to be careful. And I guess she thought there weren't any bullets in the gun. That's what me and Jose thought, too. Mom thought it would be funny, you know, Daddy seeing her with a gun—so she called out to him, 'Hey honey!'" Jackie's tears had started again. "And when he looked over at her, she was pointing the gun at him. Then..." Jackie, hysterical again, put her head down on the table and sobbed.

Nobody said anything.

Semi-automatic pistols can be tricky. Like most people unfamiliar with them, neither the mom nor Jose knew enough about this type of gun to know that, unless it's physically checked, there's a pretty good chance there still could be a round in the barrel, ready to fire—even with the magazine out. Mom thought she was playing with an empty gun when she pulled the trigger. The bullet that was in the chamber struck her husband in the forehead, killing him. A careless, deadly accident.

By now, the medical examiner had arrived and done his work and *Mr. Friendly* was on his way to the morgue. When the detectives got there a few minutes later, we told them what we knew. Jim and I had compared notes — Jackie's story matched her mom's. The *Friendly* kids, quiet now as reality hit them, were taken by a patrol car to the Homicide Unit to talk with detectives. Another patrol wagon transported Jose to the Unit, while we took the mom there to be interviewed.

After dropping her off, Jim and I spent hours with the detectives doing the paperwork, giving our statements, and submitting the gun for ballistic tests.

Early the next morning, the mother was formally charged with homicide and related charges.

About the same time, Jose was booked on weapons violations.

Their separate trials were sad events — just a rehash of that horrible day, tearing off the scabs. The *Friendly* kids were there, but they were just sad, hollowed-out versions.

Because it was her first arrest and because the shooting was officially ruled an accident, the mom was given a few years' probation. Her *real* punishment, though, was living with what she'd done. *That* was a life sentence.

As a juvenile with no prior record, Jose was also placed on probation. I'm guessing his unofficial sentence, like the mom's, was also heavy.

Once the proceedings were done, I never saw any of them again.

• ● •

I rolled through twenty-four great years with the Philly PD. And, like most big city cops, I saw too many shootings and too many killings along the way. I remember a lot of them. But this one, this one hit me more than the rest. Even now, after more than forty years, once in a while, this memory still comes back to visit.

I don't know if the family stayed or moved away. But, after that day, and for the rest of my time in the 26th, no one was ever out on the front steps of 457 Carter Street again. No friendly folks to wave to me or to any of the other passing cops.

Dogs

I love dogs; always have. When I was a toddler, we had a mixed breed, Queenie. She was big and had long brown and black hair. I remember that she liked to lick my face. I liked it, too.

Then, whenever I visited my Uncle Tom and Aunt Effie on Long Island during my pre-teen summers, their fluffy brown mutt, Lady, became my best friend for those three weeks. Always wagging her big fan of a tail, we'd go for long walks on the roads bordering the nearby potato fields.

When my brothers and I were teenagers, we somehow persuaded our parents to adopt a large black dog we named King. His previous owner told us he was a purebred Gordon Setter. He wasn't. We didn't care.

Although I loved all dogs, the feeling wasn't always mutual. I can recall a cocker spaniel on my paper route chasing me through their front yard when I delivered the evening *Bulletin.* The damn thing, hiding behind a big bush, bit my leg when I opened the gate. (From then on, the paper got thrown over the fence, not placed onto the porch like before, rain or not.)

As an adult, there was my own dog, Marcus, a shaky, ill-tempered Chihuahua, who once jumped up and bit my hand when I bent down to put dinner in his food bowl. Still have the scar. I forgave those two dogs' bites, but I never forgot.

For me, the day was always better whenever I had the chance to spend a little time with a dog. There've been plenty of dogs—mine and those of friends, relatives, and neighbors. Lots more belonging to strangers – and I was happy to know them all. Well, maybe not all. There was this one dog...more about him later.

In my early years as a cop, I focused on learning the police business but never missed an opportunity to make the acquaintance of any dog that came along. I made friends with the K9 cops, figuring they were dog-lovers like me. They eventually figured out I was actually most interested in their dogs. I sometimes worried that, by playing with these amazing dogs, I might somehow corrupt their training, making them big sissy dogs (it didn't). These special animals were so tuned in to their human partners that nothing I or anyone else did could break the dedication and obedience bonds they developed during all that intensive training.

Whenever possible, I wanted to be in the area every time a police K9 went to work. Whatever the clue or trigger given by a handler that transformed the dog into a highly focused best-partner-any-cop-could-have always impressed me and I never tired of seeing them doing their job.

I was still a rookie the first time I saw a police dog in action. Responding to a silent burglar alarm with a couple other units, we had found an open front door at a multi-use factory building at 5th and Columbia, on the west end of the 26th District. The alarm company told us they were getting multiple motion detector hits on the south side of the fourth floor, then on the third. Pretty sure we had a suspect somewhere in the building, we called for a supervisor. The sergeant decided it wasn't practical for three cops to search the five-story property (it took up an entire square block). He felt it was risky and would take too long, so he called for a K9.

We waited outside so we didn't contaminate the scene with our scents. When the K9 team arrived, the cop, Al Nugent, left his dog in the Jeep and met with us to get a better idea of the building's layout and what was going on. I noticed that the dog stayed at the window of the car, alert and keeping an eye on things, making sure his partner was alright. After further contact with the alarm-monitoring company, we figured that, whoever was in there had been on the third floor for a while, probably looking through the offices.

Nugent brought his partner, a big black and brown Shepherd, Max, from the rear of the Jeep and clicked him onto a lead. As they walked toward the building, the cop was leaning down, softly talking to the dog. It almost looked like he was filling him in. Whatever was going on between them, he *was* getting the dog ready. Following the canine officer and his partner up the fire tower stairs, we stopped at the second floor. We wanted to be close enough to back them, if needed, but far enough away to not get in their way. We were trying to keep our approach quiet, but found that impossible as a bunch of us clumped up the factory's old, creaking wooden stairs.

We stood and watched as Nugent and his dog continued up to the third floor. Then, gun drawn, he slowly opened the fire door and entered the huge warehouse space. We heard the cop shout several warnings and commands: "This is the Philadelphia Police. I'm ordering you to give yourself up. Come out with your hands up."

He repeated the commands, pausing for a long minute. Then, "I have an attack-trained dog that I'll release if you don't show yourself by the count of three." This command also was repeated. He waited. Getting no response, the cop counted to three in a loud voice. Then he gave the dog his command as he turned him loose. I'd heard that the "smart" criminals gave up when they heard that a dog was part of the police response. The others, who probably thought they were smarter than the dog, were not. Having witnessed the results of several of these during my career, I know I'd never want to be arrested by a police dog.

After a few minutes, there was lots of screaming and loud growling, then barking. Our boy had found his man. We ran up to the third floor following the echoing sounds. When we found them behind a huge stack of cardboard boxes, Nugent was holding onto the burglar (a terrified teenager) with one hand and the snarling Max, who wasn't quite through with the kid, with the other. When it was over, with everybody safe and the guy secured, the handler immediately praised his K9 partner, telling him he was a good boy, playing with him and tossing him his favorite chew toy, which was all the reward that Max wanted. *Dogs are great*, I thought.

■———●●●———■

Now, to that other dog. The middle 1970s had me patrolling in a solo marked car—266—in the Fishtown section of the 26th. The area, "D" sector, was primarily residential, and most folks lived in single-family row homes or three-story buildings, many of which had been converted into apartments. The majority of these were strung along a ten-block stretch of Frankford Avenue, running from Girard to York. Scattered among the residences in my patrol area were elementary schools, two churches, restaurants, grocery stores, a playground, and St. Mary Hospital. Near St. Mary's, there were doctors' offices, a pharmacy and a funeral home. I knew many of the owners of these establishments, having met them professionally during the course of my time in D sector. I was not as familiar with most residents of the homes and apartments in the area. That was about to change.

On a sunny weekday morning, right around lunchtime, I got a call to an address about a block away from St. Mary's. "266, 1827 Frankford, check on the well-being of the occupant."

From the address, I knew this was an apartment, so I said, "266, I got it. Do you have an apartment number?"

"Negative, 6."

"How about the address of the caller?" Cops don't like vague calls. I was hoping to get a little more information than I had.

"Stand by, 266." The dispatcher sounded a little testy. Maybe I was interrupting his lunch. I parked a few spaces north of the address and waited for the dispatcher's update. "266, the caller is the daughter; she lives out of town, but she thinks it's on the third floor. Her mother's name is Mary Doherty and her daughter hasn't heard from her in over a week."

I acknowledged the call, thanked the dispatcher and turned off the car. Putting on my hat, I grabbed my baton and flashlight and got out. Walking up, I checked out the building as I approached. It didn't look familiar. There was nobody outside and the front door was closed. I took the four brownstone front steps two at a time and, shading my eyes from the sun, looked through the door glass. I saw nothing but an empty hallway. Hoping I'd see the tenants' names below the three bells lined up on the side of the front door frame, I moved closer. No such luck. I rang the top bell, guessing it was for the third floor. No response. After a few tries, I decided to start with the bottom bell, see if anybody was home to let me in.

I could hear the bell as it rang faintly inside the first-floor apartment. In a few seconds, the apartment door flew open, and a little girl was running to the door. She was a cutie, with a big smile and blonde curls bouncing as she came. I almost opened the door to go in, but as I started to turn the knob, I saw a brown flash coming right behind the little girl. I instinctively stepped back as a good-sized dog flew past the kid, leaving the ground and hitting the door hard. He was snarling at me, doing his job. The girl opened the door and I held it so it was open just enough for me to talk to her. "Honey, take your dog back into the house and tell your mother to come to the door, please."

"Mommy, it's a policeman. He wants you to call Rex back in."

Now the mom, busy doing who knows what, said loud enough for me to hear, "Tell him it's okay. Rex won't bite. Tell him he's friendly."

Well, I thought. *Rex doesn't* look *friendly.* I stood there, waiting. The kid and I looked at each other. Rex was eyeing me hard.

I yelled, "Lady, please come secure your dog. I have to go up to the third-floor apartment."

"It really is okay, officer," came the shouted response. "He'll be fine once you come in the door."

I *knew* he wouldn't be *fine*, but I hoped there might be some unspoken vibe between me and Rex that would let him know I was okay. I hoped he would sense that I was a dog lover. I was *so* wrong.

As soon as I got into the vestibule, the cutie, who had dragged the dog halfway back in the hallway, was holding onto to his leather collar with both hands and trying to pull him back so I could pass. I figured Rex outweighed the girl by at least 60 pounds. As soon as I closed the door, the dog made his move. Breaking away, he came full speed, to say hello. But not in a good way. As he left his feet, I stepped back, trying to get back out the door, but I wasn't fast enough. I was trapped. Rex lunged and chomped down, making firm contact about three inches below my pants' zipper. He held on as the poor little girl screamed for her mommy. Meanwhile, I could feel Rex's teeth in the upper part of my right leg. Now, *I* was screaming for her mommy, too.

She finally came hurrying down the hallway, wiping her hands on a towel. "Sorry, officer, he's never bitten anybody before. Are you alright?" I wasn't sure. I was a little better when she dragged the still determined Rex back down the hallway.

I checked out Mrs. Doherty on the third floor, who appeared to be fine. The old lady told me that she couldn't always hear the phone, especially if she was asleep in the bedroom. I nodded my understanding and asked her to call her worried daughter, which she did while I stood there writing my report. The pain in my leg was worse. After the phone call, I wished Mrs. Doherty a good day and quietly made my way downstairs, keeping a lookout for Rex. I had to make a stop and quick.

Cops and Emergency Room nurses. We got along great—perhaps it's the similarity in the work. So, when I walked into St. Mary's and discreetly told the ER head nurse, Fran, what had happened, her reaction was kind of what

I expected. We had known each other for years; so, once she determined I wasn't dying, the story became especially amusing because she laughed out loud, then proceeded to share my news with her co-workers in a voice that I thought was louder than necessary. My icy stare made her regain her professional demeanor and giving me a hospital gown, pointed me to an exam room to get checked out. Thankfully, Rex hadn't broken the skin. It still hurt like hell.

A few months later and at my request, I was reassigned to the west side of the district. It had nothing to do with my meeting with Rex. I wanted to patrol in an area that was busier with more crime and more calls for service. I enjoyed the excitement of the streets, and the west side was where it was happening.

Years passed and I got into a groove as I got to know the good people and trouble spots in my new area. Then, one afternoon, with nothing going on in my sector, I heard a call come out: "266, Frankford and Palmer, meet the complainant."

I was pretty close, so when 266 didn't answer the second time, I picked up the call. "2610, I'll get that." I liked keeping busy.

"Okay, 10."

It had been a long time since I'd worked in Fishtown. But nothing was happening on my end, so I was looking for something to do. When I was a couple of blocks away, the dispatcher called and gave me an update with an address; the complainant had gone home to a nearby apartment and would meet me there.

I acknowledged the call and arrived in a few minutes. As I walked up to the house, it wasn't too familiar; it didn't register. The front door was partially open; I rang the bottom bell, and pushed it open, calling, "Hello, police!" Here came Rex, full speed down the hall. Before quickly slamming the door, I yelled out, "Lady, get your dog."

"Oh, it's okay, officer," came a woman's voice from the apartment down the hall, "he don't bite."

The Good Samaritan

The light turned red just before I got to the intersection. And this was one of those long ones — a five way-er. It was okay; I wasn't in a hurry. Sitting there, third in line, waiting, the strong smells of fried food wafted in the car windows like a heavy cloud. I turned to look at the joint on my right— "Delicious Steaks, Chops, Seafood." *Don't think so.* The faded blue plastic letters were peeling off the weathered wooden sign that hung over the big, greasy window of the OK Restaurant.

The restaurant—and the sign—had been up there forever, even since I'd been a boy, growing up in this neighborhood. Just below the sign, a tacked-on plastic streamer, boasting that the place was the "Home of the Texas Tommy," beckoned hungry locals. On the equally slimy glass front door, a red and white plastic sign, stuck to the glass with four suction cups: "OPEN 24 HOURS." The place was the last holdout of several area eateries. One by one, the others had gone belly-up, leaving the OK the last one standing.

I'd only been in the place once or twice and only for coffee. I remembered that it looked too 'greasy spoon' for me. Still, the mystique of the Texas Tommy was calling me; it sounded perversely appealing. *I'll probably have to try one someday,* I thought as I sat in the patrol car, waiting for the red light to turn green. I squinted, looking through the *OK's* smeary window. There were a few people scattered around the counter–all hunched over their food. Looked like a pathetic, distorted version of the diner in Edward Hopper's *Nighthawks* painting.

I thought back to the last time I'd been in the place: As I'd waited for the waitress to get me a cardboard cup of coffee, the cook came out of the kitchen, long-ashed cigarette sticking out of his unshaved face. I recalled his greasy whites and an apron sporting way too many stains that may or may not have been of culinary origin. Which told me the guy had either been *very* busy that day or hadn't changed his work clothes for a while. *Ewww.* Since I'd never seen the place busy... *On second thought, I'd have to be pretty damn hungry to take a chance on anything from the OK, even a Texas Tommy.*

Then, jinxing myself, I thought about how quiet the shift had been so far. Guess I'd never learn—because what happened next would keep me busy for a while.

It started with the unmistakable crashing and clattering sound of breaking glass. It wasn't a bottle breaking. It was bigger, like a window or a door. Then, about ten seconds of quiet. Followed by a blaring burglar alarm bell—loud and urgent. And it sounded close, like just around the corner. The trestles that supported the elevated train formed a steel and concrete tunnel, which bounced and echoed every sound down here at street level.

The light was still red, so I clicked on my dome lights and chirped my siren twice to alert the cars sitting in front of me. They pulled up, moving left or right, opening a barely-wide-enough path that I was able to snake through. I thought the sound had come from my right, Kensington Avenue, so I headed that way.

Now, let me make something clear: Movies and television cop shows are notorious for giving bad information. People mistakenly believe that many sight arrests—when an officer witnesses a crime resulting in an immediate arrest—are usually the result of uncanny powers like telepathy. But ask any cop and, if he's honest, he'll tell you that a lot of these pinches are mostly luck—being in the right place at the right time. This was one of those.

Wheeling around the corner, heading north, I saw him right away; closer than 25 yards. He was coming out of the place through an aluminum door. The full-pane glass window was mostly gone now. When he heard my revving engine, he turned and saw the red and white car coming his way, full speed. Like a deer in the headlights, he stood there, frozen for just a second, one leg inside the place and the other out. The guy hopped as he pulled the inside leg out, his shoe catching on one of the jagged shards still stuck in the frame at the bottom of the door, tinkling it to the sidewalk as he ran away, heading north, away from me. As I reached for the radio mike, my mind organized a description: race, age, size, height, weight, clothes. I said, "266, priority!"

"All cars stand by! Go ahead 266," came the dispatcher's reply.

"I'm in pursuit of a male running north on Kensington from Boston. He's a white male, about 20-25, about 5-10, 150 pounds, wearing jeans and a dark jacket." I was paralleling the guy with the car, keeping just a little behind him.

"Reason for pursuit, 266?"

"He just broke into a property at Kensington and Boston." By now, we were approaching Cumberland Street. As we went, I kept updating Radio with locations, surprised he didn't turn onto a side street or double back. Then, after about three blocks, the guy just stopped and knelt down on the sidewalk. It looked like he was giving up. I got out and ran over and grabbed him and placed him prone on the ground. He didn't resist. With one hand on his back, I checked for weapons. I found none. He was completely out of breath. After handcuffing the guy, I stood him up and looked at him. He wasn't familiar. *Hey pal,* I thought, *if you're going to be a burglar* and *a sprinter, you'll need to be in better shape.*

"Officer, why're you arresting me?" he asked, flushed and still panting hard.

"Oh, I don't know," I said. "Nothing better to do. What were you doing inside that building?"

"I wasn't inside any building."

I gave him a look that said, *That's the story you're going with?*

By now, other cops were there and I asked one of them to tell the dispatcher that the male was in custody and that everything was under control.

As we waited for a patrol wagon to transport the guy to detectives, I checked him over and asked him, "Are you hurt? Did you get cut?" If he was, we'd have to take him to the hospital for treatment first. He looked okay.

"I'm not hurt, officer," he said. "Can you loosen these? Lifting his arms slightly. They're too tight; hurting my wrists."

"No."

"Listen officer, you got the wrong guy."

So we're back to that. "Yeah, I know," I said. "I always get the wrong guy."

"No, really. I didn't do nothin'. I was just walking by and I saw...."

"Stop!" I said, "That's all." I didn't want him blurting out something significant about the crime before he was read his rights. And I wanted to leave that for the detectives. Besides, I knew what I'd heard and seen. Plus, the guy had stuff in his pockets that looked like office supplies. And he sure didn't look like a secretary. This was a slam-dunk, a solid arrest.

The wagon had arrived, so I walked him over and turned him over to the crew. I told them I'd meet them at Front and Westmoreland, where East Detectives was located.

"You got it, Skouf. How'd you get him? I didn't hear the call," said George Cooper, one of the wagon guys.

"No call, George, I was sitting at the light at Kensington and York — just around the corner and heard the guy smashing the glass, and then the alarm. Just lucky," I said.

"Good job. It's hard to get a sight burglary pinch."

Isn't it pretty much all blind luck? I thought. *Right place, right time?*

After they left with my prisoner, I drove back to the building. I had to find some emergency contact information—owner, manager, somebody—and call them to come out here and secure the place. Otherwise, we'd be posting some poor foot beat cop there till somebody showed up, which could be all night.

The place was a real estate office. It was a converted row house so it was narrow and long. There were a few cubicles up front and a closed office in the back. At first, I thought my guy had bypassed the cubicles and headed straight for what looked like the manager's office, in the rear. It looked like some stuff was thrown around, a couple drawers pulled out. I couldn't tell if anything valuable or otherwise was missing. I figured he was looking for money or small electronic stuff—radios, typewriters facsimile machines—anything that could be carried away and quickly sold. Then I noticed that some of the electric typewriters had been unplugged and would've probably gone out the door if the alarm bell hadn't scared the guy away.

There was no emergency number posted anywhere, so I called the alarm company and got the name of the owner. They told me they had already called him; he was on his way. They also said they were sending a technician to reset the alarm and check that the system was working okay.

As I poked around looking for evidence, I heard someone calling from the front. "Hey, Skouf, find anything?" asked Sergeant John McCabe, standing outside on the sidewalk, looking in through the broken front door.

I walked up. "Yeah, Sarge, the alarm company already called the owner. He's enroute".

"Good. I have (Officer) Mark Jessup coming over from Beat 1 to stand by the property. When he gets here you can head up to East (Detectives).

"Okay, boss. Man, for only being in here for a short time, the guy sure messed the place up. I didn't find much stuff on him, a baggie with some change and a couple boxes of Bic pens. But he had these ready to go," I said, pointing to the IBM Selectrics.

He nodded. "Probably a junkie," said McCabe, walking through the door, looking around for a phone. "They'll take anything they can sell for a fix." After the sergeant phoned Police Radio and told them what the arrangement was for securing the place, he left.

The owner, Joseph Sawyer, arrived about ten minutes later. He was freaked out when he saw the front door. I explained that we'd gotten the guy and he calmed down a little. It started all over again when he saw the mess in his office. I let him rant.

Trying to get him focused, I said, "Mr. Sawyer, if you'd like, I can give you the numbers of a couple of glass replacement companies that'll come out and board up the door for you."

"Yeah, that'd be great, officer. Are they local?"

I nodded, pulled out my notebook and gave him the numbers. Then I left, headed for the detectives to write my reports. On the way, I advised Radio that the owner had arrived and that Officer Jessup wouldn't be needed to stand by the open property. When I got to Front and Westmoreland, Pat Hardy, the assigned detective, was waiting for me. He was smiling his usual Irishman's smile and looked like he couldn't wait to share what was so amusing. With a few years on the job, I'd heard a lot of stories and a lot of excuses. But the one this guy told was an original.

Detective Hardy got the guy out of the detention room and sat him down on an old metal chair between us. "Tell the officer what you told me, sport."

The guy looked at him, then me. Looked like he was thinking fast, trying to keep his story straight. "I told the detective that I was walking by the building and I saw the broken glass and heard the alarm," he said.

We waited.

"I didn't know who broke the window, but it wasn't me," he said.

We waited some more.

Then he said, "I thought I'd go in and find out who the owner was and call them."

"Why'd you run? I asked.

No answer. He just shrugged and didn't look at either of us. I knew he was lying. "You told me you weren't inside that building, remember?" I reminded him.

"Honest to God, I didn't break in; I was walking by and saw the broken door and…"

I looked at him. He looked back. He was going to run with this version of events.

"What's your name, pal?" I asked.

"Leo Murphy, sir."

"Where do you live, Leo?"

"1800 Auburn Street."

"Well Leo," I said, inching my chair a little closer, "what were you doing on the 2400 block of Kensington Avenue? Pretty far from home, weren't you?"

After a pause to think, he came up with: "I was goin' to meet my buddy. We were supposed to go to the Kent to see a movie."

"What movie were you going to see?" I asked.

Up to his knees in his own bullshit, Mr. Murphy decided he'd said enough. He leaned back and crossed his arms. We were done.

I finished up my paperwork, including the property receipt for the pens and bag of change I'd found on Murphy. I was good to go.

On my way back, I stopped at Kensington and Boston and was glad to see that the door had been boarded up. I'd still have to keep an eye on it and give my relief a heads-up.

About a week later, I went to Front and Westmoreland for the preliminary hearing. The room was crowded, but I spotted Mr. Sawyer, the business owner, and I waved. I was gonna be here awhile, but I didn't mind: it was overtime.

When they called my case, Sawyer and I walked up to the Assistant District Attorney (ADA) and introduced ourselves. He was reading the arrest report and held up a finger, telling us to wait. A minute later he turned to me and said, "Wow, they don't get much simpler than this, officer. Pretty cut-and-dried." I agreed and went over the particulars in my head, preparing to testify.

The prisoner was brought out from the holding cell and unhandcuffed.

Preliminary hearings have one purpose: to determine if there is adequate probable cause to move the case to a trial. If not, the case is dismissed right then and there. It's a formality and part of the criminal justice process in Pennsylvania.

Mr. Sawyer was up first. The ADA asked him only two questions: Did he know the defendant? No, he didn't. Did he give the defendant permission to be inside his place of business? Same answer.

Then me. After providing my name, badge number and assignment on the day of the incident, I provided the short version of what I'd heard and seen and the details of the pursuit and arrest. Murphy's lawyer had no questions of me or Mr. Sawyer, so the hearing was over quickly.

The judge, having heard enough, stated that there "…exists sufficient probable cause to hold the case for trial." And so, the defendant was cuffed up and returned to jail. He looked dejected, like he'd lost a game he was sure he'd win. I had to hand it to him — he was an optimist.

Because the Philadelphia court system is so busy, cases take months to be heard. It was seven or eight months later when I received a court notice for the Murphy burglary. I arrived at City Hall early on a rainy morning, signed in with the Court Attendance clerk and got in line with a bunch of other cops at the coffee kiosk. Chatting with a few guys I knew, I felt good about today. I still didn't get Leo Murphy. To me, he didn't look like the typical burglar. But hey, I'd seen him coming out of the building right after the glass-breaking and the alarm. And his story was all over the place, changing every time he told it. Well, maybe the judge will give him a break, especially if it's his first time.

When the case was called, I saw Murphy get up and move to the front, taking a seat at the defense table. He was looking cleaned up, sporting a nice suit, a tie and a new haircut. I didn't recognize the defense attorney he sat next to, an intense-looking young guy who didn't appear to be the typical Public Defender. He was here for this case only, it seemed.

Hmmm, I thought, *Mr. Murphy's got himself a real-deal lawyer. Interesting.*

The trial started out pretty much like the Preliminary Hearing had: The ADA (Richard Heilman) asked Mr. Sawyer the same questions that'd been asked at that proceeding. Same answers. This time, though, Leo Murphy's attorney had his own questions. The defense lawyer, who introduced himself as Howard Franks, started out nice and easy, asking Mr. Sawyer about his business, how long he'd been there, just warming him up, getting him to relax. I'd seen this tactic before, like a shark swimming up, acting like a friendly dolphin, right before he bites the witness on the ass. When he was finished, the lawyer had questioned Sawyer's security system, the trustworthiness of his employees, asking if he'd done background checks on everyone who worked for him. He even suggested the possibility that one of those employees had broken into the property. Mr. Sawyer, not expecting to be on trial himself, was clearly defensive and it showed. The ADA tried to bolster up Sawyer's testimony by revisiting some of the questions he'd asked earlier, but it didn't help much. Sawyer was frazzled. He left the witness chair shaking his head.

It is important to note that the job of the defense attorney is not necessarily to prove his client innocent. Not at all. He is there to create "reasonable doubt," which means doubt that a reasonable person would have, based on the facts presented, that his client committed the crime he's charged with. The main goal is to create such doubt in the minds of the jury or, as in this case, the judge. If that means discrediting a victim or another witness along the way, so be it.

My turn. But I wasn't Joseph Sawyer. And this wasn't my first rodeo. I'd seen his kind before; I was ready for Mr. Franks. He'd taken advantage of Mr. Sawyer, the victim in this case. That wasn't going to happen with me.

After I gave the usual introductory information, the ADA walked me through the whole incident, making sure I testified that I heard the glass breaking *and* the burglar alarm in quick succession. We went step by step through what had happened next: my observation of Murphy inside the property, his flight, the packaged office supplies and coins in his jacket pocket, his changing story. It was pretty tight. When the prosecutor was finished, I thought we had created a pretty clear picture of a crime in progress and the apprehension of the perpetrator. No doubt about it. The case was solid.

Franks sat there and asked me about my career: how many years on the job (seven at that time); how many "sight arrests" I'd made (I didn't remember). "Can you guess, officer?"

"No, I can't."

"Okay," he said, "Did you see my client break into the property in question?"

"No, but I heard…" I didn't get to finish the sentence. Franks interrupted, shouting "Objection! Your Honor, please direct the witness to answer the question, and not expand on what he thinks he heard."

"Sustained," said Judge Marcus Williamson.

That was surprising. But then this judge had a reputation for being a little eccentric. *Doesn't matter though,* I thought. *The ADA had already gotten my observations on the record.*

We went on and on and on. Mr. Franks was tenacious, trying to get me to say something—anything that might contradict what I'd said in my reports. He asked about another guy who might have been inside, dressed like Murphy, who'd been the actual burglar. He questioned my arrest procedures, suggesting that I roughed up his client. He even tried to get the judge to believe that I'd planted the office supplies on Murphy. I knew what he was trying to do. I just wasn't going to let him. I got it; I knew he was doing his best. But, hey, pal, this is a slam-dunk case. You gave it a good try. Now let it go.

Finally, he was finished with me. The ADA came back with a few questions, reasserting the facts I'd stated before, making sure to include the unshakable fact that I'd seen Murphy actually coming out of the place, seconds after the glass broke and the alarm sounded.

Like most, these kinds of cases usually resulted in plea bargains—agreements between prosecutor and defense attorney, a compromise. Not this time. Murphy wanted to get off.

Surprisingly, Franks called Leo Murphy to the stand. *This should be good,* I thought. I settled back in my chair, waiting.

The defendant slowly walked up and took his seat in the witness stand. He looked nervous. His lawyer walked up, gave him a smile and started. Once the preliminary information (name, age, address) was provided, Franks asked him if he'd been in the 2400 block of Kensington Avenue on the date in question. He said yes.

"Mr. Murphy, did you break into the property at 2419 Kensington Avenue?" That was the address of Joseph Sawyer's real estate office.

"No, sir, I did not."

Franks asked him if he'd ever been in the property.

"Yes sir."

I sat up straighter. *Where's this going?*

Murphy explained that he'd been walking by the place, heard the alarm, and went in to look for the owner's information so he could call him. He went on to say that he hadn't found anything and was leaving when I came around the corner.

"Why did you run away, Mr. Murphy?" Franks asked.

"I was scared and I knew it looked bad, so I ran."

"No further questions, your Honor," said Franks, turning the witness over to the prosecutor.

ADA Heilman's first question was asked before he was fully standing. "Mr. Murphy, did you hear glass breaking when you were in the area?"

"No, I didn't."

"Did you see anybody else in the area?"

"Yes, I saw a guy about my size and age. He ran away toward York Street."

I see; he was running my way, and I missed him? Really?! I thought, shaking my head. Heilman continued. "Tell us how long you were inside 2419 Kensington Avenue."

"Not long, about three or four minutes, tops."

"Three or four minutes?" asked Heilman.

"Yes, sir, that's about right."

When the ADA showed Murphy the two unopened boxes of Bic pens I'd found on his person, the defendant said he'd never seen them before. He added that I'd never taken them from his pocket.

Ballsy, I thought.

"Mr. Murphy did you consider calling the police when you were inside the building? Did that ever occur to you?"

"It did, but I know they're usually busy so I figured I'd just call the owner myself."

"So did you ever get hold of the owner?"

"No."

"So, you're telling the court that you were walking along when you heard an alarm bell ringing at this building, saw that the door glass had been broken out; yet you still went inside?"

"Objection, your Honor," said attorney Franks. "He's badgering the witness."

"Sustained," said Judge Williamson. "Mr. Heilman, please continue."

"I have no further questions, your Honor."

"Okay," said the judge. "The witness can step down." Murphy quickly returned to his seat, looking relieved.

The judge called a 15-minute recess, during which I sat with ADA Heilman trying to get his read on the defense strategy.

"It's crazy," he said. I can't believe he put Murphy on the stand and the guy actually admitted being inside the place. And what the hell's the judge thinking up there?"

"Yep," I said.

When the trial resumed, the judge pounded the gavel and announced his verdict.

"Based on the testimony presented, I find the defendant not guilty."

Good thing I was sitting down. *He can't be serious!* I thought.

The ADA was speechless.

I ran into Heilman a few months later and I asked him about the case. He told me he'd talked with Judge Williamson—off the record—and the judge had said that he believed Murphy's story. He said it wasn't that we didn't prove our case beyond a reasonable doubt, he just believed Murphy over Joseph Sawyer and me. *Wow!* So much for a slam-dunk. The judge, thankfully, retired soon after that.

Oh, and I *did* see Leo Murphy again, later that year. I was part of a wagon crew that was called to a hardware store to transport a prisoner to detectives. The place had a silent alarm that went off when the guy broke in. This time, Leo Murphy, exceptional Good Samaritan that he was, had been caught *inside*, hiding in a bathroom. I was smiling a little as I led him to the back of the wagon and said hello. He was surprised I knew his name.

The Man

Placing the manila folders into my briefcase, I shook the young woman's hand and thanked her for her time. We had been talking for about two hours as we'd gone through the case file. I explained that I would contact her as soon as my report was completed.

"Will I get a copy?" she asked as I explained the process.

"Yes, ma'am," I said. "It'll take about two to three weeks, okay?" I wasn't sure if she was okay with that part, but she nodded her head. Behind her, her pretty little girl, shy when I'd gotten there, was now smiling at me and waving goodbye. Nice family.

The interview had gone as I thought it would. The investigation I was here for involved a complaint against a police officer. In my few months as an Internal Affairs Division (IAD) supervisory investigator with the Philadelphia PD, I'd learned that the complaints about verbal abuse were the most common. They were very time-consuming and were also the hardest to substantiate, especially when there were no other witnesses—just the complainant and the officer. These became 'he said' and 'she said' situations.

Anyway, I was now officially done for the day. I was worn out from a bunch of interviews that had taken me all over the city. They had all gone pretty well, considering, and I couldn't wait to get home, get showered, changed, and enjoy a cold beverage. I got into my unmarked squad car and headed toward Broad Street and the Roosevelt Boulevard.

The eastbound traffic on Diamond Street was unbelievable, especially for this time of the afternoon. I was stuck behind six or seven cars at a traffic light. Of course. We weren't moving. I soon saw why: the traffic signal was not cycling and nobody could figure out what to do. I radioed the dispatcher and reported the problem. I loosened my tie and unbuttoned my shirt. Then I sat and waited for the traffic to move.

That's when my day became very interesting.

I didn't see her coming. She was just there, all of a sudden. Then she was leaning in my car window.

She was tall and looked between 20 and 30. She fidgeted a lot, which gave the impression that her business with me was urgent. She just couldn't stand still. She was skinny and had shiny, dark tan skin and the glassy, unfocused eyes of a junkie. Her ratty blonde wig had been donned in a hurry and made her look like a sad doll with borrowed hair. Her makeup was extensive but not done very well, which gave her the appearance of a pathetic she-clown. She was wearing a shiny, very, very short red party dress. And I was about to find out why.

Now, almost anybody who's lived or visited the city, any city, or watched TV detective or reality shows can tell an unmarked police car a mile away. They either watch them hoping for a vicarious thrill or, if they're "wanted" or up to no good, they quickly depart the scene. Not this little lady. Nope. Imagine this: here I was, a very white guy in a predominantly Black neighborhood, sitting in a late model Plymouth Gran Fury, 4-door, black-wall tires, antennas on the roof. But the most obvious tip that this wasn't just *any* Plymouth Gran Fury—there was a police radio sitting conspicuously on the floor between the front seats, lit up and crackling and beeping loud and clear with urgent police messages. I watched her as she stood there and waited for her *aha* moment. Nothing. She definitely was not tuned in.

Unfortunately, I wasn't going anywhere. Besides, my new lady friend was practically halfway through the window by now, leaning in so I could get the full effect of her up close—strong perfume trying to mask unpleasant body odors, nails as red as her hastily applied lipstick, and heavy-lidded eyes that she seemed to be struggling to keep open. I'd have to proceed carefully when I could finally escape.

Then, in what I supposed was the most seductive voice she could manage in her altered state, she asked me if I wanted a date. I politely said, "No, ma'am, but thanks anyway." Turning in my seat to face her now, I added, "Listen miss, can you hear the police radio?" hoping she'd realize her case of mistaken identity and move on. I emphasized this by holding up the microphone and pointing to the Motorola that was still going strong. "They're calling me; I've got to go." Nothing. She just looked at me with that stare. I wished I had taken another street, *any* other street. Great! Now, she was touching my new suit jacket. Then, I spied an escape route as a parked car moved away from the curb, creating a small opening in the stalled traffic. Too late. Another car came from behind me and took the spot.

I was looking around, hoping I'd see a uniformed cop in a marked car, but no. *Never a cop around when you need one!* It would've been great if a patrol car had come by then. I think that even in her stupor, she would have moved on. If not, the cop could have detached her from the side of my car, even threaten to lock her up (not that that we'd do that as it wouldn't be worth the time and effort). Anyway, my calvary wasn't coming. I was stuck.

By now, she was going through her whole routine, trying to be *very* specific about what pleasures awaited me on our "date." I must admit, I didn't understand most of what she was saying, so I'm guessing her marketing pitch wasn't very successful. Finally, frustrated, I looked at her and gave her my hard-cop look, hoping I might be able to will her away. Not a chance. Then, I had another idea: since my new wannabe friend wasn't understanding me, I'd try communicating with her using street vernacular. She'd surely get that. So, I flashed my badge in her face and in the most authoritative voice I could muster, I said, "Lady, I'm the *MAN*!" She stood there, letting the words register.

"That's good, baby," she slurred, rocking on her spike heels, now apparently more energized. She shouted, "And I'm *THE WOMAN*! Let's party!" as she put her hand on my arm. I couldn't believe it. She never missed a beat. This lady was on a mission. She was amazing; clueless, but amazing. I looked at her some more and she looked back, giving me what she was hoping was her sexiest smile as she teetered back and forth, waiting for my next move.

Just then the car ahead of me zoomed across the intersection. "Excuse me, miss." I firmly nudged her bony hands from the side of my car and drove away as fast as I could.

A few blocks later, I had to pull over. I sat there laughing at the situation, the fact that she just could not get who I was, and at myself for feeling so absurdly uncomfortable. *Okay,* I thought, *it's funny but it's not funny.* I watched her in my rearview mirror as she made her way down the street, I wondered what would become of her.

The Station Bar Caper

They say cops have an extra sense, one that keeps them safe. I'm pretty sure that's true. But, if there *is* such a thing, I believe it only applies to the physical aspects of the job. It almost never works with the administrative crap and bad decisions made by those who have the power—but not always the brains—to make them. And even if the extra sense *did* kick in to raise the cop's antennae in such situations, very little could be done to avoid the fallout that usually followed.

It's been my experience that most Philadelphia police supervisors are great. Really. I can honestly say that I was fortunate to have worked with some of the best bosses in the department. Still, I've known some who were bullies — and worse — and a few who'd had a lucky Saturday or two *(a reference to the weekend written promotional tests some guys passed, defying all logic)*. But overall, the sergeants and lieutenants who ran the squads, and with whom I'd worked, taught me a lot of things that expanded my cop sense and helped get me through my career safely. Later, after making rank myself, one of the rules I lived by was to never forget where I came from. I believe it helped me be a better boss.

Police departments, like the military, have a rank structure which relies on absolute compliance with orders given from above. Unlike soldiering, police work does not typically involve actual combat. So, in situations where an order is given and the orderee believes he has legitimate misgivings about the order, there is *sometimes*—very rarely—an opportunity for a discussion — give and take between subordinate and superior — that may or may not result in a modification of the order. At least that's what I'd *heard*. Sometimes, these guys who wear stripes or bars on their uniforms seem to have traded them for common sense. And this can lead to orders that don't compute. Sometimes, they actually violate departmental policy and may even place citizens and officers at risk.

When I was a patrol supervisor, I never thought I knew it all. In fact, I sometimes relied on the cops under my direction—maybe with more experience or more familiar with a situation or issue than I to provide feedback. Better to know than to guess. Besides, it was important to them and to me that we talked about the work we did together. That's not to say that it was a democratic relationship. No. That wouldn't work. Oh, but I wish it had been on that cold March night.

The whole thing happened on the dreaded midnight to 8:00 a.m. shift. Like most cops, aggressive patrol work was what I loved to do: when not responding to calls for crimes or service, I would check properties, look for bad guys, monitor traffic, back up other officers and generally keep watch over my sector. Like many officers, doing these became more challenging for me on the overnight shift. This was partly because of the greatly decreased activity (most people were home, sleeping). Another reason was the constant struggle to stay awake.

On this night, I was lucky enough to be assigned to Emergency Patrol Wagon 2603 with Art Duncan. Neither of us was regularly assigned to 2603 or any other wagon; we normally worked solo cars. So, for me, tonight was a bonus. Having a partner to talk with all night was great. And we would typically be busier since wagons usually got more calls than patrol cars did: for hospital cases, prisoner transports and calls like disturbances that required a two-man response.

The shift started off great. After roll call, we stopped for coffee at the Paradise. Not the greatest place, just the only one open. Then, I parked us at Front and Girard, a busy El train stop, at least till about three am, when the crowds returning from downtown slowed, then stopped. Art and I sat sipping the hot mud and discussing the Eagles and their upcoming game with the dreaded Dallas Cowboys. We agreed that the Eagles would kick the Cowboys' asses; I wasn't sure if either one of us believed that.

Across the street from the El stop was the Station bar—a sleazy, hole-in-the-wall dive that attracted a lot of desperately hopeful men of all ages. They thought that, you know, maybe, one of the dancing girls would be their "date" after closing time. My take? I guess it's good to be optimistic. Also, *careful what you wish for*!

To get ready for such a hopeful, yet unlikely occurrence, the guys would get there before the entertainment began to take advantage of the happy-hour drink specials, usually cheap beer and watered-down booze. So, by the time the girls came on, much later, most of the guys were adequately polluted and feeling chippy. And not really caring much about what the dancers looked like. The not-caring part was both a good thing and a bad thing.

Pretty much every cop in the 26th had been called to the Station for *something*. Usually for fights between a couple of Romeos or the resulting hospital cases. In the fight scenarios, the loser would sometimes go to the hospital, the winner, to a cell, to cool off and sober up. It's a neighborhood bar, like dozens of others in north Philly. But the Station had some special attributes: first among them was that the place stunk. Literally. The mixed fragrances included sour old beer, stale smoke and sweat. Very conducive for romantic activities. It was a seedy dump—a questionable enterprise that enticed eager lads, young and not so young, with cheap drinks, then put them up close to equally desperate and barely-clothed…uh, dancing girls.

In my opinion, the bar owners had a pretty good, but thoroughly shady, gig going on. Liquor 'em up, then tease 'em with what they advertise as "sTOPLESS" dancers. (Really! That's what the flickering red neon sign in the window promised.) It's no wonder that there'd be lots of calls for fights at the place, especially on the weekends.

Art Duncan and I finished our coffee, then drove slowly around our three sectors and started our security checks. We shone our wagon spotlights in the windows of drug stores, a small state-owned liquor store, a half dozen factories and the new small business area on the 900 and 1000 blocks of Marshall Street. We took turns getting out to pull on some doors to make sure everything was tight.

There was nothing going on. We drove slowly up and down the small streets looking for cars parked on fire plugs. Negative. We looked for stolen, abandoned vehicles. Nothing. And there were hardly any cars driving around. Guess the cold weather was keeping people indoors. Even the bad guys.

So, we picked up a couple more cups of super-strong Paradise coffee and I drove us back to our spot across from the Station. "Might as well sit here," I said. "The bar'll be closing pretty soon. Maybe our being here will persuade them to just go home instead of beating on each other."

"Yeah, good idea," said Art, leaning back in the worn and torn vinyl bucket seat, settling in, getting comfortable. We had our windows rolled down and were being assaulted by the blasting sounds being spun by the bar's deejay. The barroom door was closed. Still, out here, across the street, the music pounded. Especially when the door opened when someone came or went. I couldn't imagine how anybody could stand being in there with all that cranked up noise. *Wait. I got it: Must be the alcohol and the lovely ladies.*

Before we could experience the exodus of the guys from the bar in all their inebriated glory, we got a call to St. Mary Hospital for a disturbance in the ER. "2603, we got it," said Art to the dispatcher, turning on the interior light to log the call. One of the good things about night work was the lack of traffic, so we'd get there fast. I made a quick left onto Girard, then another left on Frankford. A minute later I pulled onto the ramp at the back of the hospital, parking next to 266, the area sector car, who'd also responded. As we got out, the cop, Mike Caplow, came out of the ER's automatic doors with a 20-something guy in cuffs.

"What's up, Mike?" asked Art as we opened the back doors of the wagon. Before putting him in, I got my light from the front seat and looked the young man over. I noticed some blood on his head.

"This guy's brother's here for a gunshot," Mike said. "The nurses told this knucklehead that his brother was going into surgery and that he couldn't wait in the ER. Come back later. They even said they'd call him when his brother was out of the OR. Anyway, he wouldn't leave and insisted on going upstairs. When one of the nurses tried to stop him, he pushed her down and was heading to the elevator when I got here. He wanted to fight me too, so I had to smack him. He's okay now, calmed down." The guy was standing there, quiet, maybe realizing that hitting a cop wasn't a good move.

"Mike," I said, pointing to the young man's forehead, "let's take him back inside and get the cut over his eye looked at. The detectives won't take him if he's bleeding, right?"

"Okay," said Mike, grabbing the guy by his arm and heading back inside. "I didn't realize he was cut." Art and I followed Mike and his prisoner inside and stood by with them. We waited as the doctor checked the guy out. His injury turned out to be just a scrape. The small wound was cleaned up, bandaged, and took less than 15 minutes.

We took him out and locked him in the back of the van, then headed to the detectives at Front and Westmoreland. When Caplow got there, the guy would be charged with Assault on Police or, if Mike was feeling sorry for the guy, they'd ask him to apologize, then let him off with a warning. Even so, the detectives would definitely be pissed off at us for bringing in a prisoner in the middle of the night. *Such are the hazards of war,* I told myself. It was something an old-timer had said to me once during my first six months on the street when I complained about some job- related thing I had to do. I liked it.

At the detectives, we quickly secured the prisoner in one of the detention rooms, exiting quickly before the detectives could start their shit. We ran back down to our truck and got out of there, heading back to the 26th. When we hit the district's northern boundary at Lehigh Avenue, Art notified Police Radio we were back in service. At least we'd had some excitement for a little while. Anything to make the night shift hours go by. It was good. Unfortunately, the good didn't last. We weren't two blocks into the district when we got the call.

"2603, Front and Girard, meet 26B with a prisoner." Art acknowledged the call and told the dispatcher where we were—still pretty far away—so they'd send 26B, our supervisor, a backup, if he didn't already have one. We didn't want any cop, especially the sergeant, standing alone with a prisoner. But, since we were the only wagon working tonight, it was our assignment. We had to hustle to get to the south end of the district, about a mile and a half away. 263 car was called to back 26B until we got there.

I raced south on Front Street and got there in less than five minutes. We pulled up behind the two cop cars, both parked facing the wrong way, strobes flashing. "Whaddya got, sarge?" asked Art, as we walked up to the two cops. The sergeant, Brian Harris, was talking with an older man. And Officer "Big Joe" Gilman, of 263 car, stood nearby holding on to an unsteady young man who was handcuffed.

"Hey guys," said the sergeant, "this is Mr. Wilson," pointing to the older man. "The guy in cuffs is his nephew, Brett. Brett and his cousin got into a fight over a girl in the bar and their uncle broke it up. Brett, though, still doesn't want to quit and he's giving his uncle here a hard time. Wants to fight; won't go home."

"So, where's the other cousin?" I asked, looking around.

"He left on his own; he wasn't as drunk as Brett," said Mr. Wilson.

"Just take him in and DK him *(lock him up for drunk and disorderly),*" said Sergeant Harris, nodding in the direction of the almost- falling-down-drunk Brett.

"Got it, sarge," I said. Art and I each grabbed an arm and walked the staggering fellow to the back of the truck, unlocked the doors and, after frisking him, carefully sat him down on one of the wooden benches inside the truck. Then, we got into the wagon, ready to go.

"Skouf, uh, hold up, wait a second," said the sergeant. Then, "Can you guys come here a minute?"

We got out and walked over to the sergeant who was still standing with Mr. Wilson.

"Yes, sir?" I said.

"Do me a favor and take Mr. Wilson into the district too. He wants to wait around for a few hours till his nephew sobers up. The kid is from the suburbs and his uncle is gonna drive him home when he gets out."

When somebody, especially somebody in charge, asks me to do him *a favor*, I get really focused. "Sarge," I said moving off to the side, away from Mr. Wilson, "can I talk to you?"

"Sure."

"Uh, Sarge, can't Gilman transport the uncle in '3' car?" I asked. "I'd rather not put the guy in the back of the truck with a kid who's a fighter."

"It's okay, Skouf, it's his nephew. Besides, it's only a few blocks to the district. No problem."

No problem. I hate when people say that. This whole thing just didn't feel right.

"But sarge, Joe's not doin' anything now," I continued, looking over at Joe Gilman who was standing by. "Besides, when he drops off Mr. Wilson, he can get his cuffs back." I thought that was a sensible alternative. And I *really* didn't want to put a non-prisoner civilian in the back of a wagon with a prisoner, regardless of who they were. Not a good idea, and by the way, a policy violation. All kinds of shit could happen, none of it good. That's why we never did it.

"Just take the man into headquarters, okay?" Now the sergeant's tone was different, strong. Official. An order now; no longer a request. He was pissed at me.

I was pissed too. So, we were even.

We drove the drunk kid and his pain-in-the-ass uncle, who actually seemed like a nice guy, into district headquarters. The turnkey, John Morgan, took Brett back to a cell to sleep it off while I explained the situation to the corporal, who asked why *we'd* brought Wilson in. "Sarge told us to,"

I said. The corporal, Jim Van Gils just shook his head, muttering something about the 'higher the rank, the lower the smarts'.

As Art and I were heading out the door back to our wagon, Mr. Wilson stopped us. "Officers, I want to thank you for helping me out. I feel responsible for Brett — it was my idea to take him out tonight—it's his birthday. Anyway, thanks again." He was nice as pie.

I noticed that the guy was rubbing his right wrist. "Are you alright?" I asked, pointing to his arm.

"Yeah, I'm fine. Just got a little twisted up when I tried to break up the two boys. Hurts like hell, but I'll be alright."

"Are you sure? We can run you over to the hospital; it's only a few blocks away."

"No, I'm really okay. Thanks, though."

When we reported off duty a few hours later, Mr. Wilson and Brett were gone. I thought that was the end of it.

———————————•●•————————————

A year or so later, I came to work on a warm and sunny summer afternoon, looking forward to a busy 4-to midnight shift. About ten steps inside the district building, I was called over to the front of the roll call room. "Skouf, the Captain wants to see you." This was Corporal van Gils, our Operations Room supervisor.

"What does he want, Jim, do ya know?"

"No, he just told me to send you in when you got here." I thought his look was saying 'man, you're in trouble.' Maybe I was just imagining it.

I thanked Jim and headed to the captain's office at the front of the building, my stomach doing flip-flops. *Shit, what's* this *about? What did I do?* Nothing I could think of. Oh, well, might as well get it over with. I walked into the captain's outer office door and was greeted by his clerk, Mary Williams. "Go on in, Officer Skoufalos," he's expecting you.

Great, I thought. *Everybody but me knows what's going on.* I tapped on the captain's half- closed door and entered. The captain, his tie down and uniform shirtsleeves rolled up, was reading a report as he sat behind his desk, which was stacked with piles of paper and folders. He looked up.

"Come on in, sit down, Skouf." He got up and shook my hand. *Hmmm, he doesn't seem mad,* I thought. *Maybe it's nothing.* "How've you been? asked Captain James Muller, leaning back.

"Good, Captain, how are you?"

"I'm fine". He paused and looked at me. "Skouf, let me tell you why I called you in." *Down to business.* "Do you remember a Henry Wilson? White male about 50 years old? It was last year." He picked up a document from one of the piles.

I thought about it. "Not offhand, Captain. Why?"

Holding up the piece of paper, he said, "Well, this is a notification from the City Solicitor's Office. Mr. Wilson is suing the city and the department for unnecessary force. You're named in the lawsuit. Do you remember locking him up?"

Sitting there, I rolled it around in my head. Didn't remember the name or anything I'd done that would lead to a lawsuit. "No, sir, I don't." Pointing, I said, "Does that letter give specifics? Is it just me that's mentioned?"

He looked down at the paper. "It also mentions Art Duncan. Does that help?"

I sat there, still drawing a blank. The captain sat there too. Waiting. After thinking about the arrests I'd made over the last year and those I'd made with Art, the name finally hit me like a shot. *Wilson! Mr. Wilson. Brett's uncle. The fight at the Station Bar.*

I took a breath. "He was *never* arrested, Captain," I said. "What's his story? Can you tell me what he says happened?"

"Sure." Referring again to the document he was holding, the captain said, "He claims you transported him to the district in the back of a wagon and, when you handcuffed him, you broke his right wrist." He looked over at me, waiting.

Really pissed off now, I said, "Let me tell you what happened, captain." And I did, hitting every detail I could remember. Amazing how much I remembered. My voice was calmer than I was.

When I finished, he just shook his head. "Well, the good news is that the City Solicitor is settling the case; there's not going to be a hearing. It's over." That's all he said. He'd just wanted to get my side of the incident, to let me tell my story. He didn't need to do that, but that was Jim Muller. He was one of the good guys who remembered his days as a street cop.

"Boss, this is so wrong," I said. "I wish we could have a hearing, or at least a meeting with the city guy so I could confront the guy face to face. Prove Wilson's a liar. Didn't they even *check* to see if he was arrested?"

He shook his head no. "Skouf, it's a done deal." Holding up the letter, he said, "This is just notification of the settlement."

I sat there, staring into space and remembering. I wasn't worried any more, just really pissed. I didn't want to get Sergeant Harris jammed up, but I wasn't ready to quit yet, so I said, "Captain, we never cuffed that guy. And once he got into headquarters, I even offered to take him to the hospital to get his arm checked out. He refused. And since he wasn't a prisoner, I didn't push it." Then I remembered something else. "Boss, when we brought the guy in, he actually told us that he hurt his wrist trying to break up a fight between his two nephews. Ask Art."

"I already talked with Art. He's been involved in city lawsuits before. He's good." He looked at me. "Skouf, is this your first case with the City Solicitor?" asked Captain Muller, his voice calm, like a father explaining an important fact of life to his son, who was reluctant to listen.

I nodded.

"Well, let me tell you how this works," he said, leaning back in his chair. "A lot of people sue the city. Thousands every year. You know, deep pockets. A lot of it—most of it—is bullshit. And they know the City Solicitor will settle a case if it's below a certain amount, like this one is. The guy knows the system and he's gaming the city."

"But we can prove he's lying." I was still focused on doing the right thing. And my reputation.

"I'm sure you can, but it's done. And Skouf, don't worry about this. You're not in any trouble."

I wasn't worried about being in trouble. I just would've liked to have a conversation with Mr. Henry Wilson; a nice, up-close conversation... I walked out of the office, heading to the locker room. I was steaming.

"What was that all about, Skouf?" asked Sergeant Harris, who saw me as I walked out of the captain's office.

I stopped and looked at him, figuring he'd been clued in by the captain. I tried to keep my voice even. "*You* know, sarge. The Station bar fight. Remember? Last March? The uncle in the wagon?" I waited for the light to go on. It didn't.

"Nope," he said shaking his head. I said okay and walked downstairs to the locker room, still pissed. I wasn't sure if Harris remembered or not. Whatever. I wasn't going to get into it with my street boss. No point. I was going to have to let it go. But it would probably take me a while. Right now, I had to put this away and get my head ready for the street.

Sergeant Harris wasn't a bad guy. He actually was a pretty good supervisor. But he'd made a bad call on this job. Messed me up. Doing a favor for someone. A favor that, along with an opportunistic and crooked citizen, had turned an intended good deed into a sham that everybody but me seemed to be okay with. Even Art Duncan, who'd been there and had been accused too!

Why should I care? I thought, as I changed into my uniform. *If this is how it's done, just go along. Accept it. Let it go.* I kept trying, but I couldn't.

I kept thinking back to one of the lessons my parents taught me and my brothers: "Always do the right thing and always tell the truth." We got that lesson early and often. It was a good one; it stuck with me. And I really believed in it. Still do.

It's been many years since that day in Captain Muller's office. And even though I got it then and still get it, about how the system works, whenever something reminds me of what happened that night—the Station Bar Caper—it still bothers me. You know, the old "right and wrong" thing.

Plan C

In early 1986, after fifteen years on the job, I came to the realization that cops involved in certain kinds of harrowing incidents need tending to in the aftermath. Most anyone, cop or not, needs outside support and perspective to help them cope with certain experiences. For a cop, these critical incidents are events such as police-involved shootings, violent crime scenes, and deaths involving children. Left unaided, some cops crash and burn after such occurrences. I had also observed those who (post-incident) say they would be able to manage on their own, but didn't realize what lay ahead. Who could know what that even looks like? And remember, we're talking about men and women charged with life and death decision-making authority over the citizens they serve. Would unaddressed stress affect their reasoning and decision-making?

The Police Department had a counseling unit at the time. Still does. Back then, I knew some of the guys who were assigned there. But when I started looking into it, I realized it was a "counseling" unit in name only. Like most departments at the time, Philly wasn't aware of the term "critical incidents," let alone their effects. Essentially, the Counseling Unit was set up to address the common problem of alcohol addiction, which was a problem in many departments and in the broader population. So, there was a group of officers assigned to the unit, many who were recovering, themselves. A good thing, to be sure. But the city and the Department were addressing only a small part of what was needed. They didn't seem to be aware of the common- sense data that showed that when cops are involved in such incidents and the matter is unaddressed, their behavior and performance suffered.

It seemed that no one was connecting the dots. So, when it came to the aftermath of critical incidents, "Suck it up," or, "This is the job. Get used to it," was the typical reaction from colleagues and supervisors. And, as it was expected, most cops did just that. They didn't talk about it. Ever. To anyone on the job, and usually not even to loved ones. So, the *what-ifs*, the guilt, regrets and despondency they felt were left unattended. Many times, these troubled officers changed—toward their families and the world, and not in a good way. They were stuck with all the emotional burdens of that one event.

As you can imagine, the police profession is a stoic business. No room for whiners or weaklings. You see attitudes and beliefs like, "Cop work is tough," or, "Death is part of life." Or, "Sometimes you've got to shoot bad guys. That's all there is to it". And so it went (and in many cases and in lots of places, so it still goes). By then, I'd seen a lot of troubled cops on the job, and it was frustrating to see so many struggling.

Another factor (and a giant pet peeve of mine) was the negative effect that the constantly changing shifts had on cops. Back then, street cops worked three shifts, six days each, with two days off in between. Bad enough, to be sure. But what made this so much worse was the sequence of the various shifts: six days of day work (8:00 a.m. to 4:00 p.m.), two days off, then six days of night work (midnight to 8:00 a.m.), two days off, then six days of 4:00 p.m. to midnight. In addition to the challenges such a schedule presented to one's lifestyle, the fact that the rotation was *backward* by design posed what has been shown to be a risk to officers' health. Not to mention their ability to function in a productive and safe manner.

The phenomenon known as *Circadian Rhythm* has to do with the body's ability to regulate cycles of alertness and sleepiness in response to light and darkness in one's environment. To learn more, I read as many scientific studies as I could find which detailed the factors of why rotating shift work was unhealthy in itself, but went on to describe how its effects were exacerbated when the rotation was counterclockwise. So, following the approved departmental chain of command, I shared my findings with supervisors and police union officials. I also suggested that the constant backward shift-changing added unnecessary stress to many officers' lives, along with my ideas on how a slightly revised schedule would benefit everyone.

I heard absolutely nothing in return. Not a word. Nothing. Like my memos had fallen into some abyss.

Because the ignorance around these issues really bothered me, I submitted a transfer request for the Counseling Unit, thinking that I could help. After all, I figured, this wasn't one of those assignments that cops were lining up for; not like SWAT or Highway Patrol, high-profile units with long waiting lists. No, if I were assigned to the Counseling Unit, I imagined there would be plenty of middle-of-the-night calls to respond to a scene where a traumatized cop needed support. *So, who'd want that?* I thought. I was a sergeant at the time in the 26th District; a supervisor who looked after his squad of officers. And I had many years and lots of street experience on the job. I thought I'd be a good fit.

After being approved by my lieutenant, captain, inspector, and chief inspector, my request made its way back to me with the "request disapproved" box checked by the Deputy Commissioner of Patrol. I was disappointed, but not surprised. The politics of the police department rivaled those of local and state governments. *That's alright,* I told myself. I went to Plan B.

I applied and was accepted to the Temple University Master's program in Education, focusing on counseling psychology. And, because I had recently been an adjunct instructor in Temple's Criminal Justice Department, I was able to easily navigate the process.

The M.Ed. program was an intensive two-year course of study which I began in the fall of 1986. It was a tough, highly-structured curriculum and each course was presented in a prescribed order. The work was interesting and complex and, as I went, I imagined how the concepts and skills I was learning could be applied when my fellow police officers needed help.

For most of the second year, one of the requirements was to participate in an externship at a facility that provided public mental health services. Mine was at PATH (People Acting To Help), located near my northeast Philadelphia home. I was assigned to Virginia Keane, a highly skilled therapist, who would be my supervisor and mentor. I owe so much to Ginny. Her vast experience along with her gentle manner when interacting with our clients (and me) modeled the skills I needed for this work.

Soon after I graduated from Temple, I again applied for a position with the department Counseling Unit. This time, I attached a copy of my degree along with a list of the classes I had completed. Surely, this would make a difference, I believed. Nope. Rejected again.

After a period when frustration, anger, and disbelief ruled, I came up with the notion that would become Plan C. Actually, it happened out of necessity. It was as a result of what happened on one of the darkest days of my career.

In late summer, 1992, two 1st District officers were shot as they responded to a call of a robbery in progress at a restaurant, in South Philadelphia. I was assigned to the 1st at the time, having been transferred there in early 1989 when I'd been promoted to lieutenant. Although these officers were not part of my platoon, I knew them both well, because our schedules resulted in some overlap between squads. Young, bright and energetic, they represented a new wave of officers ready to step into the role. Both officers were shot by the robbers. One died. The other was gravely wounded. I was off-duty at the time, but was due in the next day.

When I walked into the 1st District headquarters, it was like I'd entered a funeral. The usual ever-present banter and laughter were missing from the place. Some cops sat with heads down, others stood with a thousand-yard stare. Some were crying. I met with the captain and my counterpart lieutenant of the other squad to talk about what had happened. It was a tragedy for the officers' families, especially for the officer who had been killed. We were also concerned for the survivor; his injuries made his condition critical, and there was a time we weren't sure if he would make it.

The three of us sat and discussed what needed to be done: prepare for a funeral, provide for an ongoing security detail at the injured officer's hospital room, review the incident top to bottom, and a hundred other things we hadn't yet thought of. Then there was the support for both officers' families. It was a lot. But doing tasks helped.

I remembered that the Counseling Unit is supposed to be notified in such incidents. Not wanting to take any chances on the notification slipping through the cracks, I called them myself to confirm. After asking me for some basic information about the incident, they assured me they would send a team. On the day they were to arrive, I gathered the group of officers who had responded and waited. I was expecting a full-blown Critical Incident Stress Intervention.

The "team" turned out to be one officer, who showed up and stood before those assembled. I couldn't believe what happened next: The Counseling Unit officer stood before the group and, after offering his condolences, said that the Counseling Unit (by now also known as the Employee Assistance Program [EAP]) was available to provide counseling to individual officers who felt the need to seek such counseling. He ended his short presentation by announcing he was providing a number of business cards with information about the EAP and its services. He placed the cards on a table. Then he was gone. Nothing about meeting with the group; nothing.

Silence. People looked at one another. I was stunned. What had just happened? Nothing, really. That's when I knew I had to step up. Time for Plan C. Looking around the roll call room with about twenty cops sitting there, I hoped I knew what I was doing, that what I was saying was right. A few seconds later, I *knew* it would be right. Something had to be done. *I* had to do something.

I stood before the dejected group and began by telling them that I wanted to conduct a Critical Incident Stress Debriefing. More of the looking around at each other. Nobody knew what I was talking about. I explained that what had happened with their two colleagues affected everyone differently. That those who were more directly involved likely would have the strongest reactions. I described the steps we would take: first, the following day we would have a meeting with all those who responded. There would be later meetings with others who felt the need to talk. And we would continue to listen and offer support as long as needed.

I explained the process. At the start of the session, the other lieutenant and I would summarize the incident based on the known facts. This was done to address any misinformation that might exist. Next, all attendees would be given an opportunity to talk about how they were feeling about what had happened. After that, anybody could ask questions regarding the incident. Importantly, the group would be limited to only those who had participated in the actual event, as well as others who had been directly involved.

After those steps were completed, I would meet with all 1st District supervisors and ask them to be alert for any behavioral change indicative of possible reaction to the incident. I also asked them to provide care and support of the officers under their command, including one-on-one assistance (aka psychological first aid) if needed.

Next, senior supervisory officers would draw up a plan of action to address the needs of officers, including referral to professional mental health providers, if needed.

We identified the core group that would be invited to the meeting: responding officers, police radio dispatchers who were involved in the assignment and any hospital personnel who provided emergency care to the injured officers. Notifications went out that the meeting would be held the next day at 3:00 p.m. in the 1st District roll room.

After I advised the captain of the less than satisfactory response from the Counseling Unit/EAP, it was agreed I would lead the debriefing.

What the hell are you doing? I kept saying to myself. This is heavy shit. Then I thought, *this has to be done right away.* Somehow, I convinced myself I *could* do what I had already agreed to do.

When I arrived at the district the next day, still a little nervous, I was amazed to see twenty-some people who'd been invited seated in the roll call room. Chairs had been arranged in a large circle and all but a few chairs were filled. At three o'clock sharp, we started.

We went through the steps. To begin, the other lieutenant and I related the facts of the incident to make sure everyone had the most accurate information.

Then it was time for the others to have their say. Most of them participated. Some of the responding officers expressed frustration and anger at themselves because they didn't get there more quickly. Some officers didn't say anything. Others sat there, heads down, nodding once in a while. Supervisors who'd been there spoke up, assuring these cops they had done everything they could have; that their quick response had been critical in providing "flash" information about the perpetrators and in securing the crime scene.

The radio dispatchers were next. These were civilians and, although they weren't "out there" with the cops, a strong bond existed between the two, a truly symbiotic relationship. They lamented that they weren't able to have more officers on the scene sooner to provide more help for the officers. They felt that they had failed. To this comment, multiple officers spoke up, saying that they thought the dispatchers had done a great job managing the response.

Several ER nurses and a doctor spoke up. With tears in her eyes, one nurse told the group that she remembered the urgency of the team as they worked on the officers, both of whom they knew, and that she'd never forget seeing the blood on her white shoes after it was over. Shaking his head, the doc just said he was sorry he couldn't have done more.

Once everyone who wanted to speak had done so, the captain joined the group. We explained that the feelings they were having and would have were normal, expected. They were told that *not* talking about it wasn't the best way to handle what they were feeling. We answered any other questions they had. Then it was over. It had lasted a little more than an hour.

For some, the follow-ups took longer, months, even years. I fear that it may never end for a few of them. Unofficially, I made myself available to listen and talk with those who wanted to. It took a while, but the officer who had nearly died eventually recovered from his physical wounds. The invisible ones persisted. I kept in close touch with him and, eventually, his family, whose loving care kept him going. Not surprisingly, he suffered greatly from survivor's guilt. I saw him years later and barely recognized the young man I'd known back then, who now was white-haired and seemingly distracted and distant.

My debriefing following the incident in the 1st was not sanctioned by the department. I'm certain some of those in charge were aware of it, but I never was told to stop. For that I'm grateful. And I truly hope that the Counseling Unit or EAP or whatever it's called now has evolved into what the men and women of the department and the larger community need and deserve.

I left the 1st shortly after that, ending up as Executive Officer for the Deputy Commissioner of Training. Even now, decades later, I'll read something or talk with someone from back then that causes me to recall my bittersweet time in the 1st District. My thoughts go to the good folks with whom I spent those few but profoundly memorable years.

There were other critical incidents in other places with which I became involved, although none affected me so deeply as that first one. I learned of them through other cops, and usually through hearsay. And because they were in other districts, places where I had no official jurisdiction, I went directly to the officers, introduced myself and offered to listen, to help. In a few of these incidents, cops who'd been involved in legitimate and justified shootings were understandably overwrought. The toll it took on them was so heavy and persistent, it sometimes affected the officer's entire family.

I'm often reminded of that terrible incident in late summer, 1992, that changed so many lives of friends and colleagues. More than anything, I hope they all have managed to find some peace.

Postscript: Can a modicum of "closure" help people heal after such critical incidents? When a murderer or criminal is caught and brought to justice, does this give comfort to those directly affected by the traumatic experience? For the case above where two officers were shot, the perpetrator(s) were not soon apprehended. During the crime scene investigation, officers discovered several pieces of evidence which were left behind by the suspects: a crowbar, the newspaper in which it was wrapped and a baseball-type cap. These items were secured by Philadelphia PD Crime Scene Unit police officers Jim Bushman and Jim Caldwell. Officer Bushman developed a partial fingerprint from the newspaper and the plastic adjustable band on the rear of the baseball cap. These items were sent to the Pennsylvania State Police who assisted in the identification of the fingerprints.

Here's where the story gets almost miraculous. The State Police analyst (name unknown to me) made several attempts to identify the partial fingerprint on the cap. I learned from officers who were familiar with the case that he was retiring at the end of 1992. It really bothered him that he had been unable to ID the print. He decided to give it one more try before he left the job. Incredibly, on his last try, he was able to identify one of the suspects from the partial fingerprint!

Based on that evidence, the two perpetrators, brothers from Philadelphia, were soon arrested. They both made statements, admitting their involvement in the incident.

As amazing as this development was, there was still more great work ahead. In January,1993, based on the statement of one of the shooters detailing where the gun had been dumped, police conducted an unsuccessful search for the firearm in Cobb's Creek. At that point, the investigation took an unusual turn. Having heard of a local treasure hunting group who might be interested in helping, the police contacted them and they quickly agreed to assist. Soon after, the group showed up at the creek and, within minutes, the gun was located.

Back at the lab, the cops from the Philly PD Firearms Identification Unit (FIU) treated the firearm with oil to stop any further rust damage that had been done to the revolver. Incredibly, doing so revealed a fingerprint on the gun's cylinder, which was identified as that of one of the brothers.

Both were tried and convicted of first-degree murder and sentenced to life in prison.

Clearly, persistence paid off in this case.

A final note: Serendipity. Between 2008 and 2013. I had the pleasure of working with two officers who had been directly involved in the investigation of the case and whose efforts helped lead to the apprehension of the two men who were responsible for this crime.

While working at Drexel University to help with the startup of the then-new Drexel University Police Department (DUPD), I met two of the officers who had been instrumental in the successful resolution of the case: Detective Robert Lis had been the assigned detective in South Detective Division and was detailed to the Homicide Unit for much of the investigation. Bob and I had known each other when I had worked in the 1st District. He is now the Captain of Detectives with the Drexel Department of Public Safety.

During DUPD's early days, I also met Jim Caldwell, who. along with James Bushman, were the Crime Scene Unit officers who responded to and processed the scene following the shootings in South Philadelphia in August,1992.

Jim Caldwell is currently a detective with the DUPD.

The Favor

My wife Monica beside me, I took the Woodhaven extension and merged onto I-95 south. It was late for a downtown excursion—about 9:30 p.m., but this wasn't a pleasure drive. We weren't going to a late dinner or to a movie. We were headed to South Philly and it was a work-related thing. I was curious, wanting to see where my new workplace was.

My recent promotion to Police Lieutenant had resulted in a transfer from the 26th District where I had spent most of my years in uniform, to the 1st District, which was geographically just about the farthest assignment from my house in northeast Philadelphia. I didn't mind, though. I would be a platoon commander in one of four south Philadelphia districts. The only thing I didn't like was that the 1st was the 'slowest' of the four. The 3rd, 4th and the 17th were far busier, with a higher volume of calls for service, something I'd gotten used to in the very active 26th. Not a problem. I was looking forward to a more administrative role, running a squad of about 20 officers.

The western part of South Philadelphia was not a place I'd been often. I used to deliver flowers down here, but that was almost 30 years prior. So, I wanted to do a quick drive-through of the area for two reasons: first, to get the lay of the land and second, to check out my new headquarters at 24th and Wolf Streets. As I crossed Broad Street and headed west through the eastern edge of the 1st District, I noticed that there were a lot of cars parked on all the streets and. they were parked everywhere. "Must be something going on at the church there." I said to my wife as we passed St. Monica's at 17th and Ritner.

"Think so?" she said. "The place is dark. There's nobody around."

She was right. Even though it was a cold January night, I figured there should have been some people out and about, but no. It was a ghost town, except for all the cars. The streets were narrow with cars parked on both sides. Not only that, but they were also double- and even triple-parked. The whole scene was strange. And there weren't just cars parked next to one another, stacked sideways from the curb to the middle of the street. Nope. Some were there with no cars between them and the curb, like they were reserved for somebody. It was so bizarre that I wondered what it was all about.

Doing a cop thing as I drove, I scanned as we passed and didn't see a single parking ticket on any of the windshields. Hmmm. In time, we made our way through the parked car obstacle course and found the district building. Mission accomplished. It was a massive old brick castle—looking thing in the dark. Now I knew where it was.

As we drove home, now on an eastbound street, through a different maze of cars, I wondered if this was the norm. I wondered if this was a Sunday night phenomenon, people visiting their families, you know, big Sunday dinners—an old South Philly Italian tradition. That had to be it. *There can't possibly be this many parked cars blocking the streets all the time,* I thought. I was wrong.

When I reported for my first tour of duty a few evenings later, I took the exact same route and found the same parked car situation. I was thinking how this must affect the patrol cops working here. I knew, after more than 18 years on the job, that parking spot shortages led to all kinds of problems, from fights to vandalism. I was wrong again. Sure, those things happened once in a while when frustration took over and people disagreed about who had the right to park where, but not so much here. That meant that, if you drove for a living, like cops did, this was your normal for eight hours a day, every day. I wondered how many auto accidents happened here.

When I asked some of the officers in my new squad about the parking, the typical answer was, "What do you mean?" When I'd explain, they'd laugh and say, "That's normal, boss, you'll get used to it."

Something I'd learned both as a soldier and a cop was that, in time, you *could* get used to just about anything. And I did. In a few weeks, (maybe it was months), I had gotten used to the mess of cars everywhere and had gotten pretty good at the weaving skill needed to navigate the district streets.

I spent a few years in the 1st, where I met and worked with some very good folks, cops and civilians alike. There were good times and some not so good, but overall, I enjoyed my stay in what would be the last patrol assignment of my career. Somewhere in the middle of that time, I became a part of a situation that challenged everything I'd known as a cop and a person. It involved an auto accident.

Like the other lieutenants, I reported directly to the captain, the district Commanding Officer. Also like the other lieutenants, I was sometimes called in to personally handle a sensitive assignment that had come to his attention. It was on a warm fall evening on the 4:00 p.m. to midnight tour of duty. I had just finished roll call when the captain's aide told me the boss wanted to see me. I walked to the front office.

"Hi, Skouf, how are you?" he asked in his calm, soothing voice as I walked in.

"I'm fine, captain, and you?"

"I'm good. Listen Skouf, I need you to do something for me. It involves a friend of mine. Maybe you know him." He gave me the name.

I told the captain I didn't know him.

"Well, he needs us to write an accident report for him. Would you take care of it?"

Now, I was certainly not above investigating auto accidents and doing the paperwork; I'd done both lots of times. But, to me, this was an unusual request. First of all, in order for a platoon lieutenant to be called on to handle such an assignment, every officer and sergeant in the squad would have to be busy with other assignments, and the accident call would have to be of an emergency nature. I had been listening to the radio and I knew that we had plenty of cops available. This was more than that. I needed more information.

"Pardon me, captain. You want *me* to handle an auto accident?"

"Yes, I do. This has to be handled properly."

So, I'm thinking: Properly. *Every cop here can handle an accident investigation. Why me? What's this really about?*

The captain must have been reading my mind. "Skouf, I'd like you to do this as a favor to me, okay?"

"Sure captain." He handed me a slip of paper with the address and off I went. As I walked to my car, I wasn't very comfortable with this assignment and the fact that the captain had framed it as he had. The captain and I had known each other for a number of years. We were friendly, but we certainly weren't friends. And not close enough for me to be doing him "favors." But I had learned to follow orders and, even though this wasn't an official order, it sure felt like one. By the time my shift was over, I'd be wondering why it had been my luck to be the duty lieutenant on this day. And then there was my probationary promotional status that came to mind.

I phoned the dispatch center and advised them that I'd be out of service with a "headquarters assignment." Then I drove the few blocks to the location, still trying to figure out what this was about.

The open front door hinted that he'd been watching and waiting for me. As soon as I rang the doorbell, a man who looked to be in his sixties opened the door and invited me in. He had that "cop look" but I didn't recognize him. I stepped into a beautifully decorated living room, taking it all in. The home was large by South Philly standards, and well appointed. The furniture was modern, with a matching blue sofa and side chairs over dark red plush carpet. The ceiling to floor drapes were a shade lighter than the rug. Very nice.

"You have a very nice home, sir" I said.

His glance in my direction was his only acknowledgement of my comments. He seemed impatient, wanting to get to the business at hand; no time for chit-chat. He was wearing a white dress shirt with the top button open and his maroon tie was loosened and pulled down. His blue suit jacket lay folded over a dining room chair, like he'd just gotten home from work.

He abruptly introduced himself, then proceeded to explain that, while parked outside near his home, his car had been struck by a hit-run driver. After jotting down some basic information and getting the vehicle registration card from the guy, I went outside to take a look. He didn't come along, which I thought was strange. Usually, the victim wanted to show and tell the cop everything. The car was parked by the left curb of the small northbound street. The vehicle was in good shape, except for the large crease on the left side, starting from the driver's door and running all the way past the rear left door. The damage looked fresh, some light-colored paint chips clinging to the car's black paint. Not wanting to assume anything, I checked the other side as well as the front and rear ends of the vehicle. The rest of the car was undamaged. I wasn't getting it. I went back to the house and asked him to confirm that the damage he was reporting was on the left side of the car. He said yes.

I had a problem. "Sir, where was the car parked when it was hit?" I asked.

"Right where it is now." All business.

"You're sure?" I was hoping for a different answer.

"What are you trying to say, lieutenant?" He glared at me. He sounded angry.

"Well, sir, you're parked on the left side of a one-way street." I stopped, hoping he'd catch on. If he did, he didn't say so. I continued. "If somebody hit your car while it was parked where it is now, the car that hit yours would have to have been driving on the sidewalk. Is that what happened?" We both knew that wasn't possible; the sidewalk was barely wide enough for two people walking side by side, let alone a motor vehicle. Still, I waited for his answer.

His look seemed to suggest that he thought I was a wise-ass. "Lieutenant, when I spoke to the captain, he said you'd take care of this. Just write it up." *Why me?* I thought again.

I looked at him. Was he telling me to make up a story? To change the facts of what had happened? Not sure; I hoped not. I stood silently for a few minutes, thinking.

Impatient now, he said, "Well, what are you waiting for? Just do the report." Now I was sure he was angry. I got the feeling he was used to people just doing what he wanted, no questions asked.

But I *did* have questions I'd had to ask. I had asked them and gotten no usable answers. I checked the report I had started and, seeing that I had all the pertinent information recorded, I told him I would give the report to the captain. He grunted something at me as I left

I drove to the Melrose Diner a few streets over and took a spot at the mostly empty counter. The waitress saw me coming and automatically placed a steaming cup of South Philly's best coffee in front of me, smiled and walked away. I sipped and thought about everything. This was a dilemma, for sure. The captain had entrusted me with this 'special assignment', and he expected it to be completed to everyone's satisfaction. My problem was that the completed accident report would satisfy the captain and his friend. But it wouldn't satisfy me. If the guy had told me that the car had been parked on the other side of the street, it would have made sense. No dilemma. But he didn't. Now I was feeling some kind of way toward the captain. He knew me, and he knew that I didn't play.

I thought of the old adage: "Go along to get along." I got it. And for the most part, I went along. But this was different. I sat there with a second cup, not really enjoying it; I was considering my next move. One of the things that popped up again was the fact that I was still a probationary lieutenant, and would be for about two more months. It occurred to me that the captain could, at his pleasure, not sign off, not recommend my permanent promotional status. Plus, he could do this for any number of reasons; he had a lot of discretion. I sure didn't want that to happen. As I sat there, I knew what I had to do. And I knew what I couldn't do. I didn't think my boss was going to be happy with me.

I finished my cup and drove to the district headquarters and parked my car in the spot next to the captain's, the one reserved for the lieutenant. I sat there a minute, gathered up the paperwork from the accident, looked it over again and went inside.

"Is he available?" I asked Betty, the captain's clerk as I walked into the outer office.

"Yes, lieutenant, but he's on the phone. You want me to tell him you were here?"

"I'll wait, Betty." I said and sat down. *I bet I know who he's on the phone with.* As I sat there, the minutes seemed like hours. Using the time, I went over everything that happened, everything that was said, making sure I had it right. Then, the captain came to the door of his office and, without a word, waved me in. He sat behind his desk and waited for me to take a seat in one of the old green cracked-leather guest chairs, facing him. Before I sat, he said, "Close the door, lieutenant." His voice was calm, his words measured. He looked at me hard. I thought, *"Lieutenant"*, not *"Skouf"*. The change in his tone was clear.

He asked me for the report. I handed him the partially completed accident report. He read it in silence, not looking up. Then, he put the papers down in front of him, and folded his hands on the desk. I felt like I was in the principal's office, only worse.

"Lieutenant Skoufalos, tell me what happened."

I explained everything: the conversations with the man, the car damage, my questions, the guy's demands.

"I thought I asked you to take care of this." It was like he hadn't heard a word I'd just said to him.

"Yes, sir. I was doing that. And when I asked your friend some questions, he got mad and started telling me what to do. Given the circumstances, I thought he was being…"

"I don't care what you thought!" he said. His face was getting red and his voice was up. He was like a different guy. "I gave you an assignment."

"Yes, sir, you did." Now *I* was a little pissed. *Wait a minute,* I said to myself. *We're both cops, right? I'll just tell him again, he'll get it. He knows I'm a stand-up guy.* I took a beat; I wanted to say this right. "Sir, you read my partial report. What do you make of it? Can I answer any questions?" I asked, trying to keep my voice even.

He picked up the report, glanced at it, dropped in on his desk. "All I know that you were given a job to do and you didn't get it done." He waited, his eyes boring into mine.

I sat up straighter. Taking a breath, I said, "Well, captain, I'm reporting the results of the assignment you gave me. My investigation showed that the statements of the complainant didn't match the facts I observed. And when I tried to clarify the discrepancies, the complainant got angry and wouldn't answer my questions." He sat there, looking at me. After a few seconds, I offered, "If you would like me to document everything that occurred, I'll prepare and submit a memorandum right away." I started to get up.

"That won't be necessary," he snapped. "*I'll* take care of it. You're dismissed. Get back on the street." I left.

I stewed for the rest of the evening, that night and most of the next day. After going over the thing again and again, I decided I was good. Maybe not with the captain and probably not with his friend. I was good with *me*, and I was feeling that quiet satisfaction that comes with doing the right thing.

There was no fallout from the incident. I made it through probation just fine. I don't know what happened with that accident report and didn't care. The captain and I never spoke of it again. I spent my time in the 1st District doing my job: leading my platoon, making sure we always tried our best to do things the right way, serving the 1st District's citizens.

•●•

After a few years, I was asked to serve as the Executive Officer for one of the department's Deputy Commissioners. As I considered my new duties, which included representing the Deputy in high-level departmental matters, I thought back to that first night I drove through the 1st District, navigating the obstacles, making my way. I remembered some of the choices I'd faced and the decisions I'd made. And, like those other times when I'd learned things during my years on the job, they too, were important lessons for me, just waiting to be discovered.

Leaving Oz

I hadn't said anything to him yet and it was bothering me. After all, the Deputy had rescued me.

"I'll do it today." It was the same thing I'd been telling myself every day for about a week. Now I sat trying to figure out how to tell him; what words to use. What would he say? Probably not much; that's his way. What would be going on in that deep, always analyzing mind of his as I explained? If there was ever a person whose thinking could almost be seen and felt, it was Deputy Commissioner John Melton. Probably one of the smartest guys I'd ever known, he was easily the most intelligent cop I'd worked with.

I hoped he wouldn't be angry or disappointed. Laying my pen down, ignoring the report on my desk I'd been reviewing, I sat back in my chair. Coffee. I always thought better with a cup in my hand. Sometimes, sipping coffee and not thinking about something head on, would give me a clue, a direction.

As I stirred powdered creamer into my Philadelphia PD mug, the boss's secretary Mrs. Hunter (Joan) walked up and poured herself a cup.

"Good morning, lieutenant," she said, smiling.

"Good morning, Mrs. Hunter," I said turning her way.

Joan Hunter was the administrative assistant that every top-level executive hopes for. She'd been with the Deputy for more than twenty years, since he'd been a captain, moving up with him as he steadily climbed the ladder of the department's hierarchy. The ultimate professional, she was his right hand and his guardian. Not that he needed guarding; it was just that her fierce loyalty to the man made her an ideal gatekeeper, along with everything else she did.

"Everything alright?" she asked as we stood there. Her gaze was soft yet strong. It was almost as if she could sense I was struggling with something.

"Yes," I answered, hoping she didn't detect anything in my voice that gave me away. She was like her boss in that way: able to drill down past the words being spoken, down to what someone was *really* saying, even thinking. I hoped that the paranoia I was feeling about my little secret was not evident.

"Okay, good," she said as she turned to go.

Today was the day. Definitely. I would tell him I was leaving.

I sat back down at my desk and thought about it. And about everything that had led up to this day.

I'd been a cop for almost twenty-four years. Now I was calling it quits. Not an easy thing. Especially now that I had what I considered a dream job: Executive Officer to the Deputy Commissioner of Administration and Training.

My time with the Deputy had started several years ago, when I, along with a group of other patrol lieutenants, had been summoned to a meeting with him. There, he told us that we were part of a task force he was forming. The mission: how to improve the preparation and management of Incident Reports— the department's basic form used to document every contact police had with citizens. Sitting in his large conference room, I remember being impressed with the man's vision, calling on us—the street patrol commanders—and not the upper echelon bosses, the captains and above, who, because of their responsibilities, were so far removed from the day-to-day activities on the street.

The Deputy briefed us on specifics of our assignment and gave us one of his famously rare smiles.

"Questions, gentlemen?" he asked as we all just sat there, trying to figure out why *we* had been selected from the hundreds of patrol lieutenants.

We all shook our heads. No one dared ask the man what we imagined would seem like a stupid question.

"Great. I appreciate your help," he said as he moved to the door. Before exiting, he stopped, looking straight at me. "Oh, Lieutenant Skoufalos, please stop by my office after your meeting," he said.

"*Uh-oh,*" I thought. "Yes sir," I said. He left.

All the others in the room were now staring at me. Their looks supported my knot-in-the-pit-of-my-stomach feeling you get when summoned to the school principal's office.

Preoccupied with thoughts—mostly scary ones—about my upcoming appointment with Deputy Melton, I wasn't a very active participant in the meeting.

I really didn't know the man; we'd never worked together. So, I concluded that I must be in trouble of some kind. *What had I done?* Rewinding the past few weeks and months, I couldn't think of anything that would land me in the Deputy's office. Still, it must be something significant; something big. *What??*

The meeting ended. I walked slowly down the hall and entered the outer office where his assistant, Mrs. Hunter, was seated.

"Good afternoon, lieutenant, the Deputy is expecting you." She got up and walked me to the open door of the largest office I had ever seen. "Excuse me, Deputy, Lieutenant Skoufalos is here."

He looked up and said, "Thank you, Joan. Come in, lieutenant, please, sit down," pointing to a chair in front of his massive wooden desk. Apparently fully aware of his intimidating reputation, he opened with a slightly brighter version of the smile he'd given the group earlier.

"Thanks for coming in."

I just sat there and nodded. Like a jackass.

He got right to the point: "Lieutenant, do you know Captain Jim Turner?"

"Yes sir," I answered, surprised that I had a voice at all. "We worked together in the 26th when he was a sergeant."

"Yes," he said. "Well, he's been my Executive Officer for a while now. The assignment is for a lieutenant and, as you probably know, Jim's recently been promoted; he's being reassigned.

Continuing my jackass portrayal, I nodded my understanding, but I still didn't know what any of this had to do with me. It was clear to the Deputy that he would have to be very specific.

"Lieutenant, I'd like you to come work with me, as my Executive Officer."

I heard the words, but still didn't comprehend.

"Pardon?" I asked.

He smiled, realizing that this had come from beyond left field. "Will you be my Executive Officer?" he repeated. Before the man finished, I was nodding like a bobble head.

"Yes sir, yes sir. I appreciate the offer. And, I-I'm grateful for your confidence in me." I stammered the words. After a bit, I managed to blurt out "This is great. Thanks!" Then, calming myself, "Sir, can you tell me why you decided to offer this position to me?"

"Well, Stratis—may I call you Stratis? You come highly recommended by some of the commanders I've talked with. Commanders who know you. You see, lieutenant, people have been paying attention; they know you and your reputation."

It wasn't until he spoke his next words that I understood.

"I know what you've been through, he said softly. "I know it's been a tough few years…believe me, you are appreciated."

We shook hands and I thanked him again as I got up to leave.

I don't remember the ride back to the 1st District; my mind was all over the place. Nor do I remember getting home. Somehow, I managed to remain cool as I walked into the kitchen and gave Monica a hello kiss. Cool. Oh yeah, I was going to play this out!

"How was your day, dear?" I asked. "Can I get you something to drink?"

"Sure, white wine, please."

After I handed my wife the glass of Chardonnay, I sat down and took a long drink from my ice-cold Yuengling. Then I leaned back, just watching her work.

"What's up?" she asked, looking over at me, turning away from the counter where she was doing something with vegetables and pasta. "You alright?"

"Sure am," I said, now the smug guy with a wonderful secret to share.

"Anything happen at work?" she asked.

That did it. *Playing it out* and *cool* just left the room. I couldn't keep anything from her.

"I might be getting transferred."

I saw her stiffen and stop working. As the Deputy had noted earlier, these past years had been tough on me—on us.

I walked up to her, put my arms around her waist, held her and whispered the good news in her ear. She was happy and relieved.

After dinner, we sat together quietly, listening to soft jazz, lost in our thoughts, enjoying our turn of fortune. I still couldn't believe it was happening.

My mind went back to a time when I thought I might have to leave the department and the job I loved. Because of what I'd done and what had come after. Even though there was no doubt that what I'd done had been the right thing.

It was the late 80s; I'd been a sergeant in the Background Investigation Unit, supervising a squad of detectives, reviewing police officer applicants, recommending those who were qualified, for hire. It was a good assignment — a *great* assignment. Until…

The lieutenant who had recruited me for the job was suddenly transferred. No reason given. But he and I thought it might have something to do with what had been going on before I'd gotten there and might still be happening. I had heard rumors that some applicants were being treated as "special cases" as they were jokingly called by one of the other supervisors in the unit. A new lieutenant was being assigned.

"Oh, they're just shortcuts," he'd said when I asked him about it. The lieutenant and I didn't buy that. Sounded more like *funny business* to me. The "shortcuts" meant sometimes ignoring things that would disqualify a candidate. Supposedly the practice had led to the hiring of some who were unqualified.

I was never much of a rumor guy, but I had also learned that sometimes rumors were true. I shared what I'd heard with my lieutenant before he left. He had also heard the same rumblings and we both started paying closer attention. Turned out, the rumors *were* true. We tightened the process, to make sure it conformed to the Police Commissioner's policies. Not everybody was happy about that.

In the weeks before the new lieutenant arrived, I began receiving some phone calls about him. Friends from around the department were telling me to *watch my back.* Wow! I'd never heard of the new guy before, but

I trusted the people who had called to warn me. My guard was up. Still, I kept an open mind.

After he'd been there a few days, I noticed that the lieutenant was paying very close attention to my work, more than that of other supervisors. Looking over my shoulder, taking notes, listening to my discussions with detectives.

"That's okay," I told myself. "I'm doing my job." I figured that maybe he was trying to learn the ropes by observing how I managed the detectives and the process. But something didn't feel right: more than once, he'd ask me why certain candidates had been rejected. Although I'd always provided valid, documented reasons, I could tell he wasn't satisfied with my answers. Looking back, some of these individuals had previously been referred to as "special cases."

Then I found out about a specific incident. It involved a female applicant—we'll call her "Ms. Smith"— I'd recommended for rejection. She had a conviction and according to our policies, couldn't be hired. But I found out Ms. Smith was being hired after all. The new lieutenant had made the decision, overriding my ruling to reject, which was certainly within the scope of his responsibilities and authority as the unit's ranking supervisor. At his request, we discussed the case again—for the third or fourth time. When I again explained that the guidelines for acceptance or rejection came straight from the Police Commissioner, the lieutenant told me he didn't agree with a policy that rejected someone because of what he termed "a minor crime." This went back and forth, I invoking the commissioner's mandate, he saying he didn't think it was fair. Finally, by the time we were finished, I thought he understood. I was pretty sure we were on the same page.

I couldn't have been more wrong.

Ms. Smith was soon hired for the next Police Academy class.

No surprise, the word got out—I still don't know or care how—and the Commissioner found out. The investigation that followed had me explaining my part in it, including my numerous conversations with the lieutenant. Apparently, his side differed. I learned that he had told the captain who was inquiring that we'd never met about Ms. Smith, never discussed her, and that I'd never fully explained our hiring process.

Soon after, I was called to a meeting with the Commissioner, who said he wanted all the details from me directly.

Ms. Smith was terminated and the Background Investigation Unit was disbanded.

Then I was transferred to Internal Affairs. Good deal.

Within months, the Commissioner retired. The mayor's appointee to replace him happened to be a very close friend of the lieutenant who had started the mess.

Almost immediately, I was transferred to a patrol district, definitely a step down. It sure felt like punishment or retribution. The lieutenant was given a command position with the elite Homicide Unit.

Back in patrol, every one of my requests for transfer, though approved through the chain of command, was disapproved by the commissioner. A couple of captains even asked for me to be transferred to their unit—a *Commanding Officer's Request*—something that was traditionally always honored. These, too, were denied. One captain confided to me that he'd been told that I was *never* going to be transferred out of patrol.

I made the best of my assignment. Patrol was something I had always enjoyed, where I'd learned the job. I was okay. Eventually, I was promoted to Lieutenant and assigned to the 1st District, geographically the farthest patrol district from my house. It felt like more fallout. No problem.

After several years, that police commissioner left the department and moved away. A few months after that, I got the offer from the Deputy.

Now I was sitting just outside his office, trying to figure out how to break the news of my retirement. Actually, it wasn't a true *retirement*. I had accepted a position as Security Director for a local university. But I'd be leaving the Philadelphia PD and the man to whom I owed a debt of gratitude. I had mixed feelings.

We met late that afternoon and I explained that I had decided to leave the police department, how I'd struggled with the decision to accept a new position. He nodded and said, "Congratulations, Stratis, it sounds like a terrific opportunity. I'm sure you'll do great." He wanted to know more about what my responsibilities would be. We talked and I started to relax. At some point, I took a deep breath, relieved that it looked like we were okay. What a gentleman. And what a great boss.

Word spread around the city and I started getting calls and visits from guys I'd worked with during the past twenty-four years: from cops I'd known in my days on the front lines and recruits I'd taught as an Academy instructor. Even a few of my academy classmates showed up. Congratulations and bear hugs, and "Let's get together for a drink before you leave." And "Hey Skouf, how about when we…" and "Remember the time…?"

I did remember. The funny stuff and the horrible things; the sadness I'd witnessed and the pride I had felt to be a member of the Philadelphia Police Department. Still feel. I realized that the memories are never far away and always would be there. I was a lucky guy.

Memories. Like that first week as a recruit officer. I was sitting in a classroom and one of our instructors, a grizzled old sergeant named Myers, said to us: "Gentlemen, when you leave the academy and hit the streets, you'll have a front row seat to the greatest show on earth."

He was right. It *was* the greatest show and I'd been a part of it.

But for me, the past twenty-four years had also been like a trip to the mystical city of Oz, where visitors gained enlightenment and self-awareness, where they learned how to help themselves and to be courageous, as well as unselfish for the good of others. I guess I saw my career that way: a tough road I'd gone down where, along the way, I had grown and learned so much. And one of the best parts of the journey had been traveling with some very good friends, friends I'll never forget.

Acknowledgements

I've liked writing from an early age. Reading, too. I remember how amazed I would be (and still am) whenever I'd read a book, a story, or an article and was struck by how the author had used words to draw a picture in my mind. To this day, I shake my head when a beautifully crafted sentence or phrase stops me in my tracks. So, to all those authors and other writers who have engaged, entertained, and informed me over the years, thank you. And thank you for introducing me to the magic of writing.

First, I am extremely grateful to Barbara Dee at Suncoast Digital Press, Inc., who took a collection of my stories and turned it into a book. Barbara, your interest in and enthusiasm for my manuscript resulted in our collaboration, which made *Shifts* possible. Thank you for your expertise, guidance, and patience. Your publishing experience and vision set the foundation for *Shifts*. Your insightful critiques, understanding and suggestions, along with your willingness to help me every step of this journey, made my dream of writing a book a reality. I truly could not have done this without you.

Many thanks to my friends and former police colleagues Bob Lis and Jim Caldwell, who were critically involved in the criminal matter discussed in "Plan C." Their dedication as part of a team of investigators helped solve the case. Bob and Jim, I appreciate your time and patience with my many questions as we went back almost 30 years to that terrible day. (After retiring from the Philadelphia, PD, Jim and Bob are still active police officers with the Drexel University Police Department in Philly.)

I owe a deep debt of gratitude to my wife, Monica, who always believed in the possibility of this book, although I admit I didn't always share her confidence. Monica, over the years of this project, you always encouraged the work and always seemed to know when to lean in, when I needed a little extra support. You sometimes provided me with a fresh look at a story with non-cop eyes, were able to see what I was saying (or trying to say) and what I may have been missing. And, sometimes, how I might say it better. Thank you, Monica, for being my first reader and critic and the love of my life.

In my time on the job, there were many colleagues who helped me and whose influence made me a better cop. If I started naming them here, I am sure I'd forget to mention someone. And yet I don't think I'll ever forget any of them and the difference they made in my life. I am proud of my association with so many fine police officers who did and continue to do the difficult work of policing. A few of them were key players and, as such, inhabit a number of *Shifts* stories.

I'd like to acknowledge the countless citizens with whom I interacted during my career. They and their personal stories became my stories and live on in my memory. Thank you for the many life lessons you taught me.

I must include here a special thanks to all the dogs I've known who have brightened my life just by being themselves and to whom I pay homage in "Dogs"—even Rex.

Finally, a salute to the men and women of the Philadelphia Police Department and to police officers everywhere. I remember. I wish you safe days and nights as you serve those who need you now more than ever.

About the Author

Stratis Skoufalos spent twenty-four years as a Philadelphia police officer, most of them on street patrol, retiring as a lieutenant. His background before that career includes his service in the US Army, 1966-1968, where he was an MP (military police).

Experiences as a Police Academy Instructor, as well as supervisory roles in Internal Affairs, Dignitary Protection, and Recruit Background Investigations broadened his career and his repertoire of stories, many of which he recorded as journal notes at the time. He also served as Executive Officer for the Deputy Commissioner for Administration and Training.

Skoufalos received numerous police commendations and community awards, including membership in the Chapel of the Four Chaplains Legion of Honor. After retiring from the department, he served as Security Director at several universities in the Philadelphia area.

He earned his B.A. in English from LaSalle University where he was recognized as the Outstanding Senior in English. He went on to earn an M.Ed. from Temple University.

With his wife, Monica, he relocated to Florida in 2003, where he taught middle school Reading and high school Criminal Justice. In 2008, he was recruited back to Philadelphia to join the management team which created the Drexel University Police Department.

Retired, but beginning a new venture as an author, he currently lives in Florida with his wife. Both are passionate about animals, especially dogs.